BOGOTÁ

ANDREW DIER

Contents

BOGOTÁ

Busy Bogotá is Colombia's cool capital—and not just in terms of its famously chilly nights. A few years ago, visitors would arrive at the El Dorado airport and spend two days maximum in the Andean metropolis before taking the next flight to Cartagena. Now people are staying awhile, and it's easy to see why.

HIGHLIGHTS

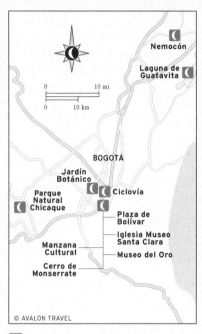

© AVALON TRAVEL

◖ **Iglesia Museo Santa Clara:** This stunning colonial-era church is decorated in the Mudejar style (page 16).

◖ **Manzana Cultural:** Colombia's tumultuous history has given rise to some noteworthy creative expression that is on display in the art museums of the city's cultural block (page 18).

◖ **Museo del Oro:** Anthropology, history, and art combine in this extraordinary presentation of pre-Columbian gold artifacts (page 21).

◖ **Cerro de Monserrate:** The views atop this hill are incredible both by day and by night (page 22).

◖ **Jardín Botánico:** Countless shades of green are on display in this lovely park minutes from downtown (page 27).

◖ **Ciclovía:** When a city can get a quarter of its population to get out and ride a bike on a Sunday, you know it's doing something right (page 37).

◖ **Nemocón:** The plaza and streets of this little-visited salt-mining town are full of charm (page 59).

◖ **Laguna de Guatavita:** This sacred lake is the source of the El Dorado myth (page 60).

◖ **Plaza de Bolívar:** Colombia's most important and most photographed plaza is named for Simón Bolívar, the man who gave the country independence (page 12).

◖ **Parque Natural Chicaque:** Minutes from La Candelaria, the cloud forests of this park seem miles away from everything (page 64).

There is the Museo del Oro, of course, undoubtedly one of the best museums in Latin America. There are precious few reminders of the Muisca settlement of Bacatá in this vast concrete jungle of today, but this museum is a stellar tribute to a people who all but disappeared within decades of the Spanish conquest.

Then there is the living museum that is the historic district, La Candelaria. Every street block has its unique story to tell: the flower vase that changed history, the loyal companion who saved the Liberator's neck, the generosity of a famous painter. Colonial churches surprise with their quiet, steadfast beauty, and grandiose buildings along the Avenida Jiménez stand as testament to the aspirations of the "Athens of South America." Red buses, glitzy shopping areas, and stunning libraries set in manicured parks are proof that Bogotá can, with a little investment and good government, overcome the formidable challenges of its recent past.

A melting pot of nearly eight million, Bogotá is home to Colombians from every corner of the country who come to study, seek opportunity, or crave the freedom and anonymity that this sprawling city of eight million offers. It shouldn't come as a surprise that it is the country's culinary and cultural capital as well. This is the place to enjoy nouvelle Colombian cuisine, with flavors from the two coasts at a host of innovative restaurants. It's the place where there is always something going on—a massive theater festival, a symphony concert, a dance marathon courtesy of a big-name DJ, a gallery opening—it's just a matter of finding out when and where. Bogotanos' reputation for being gloomy and cerebral is unfair. You only need to experience the sheer *alegría* (joyfulness) of Andrés Carne de Res one weekend night for proof.

When the sensory overload and intensity of this over-caffeinated city becomes too much, the *páramos* (highland moors), cloud forests, and mountain lakes of extraordinary natural parks beckon. Parque Nacional Natural Chingaza, Parque Natural Chicaque, and Laguna de Guatavita are all only about an hour away.

HISTORY

As early as AD 300, the Muisca people settled along the Cordillera Oriental (Eastern Mountain Range) of the Andes Mountains, forming a loose confederation. Bacatá (now Bogotá) was the seat of the Zipa, head of the southern confederation. The Muiscas had an agricultural economy but also extracted salt and emeralds, wove fine textiles, and actively traded for cotton, shells, and gold with other indigenous peoples. The names of many of their settlements—Chía, Suba, Engativá—survive, though no physical traces remain.

Lured by tales of riches, three European armies converged on Muisca territory in 1538. An army headed by Spanish conquistador Gonzalo Jiménez de Quesada arrived from Santa Marta. Another army, headed by Spaniard Sebastián de Belalcázar, arrived from the south. A third army, led by German expeditionary Nikolaus Federmann, arrived from present-day Venezuela.

By the time Federmann and Belalcázar arrived, Jiménez de Quesada had plundered the Muisca lands and had founded, in August 1538, a settlement that he named Santa Fe de Bogotá del Nuevo Reino de Granada de las Indias del Mar. In the late 17th century, the population was less than 15,000 inhabitants. European diseases had almost completely wiped out the Muisca population. Marriages between Muiscas and the Spanish formed the *mestizo* base of the city.

The city was the seat of the first provisional government established after Colombia's declaration of independence in 1810. In 1819, the name of the city was changed to Bogotá, and it became capital of the newly formed Gran Colombia. The city was not connected by railroad to the outside world until the end of the 19th century—and then only to Girardot, a port on the Río Magdalena.

The early decades of the 20th century were a period of growth and prosperity. The post-war period was a time of rapid, haphazard development that saw the establishment of many new industries. Much of the growth was unplanned, and sprawling slums developed, especially in the south of the city.

By the 1990s, Bogotá had become synonymous with poverty, crime, and urban sprawl. A series of mayors, including Enrique Peñalosa and Antanas Mockus, transformed the city. Peñalosa undertook large projects such as the TransMilenio rapid bus system, reclaimed public space, and invested heavily in education and basic services. Mockus worked to improve security and increase civic consciousness. Between 1995 and 2003, the city transformed itself.

Despite all its challenges Bogotá continues to be the economic, cultural, and educational powerhouse of Colombia. The city is a magnet for people from all over Colombia and, in recent years, even from abroad. Today Bogotá ranks as the fifth largest city in South America.

PLANNING YOUR TIME

At the minimum, give Bogotá two days. In that short time span, you can cover La Candelaria, head up to Monserrate, discover the Museo del Oro, and

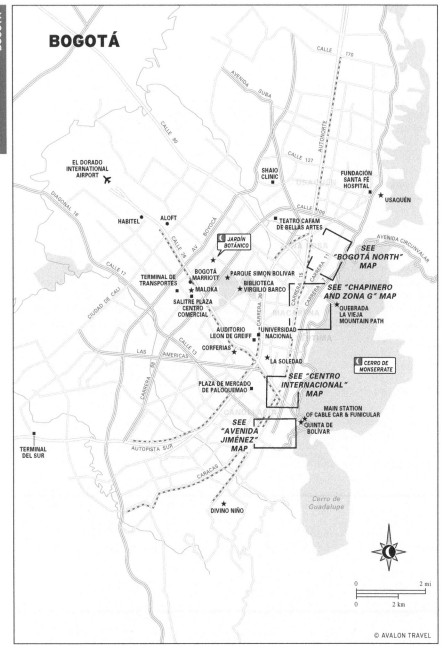

BOGOTÁ

EL DORADO
INTERNATIONAL
AIRPORT ✈

SHAIO
CLINIC ■

FUNDACIÓN
SANTA FÉ
HOSPITAL ■

USAQUÉN ■

CALLE 170

CALLE 80

CALLE 127

AUTONORTE

AVENIDA SUBA

DIAGONAL 16

CALLE 78

AV. BOYACÁ

CALLE 100

HABITEL ● ALOFT ●

TEATRO CAFAM ■
DE BELLAS ARTES

JARDÍN
BOTÁNICO ★

AVENIDA CIRCUNVALAR

SEE
"BOGOTÁ NORTH"
MAP

CALLE 17

CIUDAD DE CALI

TERMINAL DE
TRANSPORTES ■

BOGOTÁ
MARRIOTT ★

MALOKA ★

SALITRE PLAZA
CENTRO
COMERCIAL ■

PARQUE SIMÓN BOLIVAR ★

BIBLIOTECA
VIRGILIO BARCO ★

CARRERA 30

CARRERA 15

CARRERA 11

CARRERA 7

SEE "CHAPINERO
AND ZONA G" MAP

QUEBRADA
LA VIEJA
MOUNTAIN PATH ★

AUDITORIO
LEON DE GREIFF ★

UNIVERSIDAD
NACIONAL ■

CALLE 13

LAS AMERICAS

CARRERA 68

CORFERIAS ★

LA SOLEDAD ■

CERRO DE
MONSERRATE

PLAZA DE MERCADO
DE PALOQUEMAO ■

SEE "CENTRO
INTERNACIONAL"
MAP

MAIN STATION
OF CABLE CAR & FUNICULAR

SEE
"AVENIDA
JIMÉNEZ"
MAP

QUINTA DE
BOLIVAR ★

TERMINAL
DEL SUR ■

AUTOPISTA SUR

CARACAS

DIVINO NIÑO ★

Cerro de
Guadalupe

0   2 mi

0   2 km

enjoy some good meals in the Zona T, Zona G, or the Macarena.

With about five days you can explore neighborhoods like the Macarena, check out the botanical gardens, or make a day trip to the Parque Natural Chicaque or to the Laguna de Guatavita. If you're here over a Sunday, you'll absolutely have to head out to the Ciclovía.

If you are staying in Colombia for 10 days, you can try a city-country combo by adding Villa de Leyva. Or make it a city-coast combo, adding a Caribbean Coast destination such as Cartagena or Santa Marta.

Many museums are closed on either Monday or Tuesday. The Museo del Oro is closed Mondays and the art museums of the Manzana Cultural are closed Tuesdays. During the end-of-year holidays and Holy Week (Semana Santa), Bogotá becomes a ghost town as locals head for the countryside, the coast, or abroad. There is very little traffic at those times, but many restaurants are closed and nightspots are empty, especially around Christmas. Bogotá is a particularly dull place to be on New Year's Eve. Semana Santa is perhaps less lonely and can be a good time to visit, especially when the biennial theater festival is on. On long weekends, many Bogotanos skip town; those from the provinces come for a visit.

SAFETY

Bogotá is much safer than it once was, but it is no Copenhagen. The best advice is to, as Colombians would say, *"no dar papaya."* Literally, that translates to "don't give any papayas." Don't hand someone the opportunity to take advantage of you.

While strolling in La Candelaria, keep a watchful eye on cameras and other gadgets. Better yet, leave valuables—including passports—locked away in the hotel safe if possible. Private security guards and police now regularly patrol La Candelaria at night, although it may feel a little spooky after 10 or 11 at night.

You will often come across homeless people or those who claim to be displaced. Most—but not all—of these people are harmless. While ample social services do exist in the city, many of the city's destitute do not have the wherewithal to access them. When street people ask for money, you may want to have some spare change, a bottle of water, or leftover food to give out (but only if you do not feel threatened in any way).

Traveling by the city's SITP buses is safe and comfortable. The red TransMilenio buses can get crowded, so be aware of pickpockets. Private buses and *colectivos* are less safe and drivers can be reckless.

Bogotá has had a serious problem with taxi crime, commonly known as *paseo milonario*. But recent technological advances have made a noticeable dent in these crimes. Tappsi, a popular and free smartphone app, is indispensable. With this app, you can request a cab, find out the name of the driver, and have your trip tracked by a friend. Alternatively, you can order a cab over the phone. Avoid hailing cabs off the street, particularly when you are alone, when it is late at night, and near nightclubs and upscale dining areas.

If you are heading out for a night on the town, do not accept drinks from strangers. Leave credit/debit cards, your passport, and expensive cell phones at home.

During an emergency, call 123 from any phone.

ORIENTATION

Sprawling Bogotá covers some 1,776 square kilometers (686 square miles), filling a large part of the *altiplano* (high plateau) or savannah of Bogotá. In all likelihood, much of your time will be spent along the corridor that is the Carrera or Avenida 7 (most often called the Séptima). The Séptima extends, parallel to the eastern mountains, from the Plaza de Bolívar in La Candelaria through the Centro Internacional, Chapinero, and northern neighborhoods to Usaquén and beyond.

La Candelaria is the oldest part of town, dating to the 16th century. With the Plaza de Bolívar at its heart, it is a neighborhood full of historic buildings, interesting museums, and hostels.

Adjacent to La Candelaria is Avenida Jiménez, also known as the "Eje Ambiental."

northern Bogotá

This is a pedestrian street that is shared with TransMilenio. In addition to being the home of the Museo del Oro, colonial churches, the Quinta de Bolívar, and Monserrate, the area is also known for its grand early-20th-century architecture.

Farther north is the Centro Internacional. Major banks have their headquarters in this part of town, and two major museums—the Museo de Arte Moderno de Bogotá and the Museo Nacional—are two of the major tourist attractions in the neighborhood.

Just above the bullfighting ring and the iconic Torres del Parque complex is the quirky neighborhood of the Macarena, full of art galleries and cozy restaurants. The popular Parque Nacional marks the end of this area that is often considered downtown.

The Distrito Capital of Bogotá comprises 20 localidades (official neighborhoods), each with its own local mayor and neighborhood council. Chapinero is one of the largest ones along the Carrera 7 (Séptima) corridor. It extends to Calle 100, but most people consider Chapinero to include the neighborhoods from around Calle 45 to about Calle 72. Below the Séptima is a gritty commerce center that is also considered the center of gay nightlife. There are no major sights of interest in Chapinero.

Chauffeured SUVs whizzing by and bodyguards lingering about on the street are tell-tale signs that you have arrived in the swanky northern neighborhoods. The Zona G, between Calles 69 and 70 above the Séptima; the Zona Rosa, between Calles 81 and 85 and Carreras 11 and 15; and the Parque de la 93 area, between Calles 91 and 94 and also between Carreras 11 and 15, are home to excellent restaurants, famous nightspots, glitzy malls, and fancy hotels. It is the center of hedonism in Bogotá. Finally, above the Séptima between Calles 120 and 125 is Usaquén, a sleepy pueblo that has been swallowed by big Bogotá. Usaquén is becoming a trendy restaurant area and is also known for its Sunday flea market.

If you look at a map of Bogotá you will realize that this corridor from La Candelaria to Usaquén is a tiny sliver of this massive city. West of the

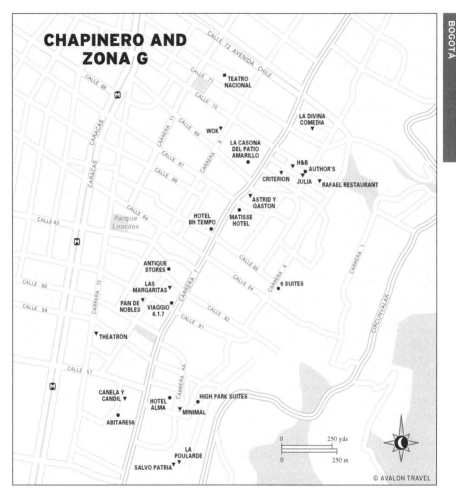

CHAPINERO AND ZONA G

CALLE 72 AVENIDA CHILE

CALLE 68

CALLE 71

TEATRO NACIONAL

CALLE 70

CARACAS

CARRERA 11

CALLE 69

WOK

LA DIVINA COMEDIA

CARACAS

CALLE 67

CARRERA 9

LA CASONA DEL PATIO AMARILLO

CALLE 66

H&B

AUTHOR'S

CRITERION

JULIA

RAFAEL RESTAURANT

ASTRID Y GASTON

CALLE 64

Parque Lourdes

HOTEL BH TEMPO

MATISSE HOTEL

CALLE 63

ANTIQUE STORES

CALLE 65

LAS MARGARITAS

CARRERA 7

CALLE 64

CARRERA 4

6 SUITES

CALLE 60

CARRERA 13

CALLE 59

PAN DE NOBLES

VIAGGIO 6.1.7

CALLE 62

CALLE 61

CIRCUNVALAR

CARRERA 1

THEATRÓN

CALLE 57

CANELA Y CANDIL

CARRERA 4A

HOTEL ALMA

HIGH PARK SUITES

MINIMAL

ABITARE56

0   250 yds

0   250 m

LA POULARDE

SALVO PATRIA

© AVALON TRAVEL

Séptima and in the center of Bogotá is the Parque Simón Bolívar, along with the Jardín Botánico and the Biblioteca Virgilio Barco. These are wonderful green spaces worth checking out on sunny days. These sights are not far from the Avenida El Dorado (Calle 26), which connects the El Dorado airport with downtown. In addition to its new TransMilenio line, this nicely designed thoroughfare is lined with hotels, shopping centers, and the fortress-like U.S. Embassy.

Southern Bogotá includes massive working-class and poor neighborhoods. Sights are few and far between. The Santuario del 20 de Julio and Paloquemao market are worth visiting and are just a few minutes south of the Plaza de Bolívar. In the huge *localidad* of Kennedy (named in honor of President John F. Kennedy, who visited the area while announcing infrastructure aid in 1961) is the fantastic Biblioteca Tintal public library. The Teatro Mayor Julio Mario Santo Domingo is in the *localidad* of Suba in the northwest of the city. Its stunning theater hosts concerts and dance performances from internationally renowned artists.

Bogotá street addresses are generally easy to figure out. *Calles* (streets) run east-west (perpendicular to the mountains), while *carreras* go north-south (parallel to the mountains). For example, the Museo del Oro address is Calle 16 No. 5-41. This means it is on Calle 16, 41 meters from Carrera 5. The Centro Andino shopping mall is at Carrera 11 No. 82-71, or on Carrera 11, 71 meters from Calle 82. The higher the number of the *calle* goes, the farther north you are. Similarly, the higher the number of the *carrera*, the farther west you go.

Perhaps because the *calle* and *carrera* system was a little too logical, the city planners have also created *avenidas* (avenues), *diagonales,* and *transversales*. Both *diagonales* and *transversales* are streets on the diagonal. To add to the fun, some *calles* are also called *avenida calles,* and likewise there are some called *avenida carrera.* Just ignore the *avenida* part of the name. Avenida Calle 26 is also known as the Avenida El Dorado. Carrera 30 (which goes past the Estadio El Campín) is also known as the Avenida Quito or NQS. Lastly, there are some streets that are called *bis,* as in Calle 70A *bis* or Carrera 13 *bis*. It's like an extra little street. Finally, addresses in the south of Bogotá have *sur* (south) in their address. The address for the 20 de Julio shrine is Calle 27 Sur No. 5A-27.

Sights

Everything you need to see in Bogotá is downtown, from La Candelaria to the Centro Internacional. Most museums have at least limited English explanations, and some have English-language tours. Photography is allowed at most sights, although the military police guarding the Casa de Nariño are sensitive about photography. Some churches and shopping centers may prohibit you from taking photos.

LA CANDELARIA

La Candelaria is a living museum. It is a reminder of Spanish power and ambition in the New World; a tribute to the yearning for freedom embodied by Colombia's founding fathers; and a reflection on the tenacity of the independent Colombian republic to persevere in the face of adversity. La Candelaria is a bustling place and has been for centuries. These days, university students, government bureaucrats, tourists, and old-timers who have lived in the area for decades pass each other along the narrow streets and frequent the same cafés.

You could spend a couple of days admiring the colonial churches and exploring the many museums in the area, but if you don't have that much time, three or four hours will give you a good sense of the area and its significance. All of the sights in La Candelaria are easily and best visited on foot. Areas above the Chorro de Quevedo (toward the eastern mountains), as well as some parts to the west, bordering the Avenida Caracas, can be a little sketchy and should be avoided.

◖ Plaza de Bolívar

Every respectable Colombian city has a Plaza de Bolívar, but none have quite the history as this one. Between Carreras 7-8 and Calles 10-11, the Plaza de Bolívar is the natural starting point for any tour of La Candelaria. Originally known as the Plaza Mayor, the plaza has had several reincarnations during its history. In colonial times, it was where the Friday market took place. It was also the setting for executions, including that of independence heroine Policarpa Salavarrieta (whose picture graces the $10,000 peso bill). Following the death of Simón Bolívar, Congress renamed the plaza in his honor in 1846. A diminutive statue of the "Liberator," the first of many Bolívar statues in the world, stands in the middle

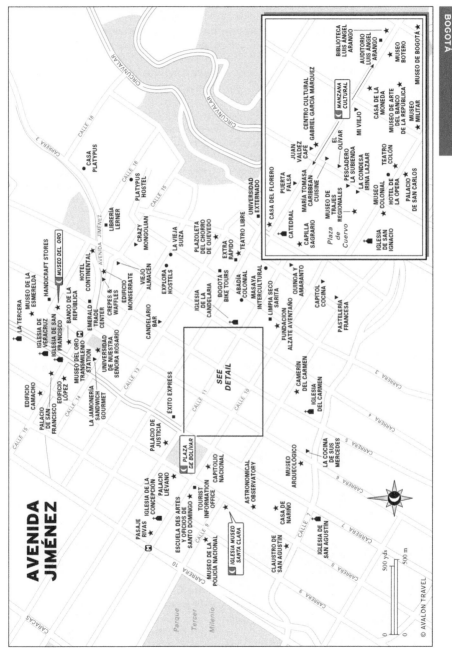

© AVALON TRAVEL

of the plaza. Today the plaza is home to political demonstrations, inauguration ceremonies for the Bogotá mayor, and concerts.

CATEDRAL PRIMADA AND CAPILLA SAGRARIO

The neoclassical facade of the Catedral Primada (mass noon Tues.-Sat., 10:30am, noon, and 1:30pm Sun.) dominates the plaza. It was built in 1807, and this is the fourth cathedral built on that same site. The tombs of Gonzalo Jiménez de Quesada, founder of Bogotá, and independence figure Antonio Nariño are in a side chapel on the right.

Next door to the cathedral is the Capilla El Sagrario (Cra. 7 No. 10-40, mass 7:30am and 5pm Mon.-Fri., 5pm Sun.). This chapel was built much earlier than the cathedral, in the 1600s, and is considered to be an excellent example of Santa Fe (as Bogotá was known) architecture. The interior is decorated with a Mudejar or Moorish-style vaulted wooden ceiling. Along the sides of the cross-shaped chapel are several large

© ANDREW DIER

the Presidential Guard

works depicting biblical scenes by Colombian baroque painter Gregorio Vásquez de Arce y Ceballos. A ceremony was held here to honor the army and Simón Bolívar following their decisive victory over the Spaniards at the Battle of Boyacá in 1819.

CASA DEL FLORERO

Across Calle 10 on the northeast corner of the plaza is the Casa del Florero (Cra. 7 No. 11-28, tel. 1/334-4150, 9am-5pm Tues.-Fri., 10am-4pm Sat.-Sun, COP$3,000), also known as the Museo del 20 de Julio or Museo de la Independencia. This small house used to be a general store run by a Spaniard, José González-Llorente. The story goes that his refusal to lend a vase to a pair of Creoles sparked the ire of either incredibly sensitive or cunning locals, who launched a protest during the busy market day against Spanish rule. Historians today dispute much of the tale, but the shattered remains of that colorful vase are exhibited today in the museum. Maybe the most interesting exhibit in the museum is a room that shows the transformation of the Plaza de Bolívar over time, with raw footage of two of the most traumatic events in recent Colombian history: the Bogotazo riots following the assassination of Jorge Eliécer Gaitán in 1948 and the siege of the Palacio de Justicia following a takeover by the M-19 guerrilla group in 1985. A free guided tour in English is given every Wednesday at 3pm.

GOVERNMENT BUILDINGS

The newest building on the plaza, completed in 1991, is the Palacio de Justicia on the north side. Housing the Supreme Court and other high courts, this building replaced the previous one, which was destroyed following the tragic events of 1985. (That building had replaced a previous justice building that was burned to the ground during the Bogotazo.) On November 6, 1985, M-19 guerrillas stormed the building, perhaps in cahoots with infamous drug kingpin Pablo Escobar, killing several justices and holding some

350 people in the building hostage. After hours of stand-off, the military counterattacked, coordinating their assault from the Casa del Florero. The fight concluded the next day with the building engulfed in flames, result of a military rocket. More than 100 people were killed. Controversy remains even today about the tragedy and the government's actions. Several victims—mostly workers in the cafeteria—were seen being escorted to safety, never to be found again. Five years later the M-19 demobilized, becoming a political movement. Today, it is telling that there is not even a plaque mentioning the tragedy. Nevertheless, clearly some wounds have healed: former M-19 guerrilla Gustavo Petro was elected mayor in 2011, with his office (*alcaldía*) in the Palacio Liéviano on the west side of the plaza.

On the south side of the square is the neoclassical Capitolio Nacional, home of the bicameral Colombian Congress. Designed by architect Thomas Reed, the Capitolio took over 70 years to build, finally being completed in 1926. Gargoyles keep watch atop the building behind the Ionic columns of the front. For about two months in 2009 the entire facade was covered with 1,300 massive ants, a project of Colombian artist Rafael Gómezbarros. The work was a commentary on forced displacement resulting from Colombia's armed conflict.

West of the Plaza
ESCUELA DE ARTES Y OFICIOS DE SANTO DOMINGO
One of the best trade schools in Latin America for woodworking, embroidery, silversmithing, and leatherworking is the Escuela de Artes y Oficios de Santo Domingo (Cl. 10 No. 8-73, tel. 1/282-0534, www.eaosd.org, 9am-5pm Mon.-Fri., free). Attracting students and teachers from around the world, this school is supported by the Fundación Mario Santo Domingo. A brief tour of the school is possible (call ahead to arrange). You will notice a warm and collegial atmosphere at the school, where some 600 students are enrolled. If you are staying in Bogotá for a while, you can inquire about taking a class. The school is housed in two lovely colonial buildings from the 1600s that are connected by a courtyard. A store—which could be mistaken for a small design museum—sells a limited number of items made by students. Many more are sold at the annual Feria de Artesanías in December.

IGLESIA DE LA CONCEPCIÓN
The Iglesia de la Concepción (Cl.10 No. 9-50, 7am-5pm daily) was completed in 1595, making it the second oldest church in the city. Along with a convent, it used to take up an entire block of old Santa Fe. The convent (which no longer exists) was built for the daughters and granddaughters of the conquistadors. The spectacular geometric designs on the ceiling and the polychromatic presbytery are among the most striking aspects of the church. If you pop in, you will no doubt see many faithful—most of humble means—in the pews, in silent meditation. This city block is called the Calle del Divorcio. This refers to a nearby residence for separated or single women who were not allowed into convents and could not live in their family's home.

Farther down the street beyond the Iglesia de la Concepción is the historic labyrinthine artisans market known as the Pasaje Rivas.

MUSEO DE LA POLICÍA NACIONAL
The grandiose Palacio de la Policía, built in the early 20th century, was once the headquarters for the national police and today is home to the Museo de la Policía Nacional (Cl. 9 No. 9-27, tel. 1/233-5911, 8am-noon and 2pm-5pm Tues.-Sun., free). Obligatory tours are given by knowledgeable and friendly cadets who are fulfilling their one-year public service obligation. The museum does have its fair share of guns, but there are also exhibits on different technologies employed by police in pursuit of the bad guys, along with tributes to police dogs. If you go up to the rooftop, you can get a unique view of the city. In the streets around the museum are dozens of shops selling police and military uniforms. Here you can pick up an official "Policía" baseball cap, but it wouldn't be a good idea to wear it while in Colombia.

Golden floral motifs adorn the nave at the Iglesia Museo Santa Clara.

IGLESIA MUSEO SANTA CLARA

It is easy to pass by the stone exterior of the Iglesia Museo Santa Clara (Cra. 8 No. 8-91, tel. 1/337-6262, www.museoiglesiasantaclara.gov.co, 9am-5pm Tues.-Fri., 10am-4pm Sat.-Sun., adults COP$3,000), but that would be a shame, as this is one of the most beautiful sights in Bogotá. Once part of a convent, the little church is an extraordinary example of Mudejar style in Santa Fe. This convent for barefoot Franciscan nuns known as the Clarisas was completed in 1647. It originally housed 12 nuns, who were descendants of conquistadors, and 12 Creole maidens. Perhaps the most stunning aspect design-wise can be admired by craning your neck and looking up: The single nave is beautifully illuminated by hundreds of golden floral motifs. The church is now strictly a museum; it often hosts edgy contemporary art exhibitions. Admission is free on Sundays.

South of the Plaza

CASA DE NARIÑO

You can have your picture taken with members of the Presidential Guard (they don't mind) at the gates of the neoclassical Casa de Nariño (Cra. 8 No. 6-26, www.presidencia.gov.co), home to Colombia's presidents. As is suggested by its name, the presidential palace stands on the site of the birth house of Antonio Nariño, who was one of the early voices for independence in New Granada, which was how the Spaniards named the territory. In 1906 Nariño's house was razed to make way for the first presidential palace, which was designed by the same French architect who designed the Palacio Liévano on the Plaza de Bolívar. The palace has served as home for Colombian presidents off and on since 1886. Minutes after the 2002 inauguration of President Álvaro Uribe, the exterior of the palace was slightly damaged by missiles fired from FARC guerrillas. Several missiles landed on humble homes in slums nearby, killing 13.

Tours are given of the Casa de Nariño, but you must make a reservation several days in advance. For more information on taking the tour visit the website. Even if you don't visit the interior of the palace, you can watch the changing of the Presidential Guard on Wednesday, Friday, and Sunday at 4pm.

Also on the grounds of the Casa de Nariño is the oldest astronomical observatory in the New World. This was the initiative of famed botanist and scientist José Celestino Mutis. It was completed in 1803. You can inquire about tours conducted by the Universidad Nacional at the Claustro de San Agustín.

IGLESIA AND CLAUSTRO DE SAN AGUSTÍN

Facing the palace, the Iglesia de San Agustín (Cra. 7 No. 7-13, 9am-5pm Mon.-Sun.) was part of the first Augustinian monastery in the Spanish New World, completed in 1668. The Franciscans and Dominicans beat the Augustinians to the punch in Santa Fe, relegating them to the far extremes of Santa Fe. It is a three-nave temple, which distinguished it from other churches at the time. San Agustín has seen its share of drama over the years. An earthquake destroyed the two towers in 1785 (they rebuilt just one). In 1861 in the midst of liberal reforms, the government took control of the church from the Augustinians. The next year the church was the scene of a presidential coup attempt during the Battle of San Agustín, as Conservatives attacked Liberals who were holed up in the church and adjacent monastery (which no longer stands). The church suffered damage yet again during the Bogotazo riots. The Claustro de San Agustín (Cra. 8 No. 7-21, tel. 1/342-2340, 9am-5pm Mon.-Sat., 9am-4pm Sun., free) didn't serve long as a seminary, and in fact was used as a garrison in which Antonio Nariño was imprisoned. During the Bogotazo rampage in 1948, international delegates in town for the 9th Pan-American Conference sought shelter from the mayhem there. Today this beautiful cloister is run by the Universidad Nacional, which puts on temporary art exhibits and hosts educational activities.

MUSEO ARQUEOLÓGICO

The Museo Arqueológico (Cra. 6 No. 7-43, tel. 1/243-0465, www.musarq.org.co, 8:30am-5pm Mon.-Fri., 9am-4pm Sat., COP$3,000) holds an extensive and nicely presented collection of ceramic work of pre-Columbian indigenous peoples. In addition there is a room on colonial-era decorative arts, in acknowledgement of the history of this 17th-century home of a Spanish marquis. A small café adjoins the museum.

East of the Plaza
MANZANA JESUÍTICA

Three important colonial buildings make up the Manzana Jesuítica (Jesuit Block). In the early 17th century, the Compañía de Jesús, a group of Jesuit priests arriving from Cartagena, was given permission by the Spanish ruling authority to build a church and school on the southeastern side of the Plaza Mayor (later to become the Plaza de Bolívar). As part of its commitment to social justice and to education, the cloister of the Colegio Mayor de

San Bartolomé (Cra. 7 No. 9-96, tel. 1/44-2530, closed to the public) was founded in 1604. The facade of the school was completed in the early 20th century and is considered an excellent example of Republican architecture. It has been in operation continuously since that year and is the oldest school in Colombia. Important figures in the Colombian independence struggle, such as Antonio Nariño and Francisco de Paula Santander were students at the school. Iglesia de San Ignacio, a church dedicated to the founder of the Jesuit order, was completed in 1643. The church has undergone a massive renovation for years, with the large cupola being restored, the roof above the nave being redone (it was on the verge of collapse), and meticulous restoration of the baroque interior, which includes paintings by many famous painters from the colonial era.

Well worth a visit, the Museo Colonial (Cra. 6 No. 9-77, tel. 1/341-6017, www.museocolonial. gov.co, 9am-5pm Tues.-Fri., 10am-4pm Sat.-Sun., COP$3,000) showcases a fine collection of art and religious artifacts from the colonial era, including the largest collection of works by Gregorio Vásquez de Arce y Ceballos. On the bottom floor is an exhibit that explores life in colonial times. The museum courtyard is quiet and green. Admission is free on Sundays.

TEATRO COLÓN

Inspired by the Teatro Santi Giovanni e Paolo in Venice, the Teatro Colón (Cl. 10 No. 5-62, tel. 1/284-7420) was designed by Pietro Cantini to commemorate the 400th anniversary of Christopher Columbus's 1492 landing in the New World. Tours of the theater have not been offered during the long restoration of the theater, but you can call or stop by and inquire about these. The best way of visiting the theater, of course, is to see a performance there.

PALACIO DE SAN CARLOS

Today housing the Ministry of Foreign Relations, the colonial-era Palacio de San Carlos (Cl. 10 No. 5-51, closed to the public) was the home of Colombian presidents from 1825 until 1908.

During the Bolívar dictatorship and the turbulent Gran Colombia period, Bolívar's companion Manuela Sáenz earned the nickname "Liberator of the Liberator" for helping him escape through a palace window—saving him from an 1828 assassination attempt. A plaque marking the exact spot draws the curiosity of passersby today.

MUSEUMS

The Museo de Trajes Regionales (Cl. 10 No. 6-18, tel. 1/341-0403, www.museodetrajesregionales.com, 9am-4pm Mon.-Fri., 9am-2pm Sat., COP$3,000), which showcases traditional costumes from the different regions of Colombia, is best known for being the home of Manuela Sáenz, Simón Bolívar's companion. The museum is next door to the Plaza de Cuervo, a tropical patio in the middle of historic Bogotá. Behind the elegant palm trees is the house where Antonio Nariño is said to have translated the Declaration of the Rights of Man from French into Spanish in 1793. After making about 100 copies of it for distribution to rouse the masses, he became nervous and started to furiously destroy them. (He got busted by the Spanish authorities anyway.)

The Museo Militar (Cl. 10 No. 4-92, tel. 1/281-3086, 9am-4pm Tues.-Fri., 10am-4pm Sat.-Sun., free, must present identification) is in a 17th-century house that was home to independence hero Capt. Antonio Ricaurte. Dozens of mannequins dressed in Colombian military uniforms keep you company as you wander the corridors of this museum. One room is dedicated to Colombia's participation in the Korean War. Over 4,300 Colombians fought in the war waged nearly 15,000 kilometers away, with 163 losing their lives. Colombia was the only country in Latin America to send troops in support of the United Nations/United States coalition. Two patios are filled with cannons, tanks, and fighter jets.

The Museo de Bogotá (Cra. 4 No. 10-18, tel. 1/352-1864, www.museodebogota.gov.co, 9am-5:30pm Mon.-Fri., 10am-4:30pm Sat.-Sun., free) may be of special interest to city planner types. A permanent exhibition examines the development of Bogotá through the years, and temporary shows have highlighted photography, historic figures in the city, and profiles of neighborhoods in the metropolis.

Manzana Cultural

The Manzana Cultural (Cl. 11 No. 4-41) of the Banco de la República is a "Cultural Block" (not Cultural Apple) that comprises the Biblioteca Luis Ángel Arango, the library's concert hall, the Museo Botero, the Museo de Arte, the Colección de Arte del Banco de la República, and the Casa de la Moneda. Without a doubt it is one of the most important addresses for visual arts in Colombia—and a required stop on any visit to Bogotá.

BIBLIOTECA LUIS ÁNGEL ARANGO

The Biblioteca Luis Ángel Arango (Cl. 11 No. 4-14, tel. 1/343-1224, www.banrepcultural.org, 8am-8pm Mon.-Sat., 8am-4pm Sun.) is reportedly one of the busiest libraries in the world, with over 5,000 visitors each day. Part of the same complex and located behind the library, the Casa Republicana (8am-8pm Mon.-Sat. and 8am-4pm Sun., free) often hosts temporary art exhibits. There is also a beautiful chamber music concert hall in the large complex.

COLECCIÓN DE ARTE DEL BANCO DE LA REPÚBLICA

With 14 galleries highlighting Colombian art from the 17th century to present day, the Colección de Arte del Banco de la República (Cl. 11 No. 4-41, tel. 1/343-1316, www.banrepcultural.org, 9am-7pm Mon. and Wed.-Sat., 10am-5pm Sun., free) is an excellent opportunity to discover Colombian art. Look for the series of "dead nuns." It was customary to paint nuns twice in their lifetimes: once when they entered the convent and once more moments after passing away. The nuns from this particular series lived at the nearby convent of the Iglesia de la Concepción.

Another highlight is the spectacular—if a tad on the gaudy side—*La Lechuga* monstrance (a monstrance is a receptacle to hold the Host). It's called

courtyard at the Casa de la Moneda

La Lechuga, meaning lettuce, because of its 1,486 sparkling emeralds, but it is also adorned by hundreds of diamonds, rubies, amethysts, and pearls. The Spaniard who created this extraordinary piece charged the Jesuits the equivalent of a cool US$2 million when he finished it in 1707. Hidden away in a vault for over 200 years, it was acquired by the Banco de la República in 1987 for US$3.5 million.

Nineteenth-century landscapes, portraits by impressionist and Bogotá native Andrés Santa María, and works from an array of well-known Colombian artists from the 20th century (including Alejandro Obregón, Eduardo Ramírez, Guillermo Wiedemann, and Luis Caballero) are other museum highlights. Free guided tours in Spanish are offered several times a day.

MUSEO DE ARTE DEL BANCO DE LA REPÚBLICA

Behind the Colección de Arte, in a sleek modern "white box," is the Museo de Arte del Banco de la República (Cl. 11 No. 4-21, tel. 1/343-1212, www.banrepcultural.org, 9am-7pm Mon. and Wed.-Sat., 10am-5pm Sun., free), which hosts temporary exhibits and has one floor dedicated to 20th-century Latin American and European art from the Banco de la República collection. On the bottom floor is the Parqueadero (2pm-7pm Wed.-Mon.)—the "Parking Lot"—a sort of laboratory on contemporary art.

MUSEO BOTERO

In the Museo Botero (Cl. 11 No. 4-41, tel. 1/343-1212, www.banrepcultural.org, 9am-7pm Mon. and Wed.-Sat., 10am-5pm Sun., free) there are still lifes, portrayals of everyday life in Colombian pueblos, and social commentaries by the most accomplished Colombian artist, Medellín-born Fernando Botero. In addition to paintings of corpulent Colombians, there are bronze and marble sculptures of chubby cats and pudgy birds. One side of the lovely colonial house, which surrounds a sublime courtyard, displays the artist's exceptional personal collection of European and

American art, including works by Picasso and Dalí. All of these were donated by the *maestro* to the Banco de la República so that Colombians of all backgrounds could appreciate and enjoy them without paying a peso—an extraordinary opportunity. Once the home of archbishops during the colonial era, the building was set ablaze during the 1948 disturbances of the Bogotazo. It has been painstakingly recreated.

CASA DE LA MONEDA
Connected to the Museo Botero and the Colección de Arte by patios and a Botero gift shop, the Casa de la Moneda (Cl. 11 No. 4-93, tel. 1/343-1212, www.banrepcultural.org, 9am-7pm Mon. and Wed.-Sat., 10am-5pm Sun., free) was where the New World's first gold coins were produced starting in the early 17th century. The museum's Colección Numismática shows the history of the Nueva Granada mint.

CENTRO CULTURAL GABRIEL GARCÍA MÁRQUEZ
Designed by Rogelio Salmona, the Centro Cultural Gabriel García Márquez (Cl. 11 No. 5-60, tel. 1/283-2200, www.fce.com.co, 9am-7pm Mon.-Sat., 10:30am-5pm Sun., free) was a gift from the Mexican government in honor of the 1982 Nobel Prize winner for literature, Colombian Gabriel García Márquez. Gabo, as he is called, has lived in Mexico since the 1960s. On the main level, where you can enjoy a nice sunset view of the cathedral, is a bookstore with an ample selection of books on Colombia. Next to the Juan Valdez Café below is a space where photography and art exhibits are often shown.

AVENIDA JIMÉNEZ

The Avenida Jiménez used to be the Río San Francisco and the extreme northern boundary of Santa Fe. For the architectural enthusiast, there are several gems on this street that stand in tribute of the city's inflated view of itself during the first half of the 20th century. Most of these historic buildings can only be enjoyed from the exterior. In 2000, in an effort to reinvent the historic Avenida Jiménez, architect Rogelio Salmona created the Eje Ambiental (Environmental Corridor), which extends from the Universidad de los Andes campus to the Avenida Caracas. Vehicular traffic is banned from the street except for the red buses of the TransMilenio. Ample pedestrian space has made this a pleasant place for a stroll.

In 2012, the city created a pedestrian zone from the Plaza de Bolívar to the Calle 26. This busy commercial area is now a fun way to check out the city's core, do a little shopping, sightseeing, and people-watching.

Historic Architecture
You don't have to be an expert on architecture to appreciate the many impressive buildings lining the entire length of the Avenida Jiménez. Most of these gems were built in the early 20th century. To the west side of the Séptima (Carrera 7) are: the neo-classical Palacio de San Francisco (Av. Jiménez No. 7-56), prior home to the Cundinamarca departmental government; the Edificio López (Av. Jiménez No. 7-65), which was built by the same construction firm that built the Chrysler building in New York; and the modernist Edificio Camacho, farther down and on the right.

It was on the southwest corner of the Séptima and Avenida Jiménez that populist Liberal Party presidential candidate Jorge Eliécer Gaitán was assassinated on April 9, 1948, which sparked the tragic Bogotazo riots. Up to 3,000 were killed. This precipitated the bloody period of La Violencia that swept the country. At McDonald's, a plaque and flowers mark the spot where the tragedy took place. A young Gabriel García Márquez, then a law student at the Universidad Nacional, lived near the Palacio de San Francisco at that time, and with his building in flames, he and his brother rushed back—to save his typewriter.

On the eastern side of the Séptima, notable buildings include the modernist Banco de la República (Cra. 7 No. 14-78); the Universidad de Nuestra Señora del Rosario (Cl. 12C No. 6-25), founded in 1653, which is housed in a colonial building that was originally a monastery; the Edificio Monserrate (Av. Jiménez No. 4-49), which was home to *El Espectador* newspaper; the fabulous restored Hotel Continental (Av. Jiménez No. 4-19), once the most exclusive hotel in town; the neoclassical Academia Colombiana de Historia (Cl. 10 No. 9-95); the 17th-century Iglesia and Convento de las Aguas (Cra. 2 No. 18A-58), where Artesanías de Colombia has a store; and finally (at the end of the Eje Ambiental) the campus of the Universidad de Los Andes, one of the top universities in Latin America, with several stunning new buildings. Los Andes has around 25,000 students.

Churches

Typical of most all colonial-era churches, the Iglesia de San Francisco (Cl. 16 No. 7-35, 6:30am-8pm Mon.-Fri., 6:30am-12:40pm and 4:30pm-8pm Sat.-Sun.) looks somber from the outside, but inside it's decorated by a fantastic golden altar, considered a masterwork of American baroque. This is the oldest of all the churches in the city, built by the Franciscans in 1557. The church is often full of working-class faithful. Adjacent to the San Francisco is the Iglesia de Veracruz (Cl. 16 No. 7-19), which is where several independence figures, executed by the Spaniards, are laid to rest.

The third church in this row is called Iglesia La Tercera (Cl. 16 No. 7-35, 7am-6pm Mon.-Fri., 11am-1pm Sat.-Sun.), and it is one of the jewels of colonial churches in Bogotá. It was built in the late 18th century, about 50 years before Colombian independence. Architecturally, the main highlight is its barrel-vaulted ceiling decorated with geometric designs and altarpieces made of cedar and walnut. Unlike other churches, the interior is not covered with gold leaf.

◖ Museo del Oro

Some visitors come to Bogotá specifically to see the world-renowned Museo del Oro (Cra. 6 No. 15-88, tel. 1/343-2233, www.banrep.gov.co, 9am-6pm Tues.-Sat., 10am-4pm Sun., COP$3,000). During your museum experience, you will see just a fraction of the thousands of treasures of the Banco de la República, Colombia's central bank, since its first acquisition in 1939. The museum tells the story of how—and why—the native peoples of Colombia created such incredibly detailed and surprisingly modern designs of gold jewelry and religious objects.

What is astonishing about the collection is the sophistication of the work. It is almost all smelted, with Muisca and Sinú peoples employing a "lost wax" technique, with various metals being purposefully alloyed. Here, rather than large, hammered pieces, as in countries like Peru, you will see intricately crafted and designed jewelry.

One of the highlights, without a doubt, is the golden raft created by local Muisca people. The raft portrays the ritual of El Dorado, "the Golden One." Another piece to look for is the collection's first acquisition, the Quimbaya Póporo. This was used during religious ceremonies. The unforgettable offering room is filled with golden treasures. English explanations are good throughout the museum (so is the audio tour). Just beyond the gift shop is a very popular restaurant that specializes in Colombian and Mediterranean cuisine. If possible try to avoid visiting the museum on weekends, when crowds soar, especially on Sunday, when admission is free.

Museo de la Esmeralda

On the 23rd floor of the Avianca building is the Museo de la Esmeralda (Cl. 16 No. 6-66, tel. 1/286-4259, www.museodelaesmeralda.com.co, 10am-6pm Mon.-Sat., COP$5,000). The museum has an impressive recreation of an emerald mine and then several examples of different emeralds from Colombia and elsewhere. Guides, fluent in Spanish and English, will make sure you know that the best emeralds do—without a doubt—come from Colombia, primarily from the Muzo mines in the Boyacá department. Although there is no pressure to do so, you can purchase all different classes of emeralds, and their jewelers can transform the emeralds you choose into rings or earrings within a day. Even if you are not interested in purchasing an emerald it is fun to check out the gems under a magnifying glass, as you learn why some emeralds are much more precious than others. The museum also has a small store on the main floor of the building that sometimes has discounted coupons for museum entry. Security at the Avianca building is stringent, and you will need to bring a photocopy of your passport and produce a telephone number of your hotel for entry.

Quinta de Bolívar

The Quinta de Bolívar (Cl. 20 No. 2-91 Este, tel. 1/336-6410/19, 9am-5pm Tues.-Sat., 10am-4pm Sun., COP$3,000) is a lovely country estate that was presented by Francisco de Paula Santander, Vice President of the República de Gran Colombia, as a gift to Simón Bolívar in 1820. El Libertador was president of Colombia from 1819 to 1830. Bolívar stayed there during his brief and sporadic visits to Bogotá, a city he did not like. He spent approximately 432 nights there, give or take. Built in 1800, it is a beautiful example of a late colonial-era house. Furnished with period pieces and set in a beautiful garden under cypress and walnut trees, it is one of the most popular touristic sights in the city. On Wednesdays there are guided tours in English at 11am (if there is a group of at least three). Reserve your spot the day before. Each day there are Spanish-language tours at 11am and 2pm, if you'd like to practice your *español*. An audio tour is available for just COP$1,000, but the narrators are a bit long-winded. Admission is free on Sundays. It is just a five-minute walk uphill from the Quinta to Monserrate.

◖ Cerro de Monserrate

Riding or hiking up to the top of this mountain, the Cerro de Monserrate, and taking in the views of the city by day or by night is a memorable one. To get to the top, take a funicular tramway (7:45am-11:45am Mon.-Sat., 6am-6pm Sun., daytime round-trip COP$15,400, nighttime round-trip COP$17,000) or the *teleférico* (cable car,

© ANDREW DIER

Cerro de Monserrate, as seen from the Quinta de Bolívar

noon-midnight Mon.-Sat., 9:30am-6:30pm Sun., daytime round-trip COP$15,400, nighttime round-trip COP$17,000).

You can also hike to the top, which, due to large crowds on weekends and holidays, is a good plan for a weekday morning. The path is open 5am-4pm Wednesday-Monday. There is no charge to make the somewhat challenging ascent on foot. Those over 75 years old, under a meter tall, or very pregnant are supposedly prohibited from making the climb, but this doesn't appear to be enforced. Going at a fast clip, the walk will take under 45 minutes. If you do decide to walk up, bring plenty of sun protection.

In the past there have been reports of bandits lingering in the woods along the path, but the security situation has vastly improved. Bored police cadets are stationed at three or four points along the trail until 4pm, and when there are no police there are plenty of vendors selling refreshments or several others huffing and puffing going up or leisurely coming down. If you feel as if you have done your exercise for the day, you can purchase a one-way ticket at the top to ride the funicular or tramway back down for under COP$8,000.

For the faithful, the white chapel atop, the Santuario de Monserrate, may be the goal of this hike. It is not of interest architecturally speaking, and it has been destroyed and rebuilt several times since the 1600s, but it is the highest church around, at about 3,152 (10,341 feet) above sea level. Inside, a 17th-century sculpture of the Fallen Christ of Monserrate attracts many believers. Some pilgrims climb the hill on their knees during Holy Week, believing that the Fallen Christ grants miracles to those who do so.

There are two pricey restaurants on the top of the mountain—a romantic setting for marriage proposals and a favorite spot for locals to bring visitors. These are French-Colombian Restaurante Casa San Isidro (tel. 1/281-9270, www.restaurantecasasanisidro.com, noon-midnight Mon.-Sat., COP$30,000) and Restaurante Casa Santa Clara (tel. 1/281-9309, www.

restaurantecasasantaclara.com, noon-6pm Tues.-Sat., COP$25,000), which serves mostly Colombian fare.

To the south of Monserrate rises the Cerro de Guadalupe, with a large statue of the virgin. It can only be accessed by road and was, until recently, unsafe to visit. If you would like to visit (the views are about the same as from Monserrate), take a microbus on Sunday from the intersection of Calle 6 and Avenida Caracas. As you enter the ticket office at the base of Monserrate, you may see an old photograph of a tightrope walker crossing the 890 meters from Monserrate to Guadalupe blindfolded. This stunt was performed by Canadian daredevil Harry Warner in 1895.

CENTRO INTERNACIONAL
Museo de Arte Moderno de Bogotá

Across from the Parque de la Independencia on Avenida 26 is the Museo de Arte Moderno de Bogotá (Cl. 24 No. 6-00, tel. 1/286-0466, www.mambogota.com, 10am-6pm Tues.-Sat., noon-5pm Sun., COP$4,000). It often puts on interesting exhibitions highlighting Colombian and Latin American artists. The cinema shows independent films and documentaries. Nicknamed MAMBO, it is another creation by the late architect Rogelio Salmona.

Torre Colpatria Observation Deck

The Torre Colpatria Observation Deck (Cra. 7 No. 24-82, tel. 1/283-6665, 6pm-8pm Fri., 11am-8pm Sat., 11am-5pm Sun., COP$4,000) offers unparalleled 360-degree views of Bogotá. The vista of the city from the Colpatria bank tower is arguably superior to that of Monserrate. At 48 floors, the building remains Colombia's tallest. At night the tower goes into disco mode, as it decks out in colorful lights.

Parque de la Independencia

The Parque de la Independencia, long a favorite for young lovers and those seeking a pleasant stroll under the towering eucalyptus and

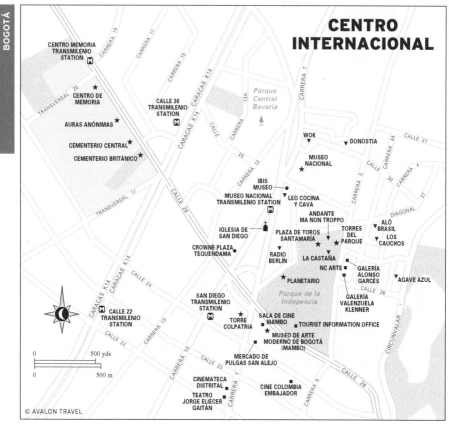

CENTRO INTERNACIONAL

wax palm trees, was created in 1910 in celebration of Colombia's 100-year anniversary of independence from Spain. The Quiosco de la Luz houses a tourist information center (Punto de Información Turística, or PIT). The park is undergoing a major expansion with the construction of a Parque del Bicentenario (it originally was to be completed in 2010). This exciting project will bring greenspace above the TransMilenio line on Calle 26.

PLANETARIO DE BOGOTÁ

On the north side of the park is the modernist Planetario de Bogotá (Cl. 26B No. 5-93, tel. 1/281-4150, www.idartes.gov.co, 10am-5pm Tues.-Sun., COP$3,000-10,000), which was built in the late 1960s and houses an air and space museum, Museo del Espacio. A statue of Copernicus stands outside.

PLAZA DE SANTAMARÍA

Next to the planetarium is the former Plaza de Toros de Santamaría, now renamed Plaza de Santamaría. The neo-Mudejar brick arena was built in the 1930s by a Spanish architect and was modeled after bullfighting rings in Madrid. Less messy events such as meditation sessions and even diving exhibitions have taken plaza in the plaza since Mayor Gustavo Petro banned bullfighting in 2012.

The Torres del Parque were designed by Rogelio Salmona.

© ANDREW DIER

TORRES DEL PARQUE

About 100 steps up from the bullfighting ring and planetarium are the iconic Torres del Parque. These three brick apartment buildings, running parallel to the eastern mountains, were designed in the 1960s by Rogelio Salmona, the most accomplished architect from Bogotá during the late 20th century. The buildings are perfectly integrated with the Parque de la Independencia and the Plaza de Santamaría. French-born Salmona studied with Le Corbusier and was awarded the Alvar Aalto Prize in 2003 for his lifetime achievements. Public space takes up almost three-fourths of the area in the towers complex, and art galleries, cafés, and bodegas are nice places to linger on a chilly day.

The Macarena

Just above the Torres del Parque, the laid-back Macarena neighborhood (also known as Zona M) is known for its art galleries and cozy restaurants. The adjective "bohemian" is frequently thrown about to characterize the barrio, which steeply slopes up from the Carrera 5 to the Circunvalar ring road. It is indeed an "artsy" place—that is most evident by the handful of galleries lining the east side of Carrera 5. While you may have to ring a doorbell to enter, gallery staff are more than happy for you to come in and check out what's on. The gallery Valenzuela Kennler (Cra. 5 No. 26-28, tel. 1/243-7752, www.vkgaleria.com, 10am-6pm Mon.-Fri., 11am-5pm Sat.) features experimental artists and, often, video art. Alonso Garcés (Cra. 5 No. 26-92, tel. 1/337-5827, www.alonsogarcesgaleria.com, 10am-1pm and 2pm-6pm Mon.-Fri., 10am-2pm Sat.) features work by major contemporary Colombian artists. It also has a nice bookstore. NC Arte (Cra. 5 No. 26-76, tel. 1/282-1474, www.ncearte.org, 10am-6pm Tues.-Sat.) is a newcomer with cool installations. The mix of intellectuals, artists, students, leftists, hipsters, and foreigners makes this neighborhood like no other in Bogotá.

Museo Nacional

The Museo Nacional (Cra. 7 No. 28-66, tel. 1/381-6470, www.museonacional.gov.co, 10am-6pm Tues.-Sat., 10am-5pm Sun., free) was designed by English architect Thomas Reed (who also designed the Capitolio Nacional) in the late 1800s to serve as the penitentiary for Cundinamarca, which was at that time one of nine states of the United States of Colombia. This prison was a cross-shaped panopticon, with a central tower from which guards could monitor prisoners housed in the three wings. It was in the late 1940s that the prison was converted into a museum. The permanent collection examines the history of Colombia from pre-Columbian cultures to the 20th century. On the top floor is a nice introduction to Colombian art. The museum often holds temporary exhibits on the ground floor. There is a pretty good museum store, and Juan Valdez Café brews coffee in the lovely courtyard.

Parque Central Bavaria

Below Carrera 13 is Parque Central Bavaria (Cra. 13 No. 28A-21), a large urban renovation project on the first site of the Bavaria brewery. The Bavaria Kopp's Deutsche Bierbrauerei was founded by German immigrant Leo Kopp and his four brothers. Bavaria is one of the few surviving—and thriving—businesses from the 19th century in Colombia. Its beers include Águila, Club Colombia, Costeña, Póker, and Pilsen. The brewery moved from this location in the 1980s and only two of the original brewery's buildings remain today, now home to several restaurants.

Parque Nacional

A center of activity on the weekends, the Parque Nacional (between Cras. 5-7 and Clls. 35-39) is the largest park in downtown Bogotá and is the second oldest one in the city. The park is set between a lovely English Tudor-style neighborhood called La Merced and, to the north, the Universidad Javeriana, which was founded by the Jesuits. On Sundays and holidays when there is

Ciclovía, free aerobics classes draw huge crowds in the park. In addition there are numerous fields and courts to practice sports, including several clay tennis courts. On the northwest corner of the park is a whimsical sculpture by Enrique Grau called *Rita 5:30.*

Cementerio Central

The most important cemetery in Colombia is the Cementerio Central (Cra. 20 No. 24-80, tel. 1/269-3141, 9am-4pm daily), where prominent political, cultural, and business figures rest. Before the cemetery was built in 1830, distinguished persons were buried in churches following Spanish tradition. Francisco de Paula Santander, who is known as Colombia's Thomas Jefferson; Gustavo Rojas Pinilla, a military dictator from the 1950s; Luis Carlos Galán, a liberal presidential candidate who was assassinated under orders of Pablo Escobar in 1989; and Leo Kopp, the German founder of the Bavaria brewery, are all buried here. Some people pray at Kopp's tomb, asking for wishes. There is also a part of the cemetery where thousands of victims from the Bogotazo riots from April 1948 are buried, many of them chillingly listed as "N. N." ("no name").

Immediately west of the cemetery is a remarkable art installation called *Auras Anonimas* by Colombian artist Beatriz González. An abandoned columbarium (structure to keep ashes) is covered with around 9,000 primitive black and white paintings of people carrying away the dead. It is a powerful reflection on the violence and death in Colombia.

CENTRO DE MEMORIA, PAZ Y RECONCILIACIÓN

A memorial to victims of violence associated with the armed conflict is adjacent to the Cementerio Central. The Centro de Memoria, Paz y Reconciliación (Cra. 19B No. 24-86, http://centromemoria.gov.co, 11am-1pm and 2pm-4pm Mon., 8am-10am, 11am-1pm, and 2pm-4pm Tues.-Fri., free) is one of the first memorials to victims of violence in Colombia—an important milestone.

© ANDREW DIER

soaring wax palms at the Jardín Botánico

CEMENTERIO BRITÁNICO

Neighboring Cementerio Central is the Cementerio Británico (English Cemetery, Cl. 26 No. 22-75, tel. 1/334-0057), which was donated by the city to the British government in 1829 in recognition of help provided by the British Foreign Legion during the war of independence. Since then it has been the main burial ground for the city's Protestants. A fence at the back of the cemetery was made with the barrels of the legionnaires' bayonets. It is a green, peaceful place—just knock at the door and the family of caretakers will show you in.

PARQUE RENACAMIENTO

The Parque Renacamiento, just west of the cemeteries, opened in 2000 and is noteworthy for its bronze sculpture *Man on a Horse,* donated by Fernando Botero.

WESTERN BOGOTÁ
Parque Simón Bolívar

Nicknamed the city's lungs, when it was built in the late 1960s the Parque Simón Bolívar (between Clls. 53-63 and Cras. 48-68, 6am-6pm daily) was in the countryside. Now, it's almost exactly in the middle of the city. Two popes have celebrated mass there: Pope Paul VI in 1968 and Pope John Paul II in 1986. The park is an excellent place for watching ordinary Bogotanos at play, especially on the weekends. Numerous festivals and concerts take place here. There are more than 16 kilometers of trails in the park. In August, traditionally the windiest month, thousands of families try their luck catching a breeze for their colorful kites.

Biblioteca Virgilio Barco

Open since 2001, the stunning Biblioteca Virgilio Barco (Av. Cra. 60 No. 57-60, tel. 1/315-8890, 2pm-8pm Mon., 8am-8pm Tues.-Sat., 9:30am-5:30pm Sun.), across the street from the Parque Simón Bolívar, is yet another project designed by Rogelio Salmona and is one of four fantastic library-parks in the city created by Mayor Enrique Peñalosa. The purpose of these mega libraries is to provide citizens access to books, Internet, and cultural/educational opportunities in a peaceful environment. While relatively plentiful in northern neighborhoods, green spaces—even trees—are few and far between in the massive lower-income neighborhoods. A bike path (*cicloruta*) surrounds the park and is popular with young inline skaters. The well-maintained grounds are a playground for the young, the old, and the canine.

◖ Jardín Botánico

Colombia is one of the most biodiverse countries on the planet, and the Jardín Botánico (Av. Cl. 63 No. 68-95, tel. 1/437-7060, 8am-5pm Tues.-Fri., 9am-5pm Sat.-Sun., COP$2,700) does an excellent job of showing off that diversity. It won't be hard to find the Colombian national tree, the towering wax palm. And inside the greenhouse, be on the lookout for the Bogotá orchid—yes, Bogotá has its own official orchid! The gardens take you on a tour of the many different climates in the country—from the *páramos* (highland moors) to cloud forests to tropical jungles. Feel free to stray from the paths and get closer. The garden has its own farm and composting station that you can wander about as well. One of the perks of working there is getting fresh organic vegetables! Run by the city, the botanical garden also runs a community garden project in neighborhoods and carries out educational projects across the city.

Other Nearby Attractions

For the romantic ones, a stroll around the Parque de los Novios (Lovers Park, Cl. 63 No. 45-10, 6am-6pm daily) might be just the thing for a sunny afternoon. In addition to renting an aquatic bicycle you can also check out the motocross track. The highlight at the Museo de los Niños Colsubsidio (Av. Cra. 60 No. 63-27, tel. 1/225-7587, 9am-4pm Mon.-Sat., COP$5,500) is an old Avianca Boeing 727 jet that kids can explore. Also for the kids is the Salitre Mágico (www.salitremagico.com.co, 10am-6pm Wed.-Sun., COP$20,000-50,000) amusement park. There you can ride the *rueda de Chicago* (Ferris wheel) or the *montaña rusa* (roller coaster).

NORTHERN BOGOTÁ

Northern Bogotá does not have many tourist sights. But the shopping and restaurant areas might be nice to stroll around on an afternoon.

The Zona Rosa (between Clls. 81-85 and Cras. 11-15), an area of shopping, dining, and nightlife, is a tribute to hedonism. Well-known Colombian designers, such as Sylvia Tcherassi, Lina Cantillo, and Ricardo Pava, have boutiques here, catering to the Colombian jet-set. The Centro Andino, Atlantis Plaza, and El Retiro—the holy trinity of shopping malls—never seem to go out of fashion. On weekend evenings the entire area buzzes with activity and anticipation. Calle 82 and Carrera 13 form a T—hence the moniker Zona T—and are pedestrian streets lined with restaurants and happening watering holes. This is where Bogotá comes alive at night.

The Parque de la 93 (between Cras. 11A-13 and Clls. 93A-B) is a manicured park surrounded by restaurants. Workers from the area stroll the park on their lunch hour. Sometimes there are big screens set up with bean bags strewn about for people to watch soccer matches. At night it is a popular dining area, but not nearly as rowdy as the Zona T.

The Parque Chicó (Cra. 7 No. 93-01) is a quiet spot in the north on an old hacienda from the colonial era. The Museo (10am-5pm Mon.-Fri., 8am-noon Sat., COP$2,500) has a small collection of pre-Columbian art, religious art, and decorative objects from around the world.

Once upon a time, charming Usaquén was its own distinct pueblo. Now, not even at the fringes of big Bogotá, miraculously somehow Usaquén has retained much of its colonial charm. It has become a dining and drinking hot spot with many restaurants and bars around the main square. On Sundays the neighborhood comes alive during its popular flea market (Cra. 5 at Cl. 119B).

SOUTHERN BOGOTÁ

If you mention going to southern Bogotá for sightseeing, Bogotanos may give you a baffled look. El Sur, the South, is synonymous with poverty and violence for many. Barrios lack green spaces, and neighborhoods are almost across the board ugly. This is where the housekeepers and the drivers for wealthy families in the north live. They can earn in a month a little more than what some from Bogotá society spend on a dinner in the Zona G on a Friday night.

But it is not necessarily a place full of despair. The middle class is growing; young people are earning college decrees; the city government is investing in TransMilenio lines, parks, and libraries; and the private sector is building malls. This is evident in all the massive *localidades* (official neighborhoods) in the south: Bosa, Ciudad Bolívar, Kennedy, Los Mártires, and Soacha, which is its own municipality.

Divino Niño

The Templo del 20 de Julio (Cl. 27 Sur No. 5A-27, tel. 1/372-5555) is one of the most important pilgrimage sites in Colombia, set in the working class neighborhood of 20 de Julio, just a couple of blocks from the new TransMilenio Portal del 20

BOGOTÁ

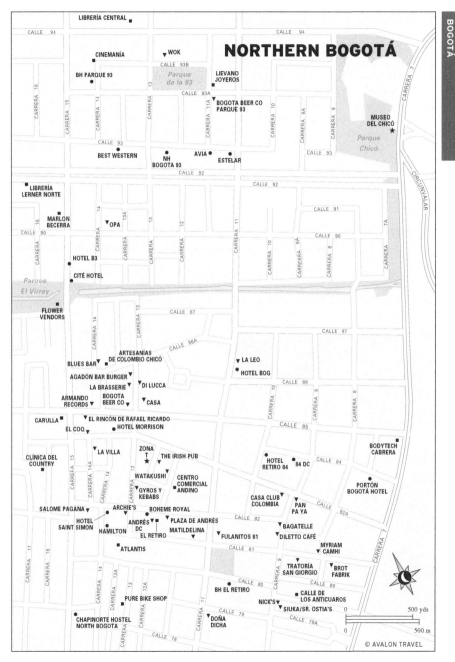

NORTHERN BOGOTÁ

LIBRERÍA CENTRAL

CALLE 94

CALLE 94

CINEMANÍA

WOK

CALLE 93B

BH PARQUE 93

Parque de la 93

LIEVANO JOYEROS

CALLE 93A

BOGOTA BEER CO PARQUE 93

MUSEO DEL CHICÓ ★

Parque Chicó

CALLE 93

BEST WESTERN

NH BOGOTA 93

AVIA

ESTELAR

CALLE 93

CALLE 92

CALLE 92

LIBRERÍA LERNER NORTE

CALLE 91

MARLON BECERRA

OPA

CALLE 90

CALLE 90

HOTEL B3

CITÉ HOTEL

Parque El Virrey

FLOWER VENDORS

CALLE 87

CALLE 87

CALLE 86A

ARTESANÍAS DE COLOMBIO CHICÓ

BLUES BAR

LA LEO

HOTEL BOG

AGADÓN BAR BURGER

DI LUCCA

CALLE 86

LA BRASSERIE

ARMANDO RECORDS

BOGOTA BEER CO

CASA

CARULLA

EL RINCÓN DE RAFAEL RICARDO

HOTEL MORRISON

CALLE 85

EL COQ

BODYTECH CABRERA

CLÍNICA DEL COUNTRY

LA VILLA

ZONA T ★

THE IRISH PUB

HOTEL RETIRO 84

84 DC

CALLE 84

WATAKUSHI

CENTRO COMERCIAL ANDINO

PORTÓN BOGOTÁ HOTEL

GYROS Y KEBABS

CASA CLUB COLOMBIA

PAN PA YA

CALLE 82A

SALOME PAGANA

ARCHIE'S

BOHEME ROYAL

HOTEL SAINT SIMON

ANDRÉS DC

PLAZA DE ANDRÉS

CALLE 82

BAGATELLE

HAMILTON

EL RETIRO

MATILDELINA

FULANITOS 81

DILETTO CAFÉ

ATLANTIS

CALLE 81

MYRIAM CAMHI

TRATORÍA SAN GIORGIO

BROT FABRIK

CALLE 80

CALLE 80

BH EL RETIRO

CALLE DE LOS ANTICUAROS

PURE BIKE SHOP

NICK'S

SIUKA/SR. OSTIA'S

0   500 yds

CALLE 79

CALLE 79A

DOÑA DICHA

0   500 m

CHAPINORTE HOSTEL NORTH BOGOTA

CALLE 78

© AVALON TRAVEL

de Julio station. July 20, 1810, is the day celebrated as Colombia's independence day. On Sundays and religious holidays, hundreds of thousands of faithful come to pray to the Divino Niño, a small statue of a smiling young Jesus in his pink robe, which is kept in a chapel behind the church. Around 30 masses are held between 5am and 7pm on Sundays to meet the extraordinary demand. It is indeed a colorful sight. Built by Salesian priests in 1942, the church provides groceries to poor families in the neighborhood who sign up for it. Nearby the church and plaza are shops selling Divino Niño statues and keychains.

Biblioteca Tintal

The Biblioteca Tintal (Av. Ciudad de Cali No. 6C-09, 2pm-8pm Mon., 8am-8pm Tues.-Sat., 9:30am-5:30pm Sun.) is a beautiful, modern public library built on the site of an unused trash recycling facility. Inaugurated in 2001, it was one of many projects conceived and built by Mayor Peñalosa. The library is easily accessed by TransMilenio (Biblioteca Tintal station). The trip there will take you through the large southwestern *localidad* of Kennedy.

Entertainment and Events

Bogotá is, without a doubt, the cultural capital of Colombia. In 2012, the city was named a UNESCO City of Music. Because it's the Colombian melting pot, all regions of Colombia are represented in their musical traditions here. Merengue, salsa, *cumbia* (traditional Caribbean music), *vallenato* (love ballads accompanied by accordion): You name it, you can hear it.

The city also attracts international artists, who perform at some of the city's spectacular theaters, such as the gorgeous Teatro Mayor Julio Mario Santo Domingo in Suba, the architectural gem of the Sala de Conciertos Luis Ángel Arango for chamber music, and the iconic Teatro Jorge Eliécer Gaitán downtown. Pop icons such as Paul McCartney and Lady Gaga perform before the masses at the Estadio El Campín soccer stadium, and nearby in the Parque Simón Bolívar, the city puts on several "al Parque" free music festivals each year. Rock al Parque is the best known, but there is also Jazz al Parque, Opera al Parque, and even Gospel al Parque.

NIGHTLIFE

The capital city is also Colombia's nightlife capital. The Zona Rosa may still dominate the nightlife landscape, but downtown hasn't completely surrendered. La Candelaria has its share of long-standing smaller bars, catering to Bogotanos and visitors alike; the non-SUV crowd hangs out in Macarena hideaways; while the party till dawn

© ANDREW DIER

the stunning Teatro Mayor Julio Mario Santo Domingo

crowd throngs the nearby nightclub Radio Berlín. Gay bars and cafés thrive in Chapinero, with massive Theatrón, as it has for over a decade, reigning as the club with something for everyone.

Most of the nightspots are, like everything else, located along the Carrera 7. To get the latest on nightlife, and find out about parties, check out Vive In (www.vive.in) or Plan B (www.planb. com.co). Many electronic music parties, attracting big name DJs, take place outside of the city towards Chía, and often the best way to find out about them is by stumbling upon posters on streetlight posts.

Bars and Clubs

Thanks to Bogota Beer Company (tel. 1/742-9292, www.bogotabeercompany.com), a successful chain of pubs with several locations throughout the city, sipping on a Candelaria artisan beer has become trendy in Bogotá. They also serve decent burgers. Try one of the northern locations (Cl. 85 No. 13-06 or Cra. 11A No. 93A-94). Sitting on the terrace and listening to rock at the always-packed Pub Bogotá (Cra. 12A No. 83-48, tel. 1/691-8711, www.thepub.com.co, noon-close daily, no cover), you're in a strategic position to watch people cruising the Zona T.

Most clubs have a cover between COP$10,000 and 30,000 (rarely). Covers usually include a *consumible* (complimentary drink). You can usually try to negotiate with the bouncer on the cover, especially if you're with a group. Finally, it's always a good idea to head out on the town with lots of smaller bills. Sometimes bartenders suffer from forgetfulness and fail to return your change. Tips are not expected at bars.

It doesn't look like much from the outside, but inside El Coq (Cl. 84 No. 14-02, tel. 1/611-2496, hours vary Wed.-Sat., cover COP$20,000), a relaxed and groovy bar in the Zona Rosa, it is pretty stylish. Also in the Zona Rosa, Armando Records (Cl. 85 No. 14-46, www.armandorecords. org, hours vary Tues.-Sat., cover COP$15,000) attracts a slightly grungy but cool crowd. The terrace is a fun (but sometimes cold) spot. Live bands

and well-known international DJs regularly play at Armando. La Villa (Cra. 14A No. 83-56, hours vary Tues.-Sat., cover COP$15,000) hosts the popular Gringo Tuesdays parties, but has all kinds of themed parties catering to locals and visitors alike.

For fans of *vallenato* (love ballads accompanied by accordion), the old-school Rincón Rafael Ricardo (Cl. 85 No. 14-55, tel. 1/530-2118, hours vary Thurs.-Sat., no cover) and flashy Matildelina (Cl. 81 No. 11-34, tel. 1/805-2933, 9pm-3am Thurs.-Sat., COP$20,000 cover) are the places to go in the Zona Rosa. Live bands from the Caribbean Coast perform regularly on the big stage at Matildelina, warming up the crowd. Salomé Pagana (Cra. 14A No. 82-16, tel. 1/221-1895 or 1/218-4076, 6pm-2:30am Tues. and Thurs.-Sat., cover COP$15,000) is a Zona Rosa staple that is your salsa and *cubana* headquarters, often hosting well-known singers and bands.

Céntrico (Cra. 7 No. 32-16, 41 floor, hours vary Wed.-Sat., cover COP$20,000) is a hot bar-restaurant where you can sip your cocktails while overlooking the city from the 41st floor. It is pretty fancy, so dress to impress.

Trampa de Vallenato Galerías (Cl. 53 No. 27A-31, no phone, 5pm-3am Thurs.-Sat.) may have the warm authenticity that you have been craving. This *vallenato* club is regularly voted as the top in the city. To hear *cubana* and salsa music, you can pop into the charming little downtown bar Son Salomé (Cra. 7 No. 40-31, 2nd floor, tel. 1/285-0547, hours vary daily) for a drink or two to unwind.

On Fridays it's often rock that the students, hipsters, and visiting foreigners groove to at classic Candelario Bar (Cra. 5 No. 3-14, tel. 1/342-3742, 9pm-3am Fri.-Sat.), but don't be surprised to hear electronic, reggae, or Latin beats. It also serves lunch during the week. Quiebra de Canto (Cra. 5 No. 17-76, tel. 1/243-1630, 6:30pm-3am Wed.-Sat., cover COP$10,000) is a classic haunt where jazz, funk, and salsa are often the order of the night. Wednesdays are especially popular in the two-floor joint. A different vibe can be found at the Viejo Almacén (Cl. 15 No. 4-30, 6pm-2am Wed.-Sun.), a tango bar named after the famous Viejo Almacén in Buenos Aires.

So, it's 6am and you still need to dance? Near the bullfighting ring and in a basement, Radio Berlín (Cra. 6 No. 26-57, 9pm-5am Fri.-Sat., COP$20,000 cover) is almost too cool for school. It's occasionally open on Thursdays. If you're looking for a late-night groove, often featuring international DJs, this is your place.

In the Macarena, cool Baum (Cl. 33 No. 6-24, cell tel. 316/494-3799, 10pm-5am Fri.-Sat., COP$15,000) attracts a fun crowd and often hosts international DJs.

LGBT

Bogotá is not lacking in gay nightlife spots. At last count there were over 100 gay establishments in the city. This is the place, after all, where many gay Colombians gravitate to so that they can escape endless questions from relatives about when they are going to get married. This isn't a gay bar town, as most people skip that step and head straight to the clubs.

On Wednesday nights the place to go is Cavú Club (Cra. 15 No. 88-71, tel. 1/249-9987, www. cavuclub.com, 9pm-3am Wed. and some week-end nights, cover COP$15,000). Here the music is *música pa' planchar* (music to iron by), and there is usually a performance by a drag queen, such as regular La Lupe. At reliable Blues Bar (Cl. 86A No. 13A-30, tel. 1/616-7126, 9pm-3am Thurs.-Sat., cover COP$15,000) you can drink and listen to cool music as you warm up around the bonfire in the patio.

As far as clubbing goes, Theatrón (Cl. 58 No. 10-32, tel. 1/235-6879, www.theatrondepelicula. com, 9pm-3am Fri.-Sat., cover COP$20,000) is a humongous disco in Chapinero. Theatrón is one-stop shopping for the gay crowd. It has no fewer than nine dance floors, featuring different types of music, including reggaetón, *vallenato*, pop, house, and trance. In the main room there is usually a drag show or contest at around mid-night on Saturdays. There are few bars and clubs specifically for women, although at Theatrón they

won't feel like second-class citizens. Theatrón occasionally puts on special parties for women. All the major electronic music clubs are gay-friendly. Salsa and *vallenato* clubs—not so much.

PERFORMING ARTS
Classical Music and Opera

You may not think of classical music when you think Bogotá, or South America for that matter, but the city is home to two excellent orchestras and an opera, and hosts talented performers year round. As is the case for most concerts and events in Bogotá, purchasing tickets in advance from Tu Boleta (tel. 1/593-6300, www.tuboleta.com) is the most convenient option.

The publicly financed Orquesta Filarmónica de Bogotá (www.filarmonicabogota.gov.co) and the Sinfónica Nacional de Colombia (www. asociacion-sinfonica.org) are the two main orchestras in town and the most important ones in the country. The *filarmónica* performs on the Universidad Nacional campus at the Auditorio Leon de Greiff (Cra. 45 No. 26-85, www.di-vulgacion.unal.edu.co); the Auditorio Fabio Lozano (Cra. 4 No. 22-61, tel. 1/242-7030, ext. 1905) at the Universidad Jorge Tadeo; and occasionally at the Teatro Jorge Eliécer Gaitán (Cra. 7 No. 22-47, tel. 1/379-5750, www.teatrojor-geeliecer.gov.co). The Auditorio León de Greiff is hard to miss: There is a huge iconic stencil of revolutionary Che Guevara on its exterior. There is often an international guest soloist at these concerts. Although tickets are available at the *taquil-las* (ticket offices) at these theaters a few hours before performance time, it is recommended to purchase tickets, which are usually embarrassingly inexpensive (usually COP$20,000-40,000), in advance at a Tu Boleta outlet (such as in Centro Andino or El Retiro).

The *sinfónica* performs at the same theaters, as well as the Colsubisidio Auditorium (Cl. 26 No. 25-40, tel. 1/343-2673) and at the spectacular Teatro Mayor Julio Mario Santo Domingo (Av. Cl. 170 No. 67-51, tel. 1/377-9840, www.teat-romayor.com), which has two concert halls. This theater, public library, and cultural center in the working class *localidad* of Suba is worth a visit regardless of whether there is a performance on. The prominent Santo Domingo family donated nearly US$31 million for the construction of this beautiful center.

At the Sala de Conciertos Luis Ángel Arango (Cl. 11 No. 4-14, tel. 1/381-2929, www. banrepcultural.org/musica, ticket office 1pm-8pm Mon.-Fri.) in La Candelaria, chamber music concerts featuring acclaimed international artists are regularly held in its spectacular, modernist theater in the Biblioteca Luis Ángel Arango. An added bonus: free *tinto* or *aromática* (herbal tea) at intermission.

The Ópera de Colombia (tel. 1/608-8752 or 1/608-2860, www.operadecolombia.com), one of few opera companies in South America, is highly regarded. They perform classic operas during their season, which usually extends from August to October. The Teatro Jorge Eliécer Gaitán (Cra. 7 No. 22-47, tel. 1/379-5750, ext. 213, www. teatrojorgeeliecer.gov.co) and the Teatro Cafam de Bellas Artes (Av. Cra. 68 No. 90-88, tel. 1/644-4900, www.teatrodebellasartesdebogota.com) host the soirees.

Theater

The largest theater company, the Teatro Nacional (Cl. 71 No. 10-25, tel. 1/217-4577, www.teatronacional.com.co), has three different theaters and performances take place just about every day. Their main theater is named in honor of Fanny Mikey, an Argentinian actress who moved to Bogotá and started its famed theater festival.

Teatro Libre (Cl. 62 No. 9A-65, tel. 1/542-1559, www.teatrolibre.org) has its main location in Chapinero and another in Candelaria (Cl. 12B No. 2-44, tel. 1/281-3516). In its 40-plus years of existence, its repertoire has included mostly classic theater as well as works by Colombian playwrights. Casa Ensamble (Cra. 24 No. 41-69, tel. 1/368-9268, www.casaensamble.com), in the cute neighborhood of La Soledad, is an alternative performance space, with avant-garde plays such as

Títeres Pornos (Porno Puppets). The theater, which sometimes feels more like a cabaret, is a project of well-known Colombian actress Alejandra Borerro. Source of neighborhood pride, the Fundación Gilberto Alzate Avendaño (Cl. 10 No. 3-16, tel. 1/282-9491, www.fgaa.gov.co), in La Candelaria, puts on theater and music performances featuring local talent year round in addition to art exhibits. Many of their events are free of charge.

Film

Most movie theaters in Bogotá, as in the rest of the country, are located inside big shopping malls. In the north that means Centro Andino, Atlantis Plaza, and Centro Comercial Granahorrar, the latter also showing more independent flicks and hosting film festivals. A couple of small cinemas in the north specialize in independent films: Cinemanía (Cra. 14 No. 93A-85, tel. 1/621-0122, www.cinemania.com.co), near the Parque de la 93, and Cinema Paraíso Café + Bar (Cra. 6 No. 120A-56, tel. 1/215-5316, www.cinemaparaiso.com.co). Downtown, go to Calle 24 at the Cine Colombia Embajador (Cl. 24 No. 6-01, tel. 1/404-2463, www.cinecolombia. com) for the usual Hollywood releases. It's across from the Museo de Arte Moderno de Bogotá (MAMBO, Cl. 24 No. 6-00, tel. 1/286-0466, www. mambogota.com). The museum often shows foreign, classic, and art films. It's best to go in person to get the schedule.

FESTIVALS AND EVENTS

While Bogotá lacks celebrations that unite the whole city, such as the Carnaval de Barranquilla or the Feria de Cali, a number of annual festivals and events have their followers.

Festival Iberoamericano de Teatro

Every two years during Easter week, theater and dance take over the city during the Festival Iberoamericano de Teatro (www.festivaldeteatro.com.co). Attracting more than 100 prestigious international troupes and companies and over 170 representing Colombia, this festival is a living tribute to Fanny Mikey, an Argentinian actress who adopted Colombia as her home. She started the biennial affair in 1988. Known for her bright red hair and distinctive smile, she passed away in 2008. With over 800 performances in the span of two weeks, it is one of the largest such theater festivals in the world. There are always theater groups from English-speaking countries, and there are typically many circus and dance performances. To take a break from the show, you can always hang out at the Carpa Cabaret at night, where you can drink and dance alongside actors from across the globe. Besides performances in theaters, there is an impressive series of free performances in parks and plazas in neighborhoods across the city and workshops for acting students.

ArtBo

More than 50 art galleries representing 400 artists from the Americas converge on Bogotá each November during ArtBo (www.artboonline.com), the Feria Internacional de Arte de Bogotá, one of the top contemporary art fairs in Latin America. It is held each year at the Corferias fairground (Cra. 40 No. 22C-67, www.corferias.com). One space is dedicated to young, emerging artists.

Feria de Artesanías

In December, and just in time for Christmas, the Corferias fairground (Cra. 40 No. 22C-67, www. corferias.com) is the setting for the fantastic—if overwhelming—Feria de Artesanías (www.ex-poartesanias.com). During two weeks, artisans come from across Colombia to showcase and sell their handicrafts. Many artisans, particularly indigenous peoples and Afro-Colombians from rural areas, have their trip to Bogotá sponsored by Artesanías de Colombia, the event's organizer. You will find that one day will not be enough to see—and buy—everything. The fair is also a great place for yummy Colombian snacks like *patacones* (fried plantains).

Music Festivals

In this city of music, free music festivals take place at the Parque Simón Bolívar during the latter half of the year. The series began in the mid-1990s and has grown in popularity ever since. The most famous outdoor music festival is by far the festival Rock al Parque (www.rockalparque.gov.co, July), the largest free outdoor rock festival in Latin America. The 2012 edition attracted 120,000 rockers. Variation include Salsa al Parque (Aug.), Ópera al Parque (Aug.), Jazz al Parque (Sept.), Hip Hop al Parque (Oct.) and Colombia al Parque (Nov.). Find schedule information online (www.culturarecreacionydeporte.gov.co).

International and national jazz and Latin jazz artists perform annually at the long-running Festival Internacional de Jazz de Bogotá. Most concerts are held at the Teatro Libre (Cl. 62 No. 9-65, tel. 1/217-1988, www.teatrolibre.org) in Chapinero. This usually takes place in early September, with tickets available at all Tu Boleta stands.

Races

If the altitude doesn't make you huff and puff along the streets of La Candelaria, maybe you would be up for the challenge of a running race in Bogotá. The Media Maratón is the city's biggest race, attracting runners from around the world. It usually takes place in August, starting at the Plaza de Bolívar and ending in the Parque Simón Bolívar. Nike sponsors its We Run 10K each year in October. The most unusual race of all takes place in December during the Ascenso Torre Colpatria race. That's when runners ascend a stairwell 48 floors to the top of the Colpatria building downtown.

Pasaje Rivas is a traditional shopping corridor.

Shopping

HANDICRAFTS

Markets selling Colombian handicrafts will likely find you before you find them. The Pasaje Rivas (between Cras. 9-10 and Clls. 10-11) dates to the late 19th century. This traditional shopping corridor—one of the few remaining—makes for a fun detour. The passages are so narrow that it is impossible to not interact with the carpenters selling their furniture and women peddling their hand-woven baskets and curios.

The Pasaje Rivas is great for atmosphere, but if you are looking for high quality, visit one of the Artesanías de Colombia (www.artesaniasdecolombia.com.co) stores. The same people who put on the amazing Feria de Artesanías every December have two stores in Bogotá. The most picturesque, by far, is at a stunningly white colonial church, the Iglesia Las Aguas (Cra. 2 No. 18A-58, tel. 1/284-3095, 9am-6pm Mon.-Fri.,

10am-noon Sat.). You can also visit the Chicó location (Cl. 86A No. 13A-10, tel. 1/691-7149, 10am-7pm Mon.-Sat.).

El Balay (Cra. 15 No. 75-75, tel. 1/347-1462, 9:30am-7pm Mon.-Sat.) is another option in northern Bogotá. While they have their share of trinkets, you might find a nice hammock or *chamba* (casserole dish).

CLOTHES AND ACCESSORIES

Looking for a cool T-shirt? Check out America del Sur (Cl. 85 No. 12-83, www.americadelsur.com.co, 11am-7:30pm Mon.-Sat.), which has mostly Colombia-themed shirts, or BrincaBrinca (Cra. 14 No. 85-26, tel. 1/530-1136, www.brincabrinca.com, 10am-7pm Mon.-Sat.). Cyclus (Cra. 7 with Cl. 54, east side, tel. 1/249-720, www.cyclus.com.co, 10am-7pm Mon.-Sat.) is a unique store that makes all sorts of messenger bags, backpacks, and wallets out of recycled tires. The slogan of this environmentally friendly boutique is appropriately "It's a round trip."

ANTIQUES

One street near the Zona Rosa is dedicated almost exclusively to antiques. Nicknamed the Calle de los Anticuarios (Cl. 79A between Cras. 7-9), this pleasant one-way street, nice for a mid-morning stroll, is lined by a handful of antique shops as well as some restaurants and, at its top, the Iglesia Santa María de los Ángeles, a popular choice for weekend weddings.

Prominent on the street are: Cinco en Punto (Cl. 79B No. 8-31, tel. 1/248-9798, 10am-6pm Mon.-Sat.), offering a range of curios from vases to furniture; Anticuario Novecento (Cl. 79B No. 7-60, tel. 1/606-8616, www.anticuarionovecento.com, 10am-6:30pm Mon.-Sat.), with a wide collection that includes religious art from colonial Colombia along with Baccarat crystal from the 1930s; and Bolívar Old Prints (Cl. 79B No. 7-46, tel. 1/695-5006, www.bolivaroldprints.com, 10:30am-6pm Mon.-Sat.), which specializes in old maps from Latin America and is owned by a French expat. The website of Asociación de Anticuarios de Colombia (Cl. 79B No. 8-49, tel. 1/248-5756, www.asociacionanticuariosdecolombia.com) has a more complete listing of shops as well as an interesting page regarding Colombian heritage pieces that are in peril of disappearing through illegal sales and transport abroad.

A smaller antique area is in Chapinero on the Carrera 9 from Calle 60 to Calle 63. Check out Librería Errata (Cra. 9 No. 61-16, tel. 1/249-6234, www.libreriaerrata.com, 10am-6:30pm Mon.-Sat.) for old books and Ayer & Co. (Cl. 62 No. 9-11, tel. 1/219-9789, 10am-1:30pm and 2:30pm-6:30pm Mon.-Sat.), which sells *de todo un poco* (a little of everything).

FLOWERS AND MARKETS

The flower market at the Parque El Virrey (Cl. 86 at Cra. 15, daily) is always colorful, and, if you

are the bargaining type, you might enjoy purchasing some flowers, if only to enjoy for a couple of days. A nearby florist, Flor Expres (Cra. 13A No. 86A-49, tel. 1/691-7335, 9am-7pm Mon.-Fri., 9am-5pm Sat.), is also good, with many unusual varieties and orchids, but there's no haggling involved. The king of all flower markets remains Paloquemao (Av. 19 No. 25-02, 3am-noon Mon.-Fri.) downtown, but to see it at its most vibrant, you have to get there really early. Best days: Friday and Sunday. Worst day: Monday. There is much more to Paloquemao, with all those exotic Colombian fruits, vegetables, meats, and more. There is a TransMilenio station nearby (Paloquemao station), but it's best to cab it if you go early in the morning.

Two popular flea markets take place every Sunday. The Mercado de Pulgas San Alejo (Cra. 7 No. 24-70, 9am-5pm Sun.) takes place in front of the Torre Colpatria. Uptown in Usaquén is the Mercado De Las Pulgas Toldos De San Pelayo (Cra. 7B No. 124-77, 8am-5pm Sun.). The crowds that go to these are worlds apart!

JEWELRY

Colombia is one of the top emerald-producing countries in the world, boasting three major mining areas, mostly located in the Boyacá department. Bogotá is probably the best place in the country to pick up one of those gems, but it would be wise to walk into jewelry stores armed with knowledge about how you can tell what is a good gem, an idea about prices, etc. Downtown, check out the Museo Internacional de la Esmeralda (Cl. 16 No. 6-66, tel. 1/286-4268, 10am-6pm Mon.-Sat.); Joyería Relojería Museum (Emerald Trade Center, tel. 1/342-2957, 9am-7pm Mon.-Fri., 9am-5pm Sat.); or the many stores on the block of Carrera 6 between Calles 10 and 13. You can also try your luck wheeling and dealing with the men milling about on the Jiménez just below the Séptima. But there, you're on your own.

Two top-end jewelers at the Centro Andino are Liévano (Centro Andino Local 157, tel. 1/616-8608, 10:45am-7:45pm Mon.-Sat.) and Bauer

(Centro Andino, tel. 1/478-5454, 11am-7pm Mon.-Sat.).

Specializing in Colombian gold is internationally recognized Galería & Museo Cano (Cra. 13 No. 27-97, Torre B, Int. 1-19, tel. 1/336-3255, www.galeriacano.com.co, 9am-7pm Mon.-Fri., 9am-5pm Sat.).

BOOKS

For English books, travel guides, newspapers, and magazines, Author's (Cl. 70 No. 5-23, tel. 1/217-7788, 10am-8pm Mon.-Sat., 10am-6pm Sun.) is the best and perhaps only place in town. Author's also has a large selection of children's books. In the north, try Librería Lerner (Cl. 92 No. 15-23, tel. 1/636-4295, www.librerialerner. com.co, 9am-7pm Mon.-Sat.), a great place to find Colombian literature, or Librería Central (Cl. 94 No. 13-92, tel. 1/622-7423, 10am-6pm Mon.-Sat.), which also has some English- and German-language books.

SHOPPING MALLS

Colombia is mall crazy, and Bogotá, with over 20 of them, is the capital of this infatuation. Symbolic of its growing middle class, glitzy shopping malls have popped up literally all across the city. The latest and largest is Titán Plaza (Cra. 72 No. 80-94, Cl. 80 at Av. Boyacá, www.titanplaza.com), proudly home of Colombia's first Gap.

In northern Bogotá, Centro Andino (Cra. 11 No. 82-71, hours vary daily, www.centroandino. com.co) was a big deal when it opened in 1993, being the first high-end shopping center. The German school, the longstanding Colegio Andino, was razed to make way for it. Colombian men's clothes brand Arturo Calle, Bosi for shoes and leather, high-end jeweler Bauer, and L.A. Cano (specializing in handicrafts) are a few of the many stores in the mall. There is a Cine Colombia movie theater as well. The food court on the top floor provides an unusual vista of the Zona Rosa, and cafés on the terrace below are popular for late afternoon *onces* (tea time).

Next door to Andino is glitzy El Retiro (Cl. 81 No. 11-94, www.elretirobogota.com, hours vary daily), home of the Plaza de Andrés restaurant; Mercedes Salazar, with whimsical jewelry; and Mundo Único, which sells skimpy men's underwear. The TurisBog sightseeing bus stops in front of the mall on Calle 81.

Finally, the Atlantis Plaza (Cl. 81 No. 13-05, www.atlantisplaza.com, hours vary daily) has a Cinemark movie theater, the swimwear shop Onda de Mar, and restaurants such as Crepes & Waffles and Hard Rock Café.

Sports and Recreation

BIKING

◖ Ciclovía

The Ciclovía is one of the best things about Bogotá. No wonder it has been copied in cities around the world—from all across Colombia to New York to Brussels. Every Sunday and on holidays (two times at night, even) about 121 kilometers of Bogotá streets are closed to vehicular traffic so that cyclists, joggers, dog walkers, skaters, and people-watchers can claim the streets. The Ciclovía started small in the 1970s as a neighborhood initiative. Today it is an institution, and really one of the few spaces in which people of all classes in Bogotá mix. On particularly sunny days, over two million people have been estimated to have participated in the Ciclovía. That's the equivalent of the entire population of Houston, Texas, out on a bike! Always be prepared for sun, cold, and rain.

While popular with joggers and others, it may be more enjoyable on a bike, especially because you can cover a lot more of the city pedaling rather than walking. The Ciclovía on the Avenida Séptima and on the Carrera 15 are two of the most popular

The Sunday Ciclovía is a Bogotá institution.

routes, but those are just a fraction of the possibilities. You can go for miles and miles. In fact, this may be a chance to explore parts of the city that you would have never considered before.

There is no need to take a guided group tour, as the Ciclovía is easy to figure out. If you ever get lost, you can always ask the helpful Ciclovía staff, patrolling the routes. Or just ask one of the hundreds of thousands of others out for some fresh air which way to go. Bring money with you so you can grab a freshly squeezed orange juice along the way. Bike repair stations are located on all routes. Keep an eye on the time, as you don't want to be far from your hotel when the cars come roaring back at the strike of 2pm.

Ciclopaseo de los Miércoles

Fast becoming an in-the-know institution is this group of over a hundred cyclists of all ages and abilities that gets together every other Wednesday night for a nighttime ride along the *ciclorutas* (bike paths) and streets of Bogotá. The Ciclopaseo de los Miércoles has been going strong for about seven years. The group meets at bike shop Welcome (Cl. 96 No. 10-57, tel. 1/256-0915) at 7pm. Find out about the next ride on Twitter (@ elciclopaseo) or on Facebook. There is no charge.

Bike Rentals

Many bike shops have begun to rent bikes specifically for the Ciclovía. Try Pure Bike Shop (Cra. 13 No. 78-47, tel. 1/476-5058, www.purebikeshop. com, daily rental COP$45,000), Eco Byke (cell tel. 311/519-2332), or Bogotá Bike Tours (Cra. 3 No. 12-72, tel. 1/281-9924, www.bogotabiketours. com). Many shops offer group bike tours.

RUNNING

Traffic in the city makes it tough to find pleasant places to run, but there are a few. The Parque Nacional (between Clls. 36-39 and Cras. 7-5), along with the cute English-style Merced neighborhood next to it, is not a bad place for a short morning jog downtown. The Parkway (Av. 24 between Clls. 45 and 34) is another option. This is a lovely strip of green in a quiet part of the

flying kites at the Biblioteca Virgilio Barco

Teusaquillo neighborhood. Of course the Parque Bolívar is also very popular, as is the park of the Biblioteca Virgilio Barco. In the north try the Parque El Virrey (Cras. 8-15 near Cl. 87). One side of the canal has a bike path, the other a foot path. In this *play* (fashionable) area, you may want to make sure your workout outfit is perfectly color-coordinated. Be careful crossing Carrera 11.

HIKING

The mountains surrounding the city are just too inviting to not explore. There are more mountain paths to conquer besides the one to the top of the Cerro de Monserrate.

Another hike in the north that is wildly popular is at the Quebrada La Vieja, a path that is operated by the Acueducto. It is open Monday through Saturday 5am-9:30am. On Sundays and holidays it is closed. It may be tricky to find the path at first. It is on the east (mountain side) of the Circunvalar at Calle 71. Most people walk up along the right side of Calle 72 and go through the tunnel under

the Circunvalar to reach the path. The hike takes about two hours total.

Amigos de la Montaña (www.amigosdelamontana.org) helps to maintain the Quebrada La Vieja. They also arrange group walks. Another group, Camino Bogotá (www.caminobogota.wordpress.com), regularly organizes hikes in the mountains around the city. Most of these excursions are accompanied by police officers. A third organization, Caminar Colombia (tel. 1/366-3059 or 1/241-0065, www.caminarcolombia.com), offers "ecological walks," usually on Sunday. These are usually outside of, but not far from, Bogotá. These walks cost around COP$40,000 including transportation. On the day of the hike, the group usually meets at 6:30am at the Los Heroes shopping center (Cra. 19A No. 78-85). The TransMilenio station there is called Los Heroes.

SOCCER

There are three professional *fútbol* clubs in Bogotá. Santa Fe (www.independientesantafe.com) is known as "Expreso Rojo" (the Red Express). Millonarios (www.millonarios.com.co) has, along with América of Cali, won the most national titles. Their color is blue. Both compete at the Estadio El Campín (Cra. 30 at Cl. 57). There is a TransMilenio station in front of the stadium (Campín station). The big match in town is Santa Fe versus Millonarios, and it can get quite heated in the stands. Note that you're not allowed to bring in belts or sharp objects to the matches.

The green team, La Equidad (www.equidadclubdeportivo.com), is the third club in the city. They are affiliated with La Equidad insurance company. Their modern, covered stadium is in the south of the city.

Tickets for all matches can be purchased at Tu Boleta (www.tuboleta.com, tel. 1/593-6300) or Ticket Express (www.ticketexpress.com, tel. 1/609-1111) outlets. You can also go to each team's ticket offices: La Tienda Roja (Cl. 64A No. 50B-08) for Santa Fe or La Tienda Azul (Centro Comercial Gran Estación, Local 2-50, Av. Cl. 26 No. 62-47) for Millonarios. The most sought-after seats in the house at the Estadio El Campín are *platea occidental alta* and *baja*. Ticket prices range between COP$20,000 and COP$70,000.

There are two soccer seasons each year. One goes from February to June and the second from June to December. Almost all the matches are on Wednesdays and on weekends.

Colombia hosted the Under 20 Soccer World Cup in 2011, which was a source of pride for the country, with the championship match (Brazil defeated Portugal) played in Bogotá. When the Colombian national team is playing a match, traffic magically disappears on the city's streets!

TOURS
Walking Tours

A free walking tour of La Candelaria is given, in English, every Tuesday and Thursday at 10am and 2pm starting at the tourist information office on the southwest corner of the Plaza de Bolívar. Spanish tours are offered every day. Stop by or call (tel. 1/283-7115) a day before to reserve your place.

Architecture buffs might be interested in taking a Rogelio Salmona walking tour, exploring some of the architect's most celebrated works. These are organized by the Fundación Rogelio Salmona (Cra. 6 No. 26-85, Piso 20, tel. 1/283-6413, www.fundacionrogeliosalmona.org). There are three different tours: Centro Histórico, the Centro Internacional, and the Biblioteca Virgilio Barco area. Tours last about three hours, each with an expert guide. English-speaking guides can be arranged. The tours are quite pricey, at COP$180,000 for two people. Prices lower substantially if you latch onto a group of at least 12 (COP$45,000).

Bus Tours

TurisBog (Parque Central Bavaria, Local 120, Manzana 2, tel. 1/336-8805, www.turisbog.com, adults COP$63,000) is a hop-on, hop-off bus tour that began operation in late 2012. The green double-decker bus makes seven stops: the Maloka science museum in Salitre, the Jardín Botánico,

the Parque de la 93, El Retiro mall, Monserrate, the Parque Central Bavaria in the Centro Internacional, and the Corferias fairgrounds near the Calle 26. Included with the purchase of your ticket is a GPS-activated audio guide in both Spanish and English, a guided walking tour of La Candelaria, and discounts to several restaurants and attractions.

Bike Tours

If you'd like the camaraderie of a group of other visitors as you get to know the city and get in a little exercise, try one of the many excursions offered by Bogotá Bike Tours (Cra. 3 No. 12-72, tel. 1/281-9924; www.bogotabiketours.com). They offer bike tours around the city and also many other walking tours, such as an unusual graffiti tour.

Tours Outside of Bogotá

Many hotels can arrange tours to attractions such as Zipaquirá and Laguna de Guatavita, or visits to these can be made via public transportation or by hiring a driver for the day. An agency that specializes in daily Catedral de Sal tours is www.tourcatedraldesal.com. These cost COP$96,000 per person.

There are some extraordinary national natural parks (*parques nacional natural,* or PNN) quite close to Bogotá, making for excellent day hikes. Sometimes these are a bit more difficult to organize without transportation and not being familiar with the area. Aventureros (Cra. 15 No.79-70, tel. 1/467-3837, www.aventureros.co) organizes mountain bike trips outside of Bogotá, for instance to the Desierto de Tatacoita near Nemocón. Ecoglobal Expeditions (tel. 1/579-3402, www.ecoglobalexpeditions.com) organizes excursions to multiple destinations throughout Colombia, including the famous Caño Cristales and hikes in El Cocuy. They also can organize day trips to parks nearby Bogotá, such as the Parque Natural Nacional Sumapaz, containing the world's largest *páramo* (highland moor), and the PNN Chingaza. Colombia Oculta (tel. 1/630-3172, ext. 112, cell tel. 311/239-7809, www.colombiaoculta.org) is a similar organization, with similar destinations.

Accommodations

As tourism has grown in Bogotá, so too have the number of accommodations options. This is evident in the Centro Histórico, with dozens of hostels catering to backpackers, and also in the north, with five-star hotels changing the landscape in upscale shopping and dining areas. Thus room rates tend to climb as you go from south to north, with Chapinero appropriately offering the most in-between options. Weekend rates are often less expensive in the larger hotels that cater to business people.

While it is probably more desirable to stay along the Carrera 7 corridor, other parts of town may be more convenient depending on your length of visit or budget. If you want to be close to the airport, many hotels, several quite new, line Calle 26 (Avenida El Dorado) in western Bogotá. This part of town is known for steel and glass, not colonial charm. There are few interesting restaurant options within walking distance at night; however, it is quite accessible to downtown during the day thanks to the new TransMilenio line (15-20 minutes) and at night by taxi. Besides being close to the airport, hotels in this area are close to the Corferias fairgrounds, the Parque Simón Bolívar area, and the U.S. Embassy.

North of Calle 100 there are many hotel options in what feels like suburbia. You might find some good deals online there, but you will be quite far from downtown attractions.

Hotel rates sometimes automatically include sales tax of 10 percent (IVA). Most hotels include free wireless Internet and breakfast (although the quality of breakfast will vary). While all the fancy hotels and backpacker places have English speaking staff—at least at the front desk—smaller hotels may not. Note that room rates usually depend on the number of persons, not necessarily on the size of the room.

Except for some international chains and upper-end hotels, most hotels will not have heating or air conditioning in their rooms. You'll have to make do with extra blankets and body heat on those chilly Bogotá nights.

A final word: *Moteles* are always, *residencias* are usually, and *hospedajes* are sometimes Colombian love hotels.

LA CANDELARIA

Travelers on a budget will find plentiful, friendly options in La Canderlaria close to all the important sights. Yet it still might feel a little desolate late at night, especially on holidays when the university students are gone and Bogotanos skip town.

Under COP$70,000

Sleek **Explora Hostels** (Cl. 12C No. 3-19, tel. 1/282-9320, www.explorahostels.com, COP$22,000 dorm, COP$50,000 d) is small with minimalist decor. There is not much common space, so you might need earplugs at night if your neighbors are in party mode (unless you join them). **Cranky Croc** (Cl. 12D No. 3-46, tel. 1/342-2438, www.crankycroc.com, COP$23,000 dorms, COP$70,000 d) is big and airy with wood floors throughout, and always has excursions and activities on offer for its guests. Private security guards make this street feel safe after dark.

La Vieja Suiza (Cl. 12 No. 3-07, tel. 1/286-9695, www.laviejasuiza.com, COP$60,000 d) is a cozy and quiet place, run by two Swiss guys, that is connected to their bakery. It's nice to be awoken by the aroma of freshly baked (Swiss) bread.

COP$70,000-200,000

Platypus Hostel (Cl. 12F No. 2-43, tel. 1/352-0127, www.platypusbogota.com, COP$22,000 dorm, COP$100,000 d) is the pioneer backpacker lodge in La Candelaria. Although somewhat worn, it is a welcoming place, where you can mix with other travelers. There are three houses in the Platypus kingdom, all on the same street. The main one, where you check in, is livelier. Platypus is just off the Eje Ambiental (Av. Jiménez).

The folks at Platypus now have gone upscale with the newish (Casa Platypus (Cra. 3 No. 12F-28, tel. 1/281-1801, www.casaplatypus.com, COP$40,000 dorm, COP$150,000 d). It is comfortable, sparkling clean, and friendly. The rooftop terrace is an excellent place to unwind with a glass of wine after a day hitting the streets.

(Masaya Intercultural (Cra. 2 No. 12-48, tel. 1/747-1848, www.masaya-experience.com, COP$22,000 dorm, COP$100,000 d) near LaSalle University offers different accommodation options depending on your budget or style, from luxurious private rooms to bunk beds. Tourists stay at this newish hostel range from backpackers to budget travelers. Staff are super friendly. Guests and students conglomerate by the bar/restaurant area in front.

The Abadía Colonial (Cl. 11 No. 2-32, tel. 1/341-1884, www.abadiacolonial.com, COP$145,000 s, COP$200,000 d), an Italian-run midrange option, is surprisingly quiet in back around the interior patio. The restaurant specializes in—surprise—Italian cuisine.

Over COP$200,000

(Hotel de la Ópera (Cl. 10 No. 5-72, tel. 1/336-2066, www.hotelopera.com.co, COP$330,000 d) still reigns as the luxury place to stay in La Candelaria. One republican-style house and one colonial house have been converted into this hotel. There are two restaurants, including one on the rooftop that has one of the best views downtown. The hotel also offers a spa.

Casa Deco (Cl. 12C No. 2-36 tel. 1/283-7032, www.hotelcasadeco.com, COP$230,000 d) is a nicely refurbished art deco building with 21 well-appointed although somewhat chilly rooms (all named by the color of their interior). The terrace is an excellent place for relaxing on a late afternoon.

CENTRO INTERNACIONAL

This part of town, once a modern and upscale commercial district, is on the rebound. The new TransMilenio line that has opened on the Séptima has been a major factor in transforming the area into a walkable and well-situated place to stay while discovering the city. There are, however, still few hotel options.

COP$70,000-200,000

In the heart of the Centro Internacional, few surprises are in store at Ibis Museo (Transversal 6 No. 27-85, tel. 1/381-4666, www.ibishotel.com, COP$120,000). Across from the Museo Nacional, the hotel has 200 smallish rooms and a 24-hour restaurant (breakfast not included). Right on the Séptima, this French economy hotel chain is a nice place to be on Ciclovía Sundays.

The 850-room Crown Plaza Tequendama (Cra. 10 No. 27-51, tel. 1/382-0300, www.cptequen-dama.com.co, COP$180,000 d) was the most exclusive address in Bogotá for many years. Charles de Gaulle even stayed there. It retains its elegance of yesteryear, with shoe-shiners in the lobby, several restaurants and cafés on-site, and smartly dressed bellboys. Rooms are comfortable, and the location is agreeable to taking in the sights downtown. Security is tight here.

WESTERN BOGOTÁ

If you are only passing through and would like to be close to the airport, you may consider staying in one of the many hotels along the Avenida Calle 26 (Avenida El Dorado). With the new TransMilenio line on the El Dorado, it is easy to hop on one of the red buses and spend the day visiting the major sights in the Centro Histórico. There's not much in the way of charm in this part of town. There is, however, a mall: Gran Estación (Av. El Dorado No. 62-47). Plus, along the Avenida and the TransMilenio line is a nice bike route and jogging path.

COP$70,000-200,000

Aloft Hotel (Av. Cl. 26 No. 9-32, tel. 1/741-7070, www.starwoodhotels.com/aloft hotels, COP$169,999 d), a member of the Starwood Hotel Group, is smartly decorated, modern, and within five minutes of the airport. There are 142 rooms in this property. It is also within about a five-minute walk of the Portal El Dorado TransMilenio station.

Over COP$200,000

The Marriott (Av. Cl. 26 No. 69B-53, tel. 1/485-1111, www.marriott.com, COP$400,000) is luxurious and is close to the Salitre business and shopping area. The two restaurants—one a cool sushi bar and the other serving Italian fare—are excellent. The hotel is within walking distance of a TransMilenio station, and it takes under 12 minutes to get to the airports. Open since in 2009, it is one of the first luxury international hotels to arrive in Bogotá in recent years.

CHAPINERO

Halfway between downtown and the Zona Rosa, the area of Chapinero between Calle 53 and Calle 72 offers quite a few midrange accommodation options. Chapinero Alto, to the east of the Avenida Séptima, is a quiet and leafy middle-class neighborhood. Below the Séptima (to the west), it's gritty. During weekdays Chapinero bustles with merchants and students, and on weekend nights the area is transformed into a mostly gay nightlife area. Hotels in Chapinero are about a 10-minute cab ride from the upscale restaurant areas in the north.

COP$70,000-200,000

The Viaggio chain has nine reasonably priced, furnished apartment buildings in Bogotá. Viaggio 6.1.7. (Cl. 61 No. 7-18, tel. 1/744-9999, www.viaggio.com.co, COP$163,000 d) is a high-rise centrally located on the Séptima. Rooms have tiny kitchenettes, but breakfast is included in the price. You can rent rooms on a daily, weekly, or monthly basis.

Classical music fills 6 Suites (Cra. 3B No. 64A-06, tel. 1/752-9484, www.6suiteshotel.com, COP$150,000 d), which has exactly that in a small house. Some packages include dinner. There is a Saturday vegetable and fruit market in a small park next to the house, as well as a round-the-clock police station.

Moderately priced, clean, and centrally located, the Abitare 56 Hotel (Cl. 56 No. 7-79, tel. 1/248-0600, www.abitare56.com, COP$113,000 d) has 28 rooms and is a great deal.

Casona del Patio (Cra. 8 No. 69-24, tel. 1/212-8805, www.lacasonadelpatio.net, COP$135,000 d) is in an English Tudor-style home, and its 24 rooms are reasonably priced despite its location near the Zona G. It has all wood floors, and there is private security on the street at night. With 10 rooms, the Matisse Hotel (Cl. 67 No. 6-55, tel. 1/212-0177, www.matissehotel.com, COP$180,000 d) is just minutes away from the Zona G in an English Tudor-style house above the Séptima.

Two hotels in Chapinero exclusively market to gay and lesbian clientele. High Park Suites (Cra. 4 No. 58-58, tel. 1/249-5149, contacto@highparksuites.com, COP$191,000 d) has four spacious rooms and is in Chapinero Alto. If you are planning on taking taxis everywhere you go, the location is perfectly fine. However, if you'd like to walk, it is on the east side of the Carrera 5 speedway—crossing the street there can be like crossing the Indianapolis 500. Warhol-mad San Sebastian (Cl. 62 No. 9-49, tel. 1/540-4643, www.hbsansebastian.com, COP$180,000 d) is on the other side of the Séptima, not far from gay mecca Theatrón and the gay-friendly gym and supermarket.

Over COP$200,000

In the leafy Chapinero Alto neighborhood, The Book Hotel (Cra. 5 No. 57-79, tel. 1/704-2454, www.thebookhotel.co, COP$273,000 d), which markets itself as gay-friendly, offers very comfortable and modern rooms, and the moderately priced adjacent restaurant with a terrace is popular with locals on their lunch hour.

NORTHERN BOGOTÁ

Uptown is a good option if comfort trumps budget and you want to be close to loads of excellent restaurants.

Under COP$70,000

A good deal within easy walking distance of all the restaurants and stores of the Zona Rosa is Chapinorte Bogotá Guesthouse (Cl. 79 No. 14-59, tel. 1/256-2152, www.chapinortehostelbogota.com, COP$64,000 s with shared bath). It's a real bargain for the north.

COP$70,000-200,000

On a quiet street in a wealthy neighborhood minutes from the Zona Rosa, Retiro 84 (Cl. 84 No. 9-95, tel. 1/616-1501 www.retiro84.com, COP$173,000 d) has 16 rooms. The breakfast area is not very happening, but the hotel is comfortable and is reasonably priced for this high-rent part of town. It's popular with business travelers in town for longer stays. Near the Atlantis Plaza shopping mall in the Zona Rosa, Hotel Saint Simon (Cra. 14 No. 81-34, tel. 1/621-8188, www.hotelsaintsimonbogota.com, COP$180,000 d) is a good value. It is a fairly nondescript brick hotel with about 60 carpeted but well-maintained rooms.

Over COP$200,000

BH (www.bhhoteles.com) is a relatively new Colombian chain of hotels, mostly catering to business travelers. All are comfortable with minimalist design. They operate several hotels in Bogotá. BH Tempo (Cra. 7 No. 65-01, tel. 1/742-4095, COP$220,000 d) has 63 rooms and is close to the Zona G. BH Quinta (Cra. 5 No. 74-52, tel. 1/742-4908, COP$280,000 d) is in an English Tudor-style house on the busy Carrera Quinta. The most expensive of their hotels is the BH Retiro (Cl. 80 No. 10-11, tel. 1/756-3177, COP$370,000), overlooking a park. It's a five-minute walk to the Centro Andino. Farther north still is BH Parque 93 (Cra. 14 No. 93A-69, tel. 1/743-2820, COP$220,000).

If you'd like to be in the middle of the action in the Zona Rosa, a few comfortable options are around or below the US$150 per night range. Near the Atlantis Plaza shopping mall is the GHL Hotel Hamilton (Cra. 14 No. 81-20, tel. 1/621-5455, www.ghlhoteles.com, COP$290,000 d) of the GHL hotel chain. Cool (84 DC (Cl. 84 No. 9-67,

tel. 1/487-0909, www.84dc.com.co, COP$248,000 d) blends in well in this upscale neighborhood. It has 24 spacious, modern rooms. Guests have some privileges at the nearby Bodytech gym.

B3 (Cra. 15 No. 88-36, tel. 1/593-4490, www.hotelesb3.com, COP$200,000 d) is one of the most striking hotels in town, due to its wonderful living facade of plants. The lobby area is a lively place in the early evening, when guests munch on tapas and sip cocktails at the bar.

Spanish midrange hotel chain (NH Bogotá 93 (Cl. 93 No. 12-41, tel. 1/589-7744, COP$240,000) is an unpretentious entry in Bogotá. It offers 137 smart rooms, a nice rooftop terrace, and a small gym.

Finally, the Hilton (Cra. 7 No. 72-41, tel. 1/600-6100, www.hilton.com, COP$250,000 d) is back in Bogotá, after having abandoned its location downtown during harsher times. This time the Hilton is in a slick black high-rise on the Séptima near Calle 72. If you book early enough, you can get a good deal on rooms.

Although it's right next door to Andrés D.C. and the rest of the Zona Rosa revelry, you'd never know it in your quiet, comfortable room at the Bohème Royal (Cl. 82 No. 12-35, tel. 1/618-0168, www.hotelesroyal.com, COP$310,000 d). You can use the gym at its partner hotel, the Andino Royal on Calle 85. Stately Hotel Morrison (Cl. 84 Bis No. 13-54, tel. 1/622-3111, www.morrisonhotel.com, COP$300,000) overlooks a nicely manicured park in the Zona Rosa. It offers spacious rooms and has a "New York style" restaurant. Guests enjoy privileges at the Spinning Center gym across the street. You may want to avoid rooms on the south side of the hotel, where you might feel the pulsating beats from nearby discos.

At B.O.G. (Cra. 11 No. 86-74, tel. 1/639-9999, www.boghotel.com, COP$420,000 d), every detail of the hotel has been thought out. An extraordinary giant photograph of an emerald in the gym area downstairs will inspire you to buy one. The most widely heralded chef in Colombia, Leonor Espinosa, has a nouvelle Colombian cuisine restaurant, and the rooftop pool is luxurious. Just a few blocks away, ◖ Cité (Cra. 15 No. 88-10, tel. 1/646-7777, www.citehotel.com, COP$400,000 d) may lack some of the finer touches of B.O.G., but its location right on the El Virrey park could not be better. The terrace of the restaurant is a popular place for Sunday brunch. They have a rooftop pool and provide bikes for guests to use on the Ciclovía, which passes by in front every Sunday and holiday.

Estelar (Cl. 93 No. 11-19, tel. 1/511-1555, www.hotelesestelar.com, COP$430,000 d) has a fabulous rooftop bar and pool, and you will be sure to get a good night's sleep thanks in part to the soundproof windows. It's close to the Parque de la 93. The discreet Hotel Portón Bogotá (Cl. 84 No. 7-55, tel. 1/616-6611, www.

hotelportonbogota.com.co, COP$400,000 d) prides itself on its tight security, making it a favorite of visiting diplomats. It has an elegant old-school feel, especially in the restaurant and lounge area, where they light the three fireplaces every evening at 7. Portón guests have unlimited access to the very close Bodytech gym.

If you have real money to burn, try the JW Marriott Hotel Bogotá (Cl. 73 No. 8-60, tel. 1/481-6000, www.marriott.com/bogjw, COP$600,000 d). The bar at this 245-room hotel can make more than 70 types of martinis—enough said. Of course, you don't have to shell out 600,000 pesos to saddle up at the bar and sip one of those martinis.

Food

Bogotá is the best city in the country when it comes to dining, with more than its fair share of excellent restaurants. Unfortunately many of these places charge Manhattan prices.

A 10 percent tip is usually included in the price, but it is a requirement for the server to ask you if you'd like the *servicio incluido.* You can say no, but that would be considered harsh. If you are truly impressed with the service, you can always leave a little additional on the table.

The Bogotá dish par excellence is *ajiaco.* This is a hearty potato and chicken soup, seasoned with the secret herb *guascas.* (Oops—there goes the secret.) On some dreary days, there can be nothing better. Heated debate can arise about what else to include in the soup. A small piece of corn on the cob usually goes in, as does a dollop of cream, but capers and avocado slices are controversial additions.

Reservations are helpful on weekend evenings, especially in the Zona G. Restaurant staff will be more than happy to order a cab for you by phone. That is a very good idea, especially at night.

Tap water in Bogotá—*de la llave*—is perfectly fine and good tasting. Besides, if you ever order a

fresh lemonade or fruit juice, you're getting *agua de Bogotá* anyhow.

LA CANDELARIA
Cafés, Bakeries, and Quick Bites

Here in coffee country, there is no shortage of tucked away cafés where you can sip a *tinto,* but if you want something more, it's best to stick to the pros. That means Juan Valdez Café (Centro Cultural Gabriel García Márquez) and Oma (Museo Arqueológico). These chains are all over Bogotá and indeed Colombia, and have a strong following. Their success is one reason perhaps that Starbucks has not yet ventured into Colombia.

If you'd like to stay away from the chains, check out the ◖ Café de la Peña/Pastelería Francesa (Cra. 3 No. 9-66, tel. 1/336-7488, www.cafepasteleria.com, 8am-8pm Mon.-Sat., 9am-6pm Sun.). This bakery/café is where locals pick up their daily baguette. They serve quiches and light lunches with a few Colombian touches as well. Inside it has a quiet, homey feeling.

The classic place for a *tamal* and a hot chocolate, the Puerta Falsa (Cl. 11 No. 6-50, tel.

1/286-5091, 7am-10pm daily) claims to be one of the oldest operating restaurants in Bogotá, having opened in 1816.

Colombian and Fusion

Capital Cocina y Café (Cl. 10 No. 2-99, tel. 1/342-0426, 9:30am-9pm Mon.-Fri., 2pm-9pm Sat., COP$17,000) is your hip little spot on the corner. Hearty lunches are reasonably priced, and the restaurant is vegetarian-friendly. Breakfast is served until noon (just on weekdays), and it's a cozy place for a nightcap. Using Andean ingredients, such as healthy quinoa, one block over is the tiny ▐ Quinoa y Amaranto (Cl. 11 No. 2-95, tel. 1/565-9982, 8am-4pm Mon., 8am-9pm Tues.-Fri., 8am-5pm Sat.), a warm little place that is a haven for vegetarians downtown. With lunches for around COP$11,000 it's an herbivore bang for your buck.

An always popular Colombian seafood joint specializing in fried fish and *cazuelas* (seafood stews) is Pescadero la Subienda (Cra. 6 No. 10-27, tel. 1/284-9816, noon-6pm Mon.-Sat., COP$20,000). El Olivar (Cra. 6 No. 10-40, tel. 1/283-2847, 7:30am-5pm Mon.-Thurs., 7:30am-10pm Fri., 11am-4pm Sat., COP$25,000), across the street, is a more upscale fusion place—and the prices reflect that. Popular at lunchtime with bureaucrats, it serves hearty soups, such as *cazuelas* based in coconut milk, and also Mediterranean cuisine. Finally, María Tomasa Caribbean Cuisine (Cra. 6 No. 10-82, tel. 1/744-9097, 9am-4:30pm Mon.-Sat., COP$25,000) is a cheerful place with a Costeño feel. Seafood dishes abound, but there are also the customary *arepa de huevo* (egg fried in corn meal) and juices that you can only get on the coast—like *níspero* (sapodilla) juice.

International

La Manzana (Cl. 11 No. 4-93, tel. 1/284-5335, 9am-7pm Mon. and Wed.-Sat., 10am-5pm Sun.) is inside the Banco de la República art complex. It's a quiet environment, overlooking a modern fountain and magnolia trees in the courtyard between the museums. This restaurant specializes in Mediterranean cuisine and pastas. They have some pretty good desserts, too.

If mushrooms are your thing, head to Merlin Café Galería Restaurante (Cra. 2 No. 12-84, tel. 1/284-9707, noon-1am Mon.-Sat., COP$20,000). They promise the best mushrooms in Bogotá. It's a funky place. Just across the way is candlelit El Gato Gris (Cra. 1 No. 13-12, tel. 1/342-1716, www. gatogris.com, 9am-midnight Mon.-Thurs., 9am-3am Fri.-Sat.). The menu has a wide range of fare, including steaks and pastas, and they are proud of their crêpes as well. Both of these are close to the Chorro de Quevedo.

Two classy international cuisine restaurants have been a part of the Candelaria scene for many years now—meaning they are doing something right. Bonaparte (Cra. 8 No. 11-19, tel. 1/283-8788, noon-4:30pm Mon.-Sat., COP$30,000) is an authentic French bistro. It's known for its crêpes as well as heartier dishes such as beef Roquefort. Bonaparte remains popular with gossiping politicians and court justices. Mi Viejo (Cl. 11 No. 5-41, tel. 1/566-6128, noon-5pm Mon.-Sun., COP$30,000) was the first Argentinian restaurant in La Candelaria, and it has a loyal following. Paradise for beef-eaters, this friendly spot has, as would be expected, an extensive Argentinian wine selection.

Cajun food is the thing at La Condesa Irina Lazaar (Cra. 6 No. 10-19, tel. 1/283-1573, lunch Mon.-Sat., COP$35,000). This American-run spot is very easy to miss, but if you are in the mood for pork chops or perhaps crab cakes, this is the place. There are only six tables, so it is best to reserve in advance. If you persuade him, the friendly owner might consider opening the restaurant for you for dinner.

Near loads of backpacker hostels, the Crazy Mongolian (Cl. 12D No. 3-77, 12:30pm-9:30pm Mon.-Sat., COP$12,000) lets you choose the ingredients in generous portions of Mongolian barbecue.

The food at the Mirador restaurant (Cl. 10 No. 5-22, tel. 1/336-2066, noon-10 pm daily, COP$35,000) on the top of the Hotel de la Ópera may get mixed reviews, but the views? Above the red roofs and church steeples of La Candelaria, they are incredible.

AVENIDA JIMÉNEZ
Cafés, Bakeries, and Snacks

For a sandwich or coffee on the go check out tiny La Jamonería Sandwich Gourmet (Cl. 12C No. 6A-36, tel. 1/283-0361, 7am-6pm Mon.-Fri., 7am-2pm Sat.). If you're in one of those moods, you can order a "Cheese Lonely" sandwich for about COP$7,000.

Brush shoulders with the locals at La Gran Parilla Santa Fe (Av. Jiménez No. 5-65, tel. 1/334-4745, 11:30am-5:30pm Mon.-Sat., COP$15,000), a no-surprises and budget-friendly Colombian restaurant downtown. They do the *comida típica* (Colombian fare) thing specializing in grilled meats. Pastelería La Florida (Cra. 7 No. 21-46, 8:30am-9pm daily, COP$10,000) is a Cachaco institution, sort of a Colombian greasy spoon diner.

Colombian and Fusion

For a hearty meal of *mamona* (grilled meat), run, don't walk, to 🄲 Capachos Asadero (Cl. 18 No. 4-68, tel. 1/243-4607, www.asaderocapachos.com, 11:30am-3:30pm Tues.-Thurs., 11:30am-5pm Fri.-Sun.), an authentic *llanero* (cowboy) restaurant. For under COP$20,000 you get a healthy portion of grilled meat tenderly cooked for several hours, fried yucca, and a *maduro* (fried plaintain). Goes down well with a beer. On weekends they have live music and dance performances. It's open every day at lunch.

For a taste of the Colombian Pacific, you can't beat the seafood lunch places on Carrera 4 at Calle 20. There are several of them, all serving about the same thing. Try Sabores del Mar (corner of Cl. 20 and Cra. 4, lunch Mon.-Sat., COP$15,000) or Sabores del Pacífico (Cr. 4 No. 20-29, lunch Mon.-Sat, COP$15,000). If you're looking for cheap fried fish or other typical dishes in a place oozing with character, try the Mercado de las Nieves (Cl. 19 No. 8-62, no phone, lunch Mon.-Sat., COP$12,000). The passage that connects Calle 19

with Calle 20 is filled with mom-and-pop restaurants serving mostly fish dishes. (A sign marks the place as Pasaje La Macarena, but few call it that.)

Is it time for a chain? You can't beat always-reliable 🄲 Crepes & Waffles (Av. Jiménez No. 4-55, tel. 1/676-7600, www.crepesywaffles.com.co, noon-8:30pm Mon.-Sat., noon-5pm Sun.), found all over Colombia. Fill up on a *crêpe de sal* (savory crêpe) for around COP$15,000, but save room for the scrumptious deserts (such as a mini-waffle with Nutella and vanilla ice cream). Also, if you have been searching the world over for a crêpe with tofu in it, the crêpe Gandhi awaits. This particular location is in the easy-on-the-eyes Monserrate building on the Eje Ambiental. Other popular locations are on the Zona T, Parque de la 93, and at the airport, where you can get a healthy breakfast before that morning flight.

CENTRO INTERNACIONAL
Cafés and Snacks

Andante Ma Non Troppo (Cra. 5 No. 15-21, tel. 1/341-7658, COP$12,000) is a long-running café that also serves breakfast, sandwiches, and salads.

Colombian and Fusion

In the Centro Tequendama, a popular spot for Cali food is Fulanitos (Cra. 13 No. 27-00, Local 101, tel. 1/281-7913, noon-5pm Mon.-Fri, COP$15,000). Another inviting place with a set lunch menu of Colombian favorites is Ruta (Cl. 37 No. 13A-26, tel. 1/751-9239, noon-10pm Mon.-Sat., COP$12,000). At Los Cauchos (Cl. 26B No. 3A-20, tel. 1/243-4059, noon-10pm Mon.-Sat., COP$25,000), preparing excellent Colombian food is a family affair. They have been around in the Macarena since 1976. Check out their plate of the day: Monday it's *ajiaco* (chicken and potato soup) and on Friday it's *puchero*, a hearty plate of chicken, pork, beef, potatoes, yuca, and corn in a tomato-onion sauce.

Leo Cocina y Cava (Cl. 27B No. 6-75, tel. 1/286-7091, noon-midnight Mon.-Sat., COP$45,000), by internationally acclaimed chef Leonora Espinosa, has been featured by *Condé Nast* magazine as one of the tops—in the world. Her empire has expanded northward with her new sleek and savvy restaurant, La Leo (Cra. 11 No. 86-74 at the B.O.G. hotel, tel. 1/639-9999, 6am-10am, noon-3pm, and 7pm-11:30pm Mon.-Sat., COP$40,000), which some say is more style than substance.

International

The Macarena is a veritable United Nations of cuisine. On a quiet street behind the Museo Nacional, Donostia (Cl. 29 Bis No. 5-84, tel. 1/287-3943, noon-4pm Mon., noon-4 and 7pm-11pm Tues.-Sat., COP$30,000) is a swanky place for Spanish-Colombian cuisine. You'll want to linger on the colorful sofas. Alô Brasil (Cra. 4 No. 26B-88, tel. 1/337-6015, noon-3pm and 6-10pm Tues.-Wed., noon-3pm and 6pm-midnight Thurs.-Fri., noon-midnight Sat., 1pm-5pm Sun., COP$22,000) serves the famous *feijoada brasileira,* a stew of beans with beef and pork. The ladies at Agave Azul (Cra. 3A No. 26B-52, tel. 1/560-2702, www.restauranteaga-veazul.blogspot.com, 1pm-10pm Sat., noon-3pm Sun., COP$70,000 set menu) have a passion for Mexican food. Tequila is an important part of the equation at this creative place—you were warned. Reservations are necessary.

In the Parque Bavaria the Mexican place San Lorenzo (Cra. 13 No. 28A-21, tel. 1/288-8731, noon-4pm Mon.-Fri., COP$23,000) packs in the banking crowd at lunchtime on the fourth floor of the old Bavaria brewery.

CHAPINERO

Cafés and Snacks

Pan de Nobles (Cra. 9 No. 60-82, tel. 1/606-7262, 7am-8pm Mon.-Sat., 9am-6pm Sun., COP$10,000) started out as a whole-wheat bread bakery. Today it has expanded into a healthy and vegetarian empire. There is a sit-down restaurant upstairs with a set menu. Downstairs on the corner is a "vegetarian express" popular with university students, who chow down on veggie burgers between classes. And the bakery still sells unusual breads, such as feijoa bread and soy arepas (cornmeal cakes).

A typical bakery/café that has packed them in for breakfast and lunchtime since 1943 is San Marcos (Cra. 13 No. 40-36, 6am-8:30pm Mon.-Sat., 7:30am-7pm Sun.). They specialize in lasagnas and pastas.

Colombian

It is hard to find a seat, especially on the terrace, at Canela y Candil (Cra. 8 No. 56-32, tel. 1/479-3245, lunch Mon.-Fri., COP$12,000). Las Margaritas (Cl. 62 No. 7-77, tel. 1/249-9468, noon-4:30pm Mon.-Fri., 8am-6:30pm Sat.-Sun.) has been around for over a century. Try the *puchero,* a meaty stew, on Thursday. The *ajiaco* (chicken and potato soup) is also good. For the best of original coastal cuisine, try friendly MiniMal (Cra. 4A No. 57-52, tel. 1/347-5464, www.mini-mal.org, 12:30pm-10pm Mon.-Wed., 12:30pm-11pm Thurs.-Sat., COP$25,000). The stingray *cazuela* (stew) is one of the more exotic items on the menu. There's also a funky gift shop where you can get one-of-a-kind, 100 percent Colombian handicrafts.

International

Hipster-ish Salvo Patria (Cra. 54 No. 4A-13, tel. 1/702-6367, noon-10pm Mon.-Sat., COP$22,000) is a happening place. There's a variety of interesting appetizers, sandwiches, meaty main courses, and vegetarian options. You'll be tempted to try a carafe of gin *lulada* (a drink made with the juice of a *lulo,* a type of orange).

To go old school in Chapinero Alto, there are two options. First, Giuseppe Verdi (Cl. 58 No. 5-35, tel. 1/211-5508, noon-11pm Mon.-Sat., noon-9pm Sun., COP$20,000) has been around forever, serving typical Italian dishes. They have added a small terrace café for more informal meals or a glass of wine. La Poularde (Cra. 4 No. 54-56, tel. 1/249-6156, noon-3pm and 7pm-11pm Mon.-Sat., 12:30pm-4pm Sun., COP$25,000) serves very traditional French dishes, such as escargot and crêpes suzette. There's a 60 percent chance of Edith Piaf songs being played while you're here.

NORTHERN BOGOTÁ
Cafés and Quick Bites

When it comes to *onces* (Colombian tea time), Myriam Camhi (Cl. 81 No. 8-08, tel. 1/345-1819, 7am-8pm Mon.-Sun.) takes the cake. Just take a look at the decadent desserts on display. The Napoleon de Arequipe and chocolate flan are favorites. While it is known for sweet indulgence, the extensive lunch menu is also nice, with many lighter dishes such as wraps and a pretty good salad bar. On Fridays Myriam serves *ajiaco* (chicken and potato soup). With a more local feel, Brot Café (Cl. 81 No. 7-93, tel. 1/347-6916, 7:30am-7pm daily) has a fiercely loyal following for breakfast and during afternoon *onces*. They are famous for their freshly baked chocolate baguettes. It's also open for lunch. Surrounded by green on their terrace it's easy to forget the chaos of the city.

Siuka (Cl. 79A No. 8-82, tel. 1/248-3765, 9am-7pm Mon.-Sat., 11am-5pm Sun.) has got it all. Well, according to its name at least. *Siuka* means "everything" in Chibcha, the language of the Muiscas. It's hard to find any fault at all with this airy, friendly, and minimalist newcomer. Suika adjoins the good Los Sánduches de Sr. Ostia high-class sandwich joint (Cl. 79A No. 8-82, tel. 1/248-3311). Instead of french fries, you can get spicy carrots! (It's by the same people as Donostia downtown.)

Nick's (Cra. 9 No. 79A-28, tel. 1/321-4108, 11am-10pm Mon.-Sat.) is a quaint place specializing in sandwiches that is popular with hipsters and advertising types. If you arrive on bike, Nick will give you a discount. Doña Dicha (Cra. 11 No. 78-78, tel. 1/629-7452, 10am-7pm Mon.-Sat.) bakes delicious bread and is a nice place for a cappuccino (always served with a spoon dipped in chocolate). Best to go there during non-rush hour, as the traffic on the Carrera 11 might spoil the mood.

Brown (Calle 77A No. 12-26, tel. 1/248-0409, www.brownesunareposteria.com, 11am-6pm Mon.-Fri., 11am-4pm Sat.) is cute as a button and has a light lunch menu (half a sandwich, soup, salad, and drink for COP$16,500) and pretty good brownies. It's a nice place to get stuck during the rain. Remember to request your coffee to be strong if that's the way you like it.

Diletto Café (Cra. 9 No. 80-45, tel. 1/317-7383, 7:30am-8:30pm Mon.-Fri., 9am-8pm Sat., 11am-7pm Sun.) often seems to host caffeinated business meetings—and they also can fry eggs. For under COP$10,000 you can have scrambled eggs, a croissant, and a cappuccino for breakfast. Pan Pa' Ya (Cl. 82 No. 8-85, www.panpaya.com.co, 7am-9pm daily) is an inexpensive bakery that everyone loves. There are many other locations, even in Weston, Florida! Plan your visit strategically: *Almojabanas* (cheese rolls) come out of the oven at 8:30am and 6:30pm; *palitos de queso* (cheese sticks) at 9:30am and 4:30pm.

Colombian

At Fulanitos 81 (Cl. 81 No. 10-56, tel. 1/622-2175, lunch daily, COP$20,000) there is always a line at lunchtime. This is Cali cuisine at its best. Try the *chuletas de cerdo* (pork chops) or *sancocho* (soup), and have a refreshing *lulada* (a drink made with the juice of a *lulo*, a type of orange), of course.

If you want a good introduction to Colombian delicacies in an elegant atmosphere that doesn't feel like the Carnaval de Barranquilla, the Casa Club Colombia (Cl. 82 No. 9-11, tel. 1/744-9077, 8am-1am, COP$25,000) is an excellent choice. In a lovely house where the fireplace is always lit, *bandeja paisa* (dish of beans, various meats, yuca, and potatoes) and all your favorites from all corners of the country are on the menu.

Andrés Carne de Res is the required stop for all visitors to Colombia. It's sort of like a shrine, but one where you can have mojitos, *patacones* (fried plantains), and a menu full of other typical Colombian dishes. This is one of the first places around that embraced Colombian culture and cuisine with gusto, convinced that it is something to be proud of. And it has worked. The food is good and the atmosphere fantastic. The original, and to many, the best Andrés (Cl. 3 No. 11A-56, tel. 1/863-7880, noon-3am Thurs.-Sat., noon-11pm Sun., COP$30,000) is in Chía, about 45 minutes away. This house seems to go on forever, and on weekend nights the slide from dinner to rumba is a slow but definitive one. Andrés D.C. (tel. 1/863-7880, noon-midnight Sun.-Wed., noon-3am Thurs.-Sat., COP$35,000) is for an urban Andrés experience—for you and about 1,199 others. Look for the windmills next to the El Retiro mall. (La Plaza de Andrés is in the mall itself (8am-10pm daily, COP$25,000). The colorful Plaza is more reasonably priced and is not the full-on rumba experience, although it does have its personality.

Welcome to Santa Marta—in Bogotá, that is. The (Gaira Cumbia Café (Cra. 13 No. 96-11A, tel. 1/746-2696, www.gairacafe.com, 9am-10pm Mon.-Wed., 9am-2am Thurs., 9am-3am Fri.-Sat., 9am-6pm Sun., COP$25,000) specializes in Caribbean cuisine. This is a special place, a tribute to music and family. It is run by Guillermo Vives and his mom. Guillo, as he is known, is a talented musician, and is the brother of Carlos Vives, the multiple Grammy Award-winning *vallenato* singer. The food is quite good, and it is popular at lunchtime. At night, Guillo and other musicians regularly perform, to the delight of the whiskey-drinking crowd. On weekends they have special activities for children in the morning. Some just go for the rumba on weekend nights, for which there is a cover.

International

Bagatelle (Cl. 82 No. 9-09, tel. 1/621-2614, 7am-10pm Mon.-Sat., 8am-5pm Sun., COP$20,000) is a long-standing French pâtisserie and restaurant. Their terrace, under the trees, is a nice place for lunch or to sip on a café au lait and nibble at a delicious bread pudding.

French restaurant Criterión (Cl. 69A No. 5-75, tel. 1/310-1377, noon-4pm and 7pm-11pm Mon.-Sat., 9am-1pm and 7pm-11pm Sun., COP$40,000) is the standard bearer when it comes to haute cuisine in Bogotá. It is the creation of the Rausch brothers, who are among the top chefs in Bogotá.

Harry's Bakery (Cra. 6 No. 69A-24, tel. 1/321-3940, noon-11pm Mon.-Sat., noon-6pm Sun.,

COP$20,000) is headed by another highly regarded chef, Harry Sassón. It serves sandwiches, burgers, popcorn shrimp, and other diner fare. Harry's mom is in charge of the decadent desserts.

Classy Astrid & Gaston (Cra. 7 No. 67-64, tel. 1/211-1400, www.astridygastonbogota.com, 12:30pm-3:30pm and 7:30pm-11:30pm Mon.-Sat., bar open until 3am Fri.-Sat., COP$35,000), direct from Lima, and stylish Rafael (Cl. 70 No. 4-65, tel. 1/255-4138, 12:30pm-3pm and 7:30pm-11pm Mon.-Sat., COP$30,000) are rivals for the top Peruvian food in town. At Astrid, try an only-in-Colombia coca pisco sour.

The little block of restaurants on Carrera 13 between Calles 85 and 86 has some great options. The vast menu of generous designer burgers at (Agadón Burger Bar (Cra. 13 No. 85-75, tel. 1/255-4138, noon-10pm Mon.-Wed., noon-midnight Thurs.-Sat., noon-4:30pm Sun., COP$20,000) will leave you satisfied. It's run by a pair of Israelis, and they even have a couple of vegetarian burgers on the menu. Casa (Cra. 13 No. 85-24, tel. 1/236-3755, noon-midnight daily, COP$22,000), in a cozy house with fireplaces and cool artwork on the walls, serves food meant to be shared. You're surrounded by *palma bobas* and other tropical plants in their patio. Across the street is elegant La Brasserie (Cra. 13 No. 85-35, tel. 1/257-6402, noon-midnight Mon.-Sat., noon-6pm Sun., COP$32,000). Oh, yes, and the Clintons have dined here.

Opa (Cra. 14 No. 90-80, tel. 1/218-9682, noon-8pm daily, COP$12,000) is a cheap and good gyros joint popular with the work crowd on dull Calle 90. Gyros y Kebabs (Cra. 13 No. 82-28, tel. 1/635-9324, noon-11pm daily, COP$15,000) does standard Lebanese food very well. It's cozy to sit by the bread oven and watch the bread guy slide pita bread in and back out, piping hot. Yes, they have an afternoon happy hour.

In Usaquén try Abasto (Cra. 6 No. 119B-52, tel. 1/215-1286, http://abasto.com.co, 7am-10pm Mon.-Thurs., 7am-11pm Fri., 9am-10:30pm Sat., 9am-5pm Sun., COP$22,000), where they use only the freshest and often organic ingredients.

Asian

Having had just a tiny Asian immigration, unlike Peru, Panama, and Brazil, Colombia doesn't have dazzling Asian cuisine, but you'll probably be pleasantly surprised at the offer in Bogotá. The pan-Asian cuisine chain ◖ Wok (Quinta Camacho, Cra. 9 No. 69A-63, tel. 1/212-0167, www.wok.com.co, noon-11pm Mon.-Sat., noon-8pm Sun., COP$23,000) is hard to beat. A second location is in the Museo Nacional (Cra. 6 Bis No. 29-07, tel. 1/287-3194). The menu is astoundingly extensive, inventive, and fresh. Hearty fish soups and curries based in coconut milk will warm you up, and there are numerous vegetarian dishes, such as a Vietnamese-inspired grilled tofu sandwich. The quality of their sushi is also good. Wok is an environmentally and socially responsible company, working with family farmers and fishers in small communities throughout Colombia. Don't let the fact that it is a chain dissuade you.

Excellent service awaits at sleek Watakushi (Cra. 12 No. 83-17, tel. 1/744-9097, noon-3pm and 6pm-11pm Mon.-Thurs., noon-11pm Fri.-Sat., noon-5pm Sun., COP$35,000), one of the many restaurants operated by local restaurant wizard Leo Katz. It is on the Zona T. Sushi Gozen (Cl. 94 No. 14-11, tel. 1/257-0282, noon-3pm and 6:30pm-midnight Mon.-Fri., noon-midnight Sat., COP$25,000) is a Colombian-Japanese restaurant popular with Japanese business people (a good sign) that has much more than just sushi. Finally, Arigato (Cl. 76 No. 12-22, tel. 1/248-0764, 11am-9pm Mon.-Sat., COP$20,000) is a family-run Japanese restaurant. The fresh fish is flown in regularly from the Pacific Coast.

There are few Indian restaurants in Bogotá, but of those, Flor de Loto (Cl. 90 No. 17-31, tel. 1/617-0142, noon-3 p.m. and 6pm-9pm Mon.-Sat., COP$24,000) is probably the best. The head chef is originally from the Punjab. The restaurant surrounds a peaceful garden. It's cash-only here.

Italian

Italian restaurants are in abundance in Bogotá. At ◖ La Divina Comedia (Cl. 71 No. 5-93, tel. 1/317-6987, noon-4pm and 7pm-11pm Mon.-Sat., COP$25,000) go for the divine *tortellata* (a mix of stuffed pastas). At unpretentious Trattoría San Giorgio (Cl. 81 No. 8-81, tel. 1/212-3962, noon-10:30pm Mon.-Sat., noon-6pm Sun., COP$22,000), Italian regulars are often found sipping wine and enjoying a multi-course meal. ◖ DiLucca (Cra.13 No. 85-32, tel. 1/257-4269, noon-midnight daily, COP$25,000) is consistently good, with both pastas and pizzas, and they deliver. The atmosphere is rather lively inside.

◖ Julia (Cra. 5 No. 69A-19, tel. 1/348-2835, noon-11pm daily, COP$25,000) serves the best pizza in town. Theirs is the irregular-shaped and paper-thin Roman crust. They also have a couple of non-cheese pizzas, which is unusual for Bogotá. It is astounding to see what the chefs manage to come up with in such a tiny—and infernally hot—kitchen. As no reservations are accepted in this tiny restaurant, it's best to get there on the early side. Second best pizza in town? That would be Archie's (Cl. 82 No. 13-07, tel. 1/610-9162, www.archiespizza.com, breakfast to late night daily, COP$22,000). This chain is all over Bogotá and in many cities countrywide. Archie's delivers.

Information and Services

VISITOR INFORMATION

For information on all things Bogotá, go to the Punto de Información Turística (PIT). In La Candelaria there is a PIT on the southwest corner of the Plaza de Bolívar (tel. 1/283-7115, daily). Other locations include the Quiosco de la Luz in the Parque de la Independencia (Cra. 7 at Cl. 26, tel. 1/284-2664, 9am-5pm Mon.-Sat., 10am-4pm Sun.), both airport terminals, both main and south bus terminals, and in the north at the Centro Comercial Granahorrar on Calle 72. The attendants will bend over backwards to help you out any way they can, providing maps and tips.

TELEPHONES

The telephone code for Bogotá and many surrounding towns is 1. From abroad, dial 57 for Colombia, then 1 for Bogotá, followed by the 7-digit number. To call a cell phone from a landline, first dial 03 and then the 10-digit number. To do the reverse, call 03-1 (the 1 for Bogotá). Prepaid cell phones or SIM cards can be purchased at any Claro or Movistar store. When in the city, there is no need to dial the 1 before the landline number.

Emergency Numbers

For emergencies, just remember 1-2-3. The single emergency hotline is 123. While some operators may speak English, that is probably unlikely. You should provide the neighborhood you are in and a precise street number.

U.S. citizens who have health, safety, or legal emergencies can contact the U.S. Embassy at 1/275-2000.

POST OFFICES AND COURIER SERVICES

Here are some of the main offices of 4-72, the national post office, in Bogotá: Centro Internacional (Cra. 7 No. 27-54, tel. 1/245-4015), Chapinero (Cl. 67 No. 8-39, tel. 1/248-7810), and Chicó (Car. 15 No. 85-61, tel. 1/621-9508). The office hours are the same at all locations (8am-5pm Mon.-Fri., 9am-1pm Sat.). Private courier services are the way most people send correspondence domestically. Two major companies are Servientrega and Deprisa. Servientrega is in the Centro Internacional (Mailboxes Cra. 13 No. 32-16) and in Chapinero (Mailboxes Cl. 67 No. 7-28). Deprisa is operated by Avianca. There are many offices throughout the city, including in the north at the Centro Comercial Granahorrar (Cl. 73 No. 9-42), near Andino (Cr. 11 No. 81-17), and near the Parque El Virrey (Cra. 15 No. 88-53). Downtown they can be found at Calle 13 No. 7-09. Hours of these offices are typically 8am-5pm Monday-Friday and 9am-1pm Saturday.

INTERNET CAFÉS

Internet cafés are plentiful, especially in La Candelaria area and Chapinero, although you may have some difficulty locating cafés in the wealthier residential neighborhoods of Chicó and Rosales.

NEWSPAPERS AND MAGAZINES

The *City Paper* is a free monthly newspaper in English with information on events, interesting profiles, and essays. It is generally distributed to hotels, restaurants, and cafés during the first two weeks of the month. Two other freebies, *ADN* and *Metro,* both in Spanish, are newspapers that are distributed on street corners in the mornings. Another fun publication is the hip and free bimonthly *Cartel Urbano,* which examines Bogotá cultural life. *GO* is a monthly publication on things going on in the city. *El Tiempo* and *El Espectador* are the two main newspapers in town, and are good sources for information. *Semana* is considered the best news magazine, and is published weekly.

SPANISH LANGUAGE COURSES

The Spanish spoken in Bogotá is considered neutral and clear, compared to accents you may have heard in the Caribbean, Spain, or Argentina. Therefore Bogotá is an excellent place to study Spanish, if you have some time to invest. The best schools are operated by the major universities in town. These include the Universidad Externado (Centro de Español para Extranjeros, CEPEX, Cra. 1A No. 12-53, tel. 1/353-7000 or 1/342-0288, www.uexternado.edu.co/cepex), the Universidad Nacional (Edificio 229, Torre Sur, Primer Nivel, tel. 1/316-5000), and the Universidad Javeriana Centro Latinoamericano (Transv. 4 No. 42-00 Piso 6, tel. 1/320-8320, www.javeriana.edu.co/centrolatino).

MONEY

ATMs are everywhere throughout the city, and this is probably your best option to get Colombian pesos. Transaction fees vary. Some ATMs on the streets are closed at night. Be discreet and cautious when taking out money.

To change money, try New York Money at the Centro Andino mall (tel. 1/616-8946), Atlantis Plaza (tel. 1/530-7432), or at the Centro Comercial Granahorrar shopping center (tel. 1/212-2123). They are open also on Sundays and holidays. Note that you'll need to show your passport to change money.

VISAS AND OFFICIALDOM

If you need to stay beyond the 60 or 90 days allowed to visitors from the United States, Canada, Australia, New Zealand, and most European countries, you will need to go to Migración Colombia (Cl. 100 No. 11B-27, tel. 1/595-4331). It is best to go there a few days before your current visa expires.

HEALTH

Altitude

At 2,580 meters, Bogotá is the third highest capital city in the world (behind La Paz, Bolivia, and Quito, Ecuador). It is common to feel short of breath and fatigued during the first two days at the higher altitude. Other symptoms of altitude sickness include headache and nausea. Take it easy for those first few days in Bogotá and avoid caffeine and alcohol. If you are sensitive to high altitude, see a doctor, who can prescribe medication to mitigate the effects of high altitude, before your trip. If you feel symptoms such as fever or gradual loss of consciousness, see a doctor immediately.

Also, keep in mind that, being so high up, you are also that much closer to the sun. When it is sunny those rays are deceivingly potent.

Hospitals, Clinics, and Pharmacies

Bogotá has excellent physicians and hospitals. Two of the best hospitals are the Fundación Santa Fe (Cl. 119 No. 7-75, www.fsfb.org.co, emergency tel. 1/629-0477, tel. 1/603-0303) and the Clínica del Country (Cra. 16 No. 82-57, tel. 1/530-1350, www.clinicadelcountry.com). The Fundación Shaio (Diag. 110 No. 53-67, emergency tel. 271-4050, tel. 1/624-3211) hospital specializes in cardiology. For sexual and reproductive health matters, Profamilia (Cl. 34 No. 14-52, tel. 1/339-0900, www.profamilia.org.co), a member of the International Planned Parenthood Federation, offers clinical services. It is steps away from the Profamilia TransMilenio station on the Avenida Caracas.

Mom-and-pop pharmacies are all over the city, and sometimes these can be less stringent about requiring physical prescriptions. The Supermarket chain Carulla (www.carulla.com) usually has an in-store pharmacy, and the Venezuelan chain Farmatodo (tel. 1/743-2100, www.farmatodo.com.co) has around 30 stores in Bogotá; some of them are open 24 hours a day.

Dental Services

Dental care is excellent in Bogotá. Americans are known to come to Colombia specifically for dental treatments and surgeries. Marlón Becerra (Cl. 91 No. 15-15, tel. 1/746-1111) has several offices in Bogotá.

LAUNDRY

Wash and dry services that charge by the pound or kilo are plentiful in La Candelaria and in Chapinero. This service is often called *lavandería,* as opposed to dry cleaning (*lavado en seco*). In La Candelaria two such services are: Limpia Seco Sarita (Cra. 3 No. 10-69, tel. 1/233-9980) and Extra-Rápido (Cl. 12 No. 2-62, tel. 1/282-1002). In Chapinero there is Lava Seco (Cra. 9 No. 61-03, tel. 1/255-2582), another Lava Seco (Cl. 66 No. 8-20, tel. 1/249-7072), and Lavandería San Ángel (Cl. 69 No. 11A-47, tel. 1/255-8116). A good dry cleaning service is Classic (Cra. 13A No. 86A-13, tel. 1/622-8759).

Getting There

BY AIR

The Aeropuerto Internacional El Dorado (BOG, Cl. 26 No. 103-09. tel. 1/266-2000, www.elnuevodorado.com) is undergoing a massive expansion. The international terminal will finally be connected with the Puente Aereo (Avianca domestic terminal).

You will need to show your luggage receipts before passing through customs. A customs agent will take one copy of the customs declaration and then you may be required to put both checked and carry-on bags through a scanner. They are mostly looking for weapons, cash, and fruits and vegetables.

There are money exchange offices and ATMs just outside of the customs area.

If you are not being picked up by a hotel shuttle or friend, it is imperative to use the official taxi services available outside the arrivals area.

BY BUS

Bogotá has three bus terminals. These are the Terminal del Sur, the Portal del Norte, and the main bus station, the Terminal de Transportes (Diagonal 23 No. 69-60, tel. 1/423-3630, www.terminaldetransporte.gov.co) in Salitre.

You can catch a bus to just about anywhere at the Terminal de Transportes. The terminal is well organized and clean and is divided into three "modules," each generally corresponding to a different direction: Module 1 is south, Module 2 is east/west, and Module 3 is north.

There are two other modules, 4 and 5, corresponding to long-distance taxi services and to arrivals. All modules are located in the same building. Each module has an information booth at the entrance with an attendant who can point you in the right direction.

The terminal has plenty of fast food restaurants, ATMs, a pharmacy, and a Dunkin' Donuts every 50 meters. You can stow your bags in a locker or check them in a storage area. Wireless Internet is available in some areas of the building, and if not, there are Internet and telephone services. To pass the time, you can win big at the many casinos in the terminal or enjoy some peace at the second-floor chapel.

In the arrivals module, there is a tourist information office (PIT), where the helpful attendants can give you a map of the city and assist you in getting to your hotel. There is also an organized and safe taxi service and plenty of public transportation options available.

During the Christmas and Easter holidays, the bus terminal is a busy place with crowds and packed buses. This is also true on *puentes* (long weekends).

The terminal website is not bad, with a map of the modules, information on bus companies with links to their websites, timetables, and price

TransMilenio bus along Avenida Jiménez

information. Prices listed online are comparable to the prices found at the terminal.

Check prices with a couple of companies, as levels of comfort can vary. Some companies even offer Wi-Fi in their buses, and most show loud, violent movies for your enjoyment.

The Portal del Norte (Autopista Norte with Cl. 174), part of the TransMilenio station of the same name, may be more convenient if you are traveling to nearby destinations. As you exit northbound TransMilenio buses, there are well-marked exits to platforms for different nearby destinations. The area for Zipaquirá (shortened to Zipa on signage) and Chía is at the far left of the platform. Destinations such as Laguna de Guatavita (COP$7,400), Sesquilé (COP$5,500), Suesca (COP$6,000), and Tenjo (COP$3,600) are straight ahead. You pay the bus driver directly for these trips.

Meanwhile, in front of the Éxito supermarket/store on the east side of the Autopista is where buses going a little farther on to places such as Nemocón, Villa de Leyva, Tunja, and Bucaramanga pick up passengers. It is not nearly as organized as at the main terminal, but it all somehow manages to work out. It's best to catch these buses during the daytime.

The Terminal del Sur (Autopista Sur with Cra. 72D) is near the Portal Sur of TransMilenio. This station serves locations in the south of Cundinamarca, such as Tequendama, and farther south to Girardot, Ibagué, Neiva, Popayán, Armenia, Cali, and all the way to Mocoa in Putumayo.

Getting Around

TRANSMILENIO

While it has become the public transport system that Bogotanos seem to love to hate, the red buses of TransMilenio have clearly transformed the city. This dedicated mass transit system began rolling along the Avenida Caracas in 2000 near the end of the Enrique Peñalosa mayorship. Today, the Caracas line moves more passengers than most subway lines. One of the great characteristics of the TransMilenio project is that, in addition to buses, a requirement has been made to create wide sidewalks, pedestrian bridges, and bike lanes alongside the bus lines. The system has been lauded internationally and copied by several cities as a very cost effective mass transit system. However, lack of investment in new stations and buses has meant that the buses are overcrowded.

How do you determine which bus to take? It's not that easy at first. The stations are divided into 12 zones. For example, the Museo del Oro is classified as Zona J and Calle 85 is Zona B. The first step may be to figure out the zone you are going to and the zone you are starting out from. Because there are many express lines, or lines that skip certain stations, figuring out the system map may give you a migraine. If you are not up for the challenge, just ask one of the attendants at the station.

You are most likely to use the Caracas line to go north and south, with buses that spur off to the Las Aguas station as a convenient way of getting to Centro Histórico attractions. In the opposite direction, that same line—bound for the Portal del Norte—will get you close to the Zona Rosa (Calle 85). The line that goes along the Avenida 30 stops near the Parque Simón Bolívar, the Estadio El Campín, the Universidad Nacional, and Paloquemao. The new line that goes to the Portal Eldorado stops at the cemeteries (Centro Memoria), the fairgrounds (Corferias), and close to the U.S. Embassy (Gobernación). Unfortunately, TransMilenio is not an option to reach the airport.

The system operates 5am-midnight Monday through Saturday and 6am-11pm on Sunday and holidays. Fares are a little more expensive during rush hours (COP$1,700 as opposed to COP$1,400). Also, Bogotanos are usually in a hurry to get where they're going. So the "local" routes—often called "Ruta Fácil"—may be less crowded. Keep your wallet in your front pocket and watch your things, especially during rush hour.

In 2012, Bogotá began replacing private buses with the city SITP buses (www.sitp.gov.co). SITP buses stop only at designated stops. You must purchase a refillable card to ride, which can be found at numerous locations. This is the best way to travel between La Candelaria and the north.

PRIVATE BUSES

They are intimidating at first, but sometimes private buses are the only way to go. The good (and bad) thing about buses is that, although they are not supposed to, they will stop just about anywhere, even in the middle of the street. In both big buses and *colectivos* (minivans), you pay the driver upon entry. It's best to have small bills and change. Exit buses at the back door. You can use the button to alert the driver to stop. Sometimes buses don't come to a complete stop (especially for young men)—they just slow down. Take precautions when exiting any bus that hasn't stopped completely. Heading downtown from the Zona Rosa or Chapinero areas, look for buses that say Normandía on them.

TAXIS

It's estimated that over a million people take a cab each day in the city. There are around 50,000 taxis (mostly yellow Hyundai vehicles) circulating the streets of Bogotá, so you will rarely have a hard time locating one. However, it's important to always order cabs by phone or the smartphone app Tappsi for safety.

A trip from the Zona Rosa area to La Candelaria costs around COP$15,000. A *taximetro* calculates units, which determine the price. The rates are listed on a *tarjetón* (large card) with the driver's information. That card is always supposed to be visible. There are special surcharges for cab services ordered by phone, for nighttime, and for going to the airport. Taxi drivers do not expect tips, but you can always round up the fare if you'd like. During the end-of-year holidays, drivers may ask for a holiday tip.

WALKING

You get a real feeling for the city—the good, the bad, and the ugly—by walking its streets. All areas from the historic district through to the Centro Internacional and Macarena are accessible on foot, and walking is often the best way to get around. The same is true for upscale shopping and residential areas to the north. All of these areas are safe to walk around, but it's never a good idea to advertise your tourist status with bulky cameras and backpacks. Old, leafy neighborhoods like Teusaquillo-La Soledad are nice to wander around during the daytime as well. The worst thing about walking in the city is dealing with drivers. Generally speaking, they have very little respect for pedestrians or cyclists. Look for stoplights at intersections to help you safely cross streets. Also, note that when traffic lights turn yellow, that means green. Finally, keep in mind that, when there is no traffic, there are apparently also no speed limits.

BIKING

Bogotá has a huge bike path network, one of the most extensive in Latin America. These are called the *ciclorutas*. For those tired of getting stuck in traffic or dealing with buses, biking it to work has become a nice alternative. But you really have to keep your wits about you. Crossing the street can be tricky, as drivers don't hold a lot of respect for bikers, unfortunately. In addition, most bike paths follow alongside busy thoroughfares like the Carrera 11, so, during rush hours especially, you could be inhaling polluted air. It's nicer on weekends or late at night. If in town for just a limited time, you may prefer to make your bike experience a stress-free Ciclovía one (Sundays and holidays), rather than having to deal with the bike paths. A map of the 344-kilometer bike lane network is available at www.movilidadbogota.gov.co. As part of the public spaces along TransMilenio routes there are always *ciclorutas*, such as along Calle 26 (Avenida El Dorado). Another long stretch from downtown to the World Trade Center on Calle 100 goes along the Carrera 11. It's strongly recommended to wear a helmet, and using a bike lock is a good idea.

CAR RENTAL

With more than a million aggressive drivers on the clogged streets of Bogotá, renting a vehicle is a horrible idea for visitors. However, if you are planning to travel to places nearby Bogotá like Villa de Leyva or would like to take your time touring parks or villages, it might be an option. National (Cra. 7 No. 145-71, www.nationalcolombia.com), Avis (Av. 19 No. 123-52 Local 2, tel. 1/629-1722, www.avis.com), and Hertz (Av. Caracas No. 28A-17, tel. 1/327-6700, www.rentacarcolombia.co) have offices in Bogotá. Your driver's license is accepted here in Colombia.

Vicinity of Bogotá

TENJO

The town of Tenjo is charming. If you would like to visit a pueblo in the green pastureland outside of Bogotá, this makes a fine day trip. The plaza is shady and compact with a colonial church on one side. People keep warm wrapped in their heavy woolen *ruanas* (ponchos) as they relax on park benches, and people sell *obleas* (wafers) and *almojabanas* (cheese rolls) to passersby.

Just outside of town are two recommended restaurants: La Granja (Km. 12 Vía Siberia-Tenjo, tel. 1/864-6148, www.lagranjatenjo.com, COP$25,000), which has a petting farm, and nearby Viveros Tirrá (Km. 11 Vía Siberia-Tenjo, cell tel. 312/397-9940,

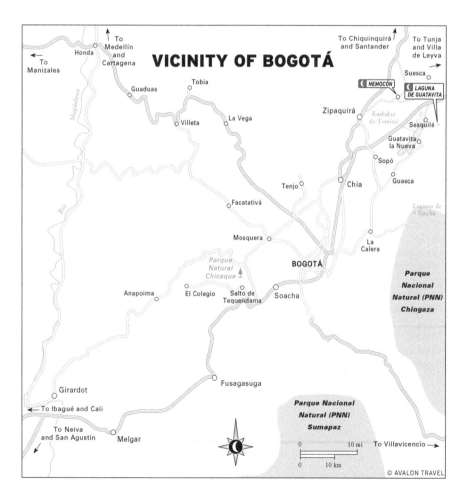

© AVALON TRAVEL

www.restauranteviverostirra.com, COP$25,000). Both of these are popular with families on the weekends.

ZIPAQUIRÁ AND VICINITY

A favorite day trip for visitors to Bogotá is the city of Zipaquirá (pop. 112,000). About an hour's drive from Bogotá, Zipaquirá is known for its Catedral de Sal—a cathedral built in a salt mine. Zipaquirá is named for the Muisca leader of the Bacatá confederation—the Zipa. The Muisca settlement was very close to the mines, and they traded salt for other commodities with other indigenous groups.

The Catedral de Sal (tel. 1/852-3010, www.catedraldesal.gov.co, 9am-5:30pm daily, COP$20,000) is part of the Parque del Sal and the top "Wonders of Colombia" as voted by Colombians. The original cathedral was built by miners in 1951, but due to safety concerns, a new and larger cathedral was built and opened in 1995. The cathedral is indeed an impressive feat of engineering. Tours are obligatory, but you can stray from your group. The tours go past the Stations of the Cross and finally there is a massive cross in the cavernous sanctuary. Masses actually do take place here in the depths on Sundays, and they attract many faithful. Other features include a museum, a rock-climbing wall, and a children's 3-D film, which you could probably skip.

The picturesque main plaza in Zipaquirá, with palm trees rising against a backdrop of green mountains, is always the center of activity in town. Here locals gather to gossip, get their shoes shined, or munch on an *oblea* (wafer) oozing with caramel. Dominating the plaza is a cathedral designed by Friar Domingo de Petrés, who also designed the Bogotá and Santa Fe de Antioquia cathedrals. Construction began in 1805; 111 years later, in 1916, it was completed and dedicated.

On the main road into town from Bogotá, there are several grilled meat-type restaurants, with teenage boys furiously waving red flags to attract customers. A local favorite for a hearty lunch of grilled fish, chicken, or vegetables is Casa Nnova (Cra. 10 at Cl. 3), across from the fancy La Cascada restaurant. A good option for overnight accommodations is Hotel Cacique Real (Cl. 6 No. 2-36, tel. 1/851-0209, www.hotelcaciquereal.com, COP$88,000 d).

Zipaquirá is an easy day trip. On weekends, families and tourists alike take the Turistren from the Usaquén station. Bands play Colombian *papayera* music as you slowly chug through the savannah of Bogotá on this three-hour trip. The train leaves in the morning and returns in the late afternoon, giving you more than enough time to visit the salt mines. You could also (and probably will want to) just take the train one way, returning by bus or taxi back to Bogotá. Otherwise, buses depart the Portal del Norte TransMilenio station every 10 minutes or so, all day long, and the fare is inexpensive. If arriving via TransMilenio, when exiting the bus take a left and you will see signs pointing the way for "Zipa" buses. The attendants can also direct you. You'll pay the bus driver directly. The trip takes about 45 minutes. You can either walk or take a short taxi ride to the Parque del Sal.

Nemocón

With only 10,000 residents, the sleepy pueblo of Nemocón (www.nemocon-cundinamarca.gov.co) is 15 kilometers from Zipaquirá and just 65 kilometers from Bogotá. It is a cute, compact colonial-era town, also home to salt mines, but it does not attract nearly the same number of visitors that Zipaquirá does. That's part of its allure. In pre-Columbian times, this was also a Muisca settlement devoted to salt extraction.

On the plaza, the church is set against a backdrop of eucalyptus-covered hills, obviously some sort of reforestation effort. There is a small salt museum on the corner, and students will be happy to give you a tour in Spanish. About a 10-minute walk toward the hills are the mines (9am-5pm daily, COP$17,000). Tours take about 90 minutes. The beautifully renovated section of the mines that you visit is no longer used for salt extraction. In the depths of the mines you will see all types of stalactites and stalagmites. The pools where salt and water were mixed to pump out the salt are a

© ANDREW DIER

the sleepy pueblo of Nemocón

highlight. The reflection of the illuminated vaults on the surface of the pools, combined with the cool lighting, is amazing. You can take some fun photos inside. Once you get back out into daylight, there are simple restaurants with names like the Venado de Oro (the Golden Deer) on the plaza or La Casa de la Gallina (the Hen House) on Calle 2 (No. 4-24). There's not much in the way of accommodations in Nemocón, but most visitors make it a day trip. Not far from Nemocón is a desert microclimate called the Desierto de Tatacoita. It's a popular mountain-biking area.

LAGUNA DE GUATAVITA AND VICINITY

Laguna de Guatavita

The El Dorado myth, which became an obsession for gold-thirsty Europeans in the New World, is based on a Muisca Indian ritual that took place here in this perfectly round mountain lake.

Following the death of the Muisca *cacique* (chief), a nephew would be chosen to succeed him. The day of the ceremony, the nephew would be sequestered in a cave. Then, stripped naked and covered with mud and gold dust, he would be rowed to the center of the sacred lake with incense and music filling the air. Once there, gold, silver, emeralds, and other tributes were tossed into the cold waters, and the cacique would dive in. Incidentally, the gold used in these ceremonies mostly came from outside Muisca territories. This was an area rich in emeralds, salt, and corn—gold, not so much.

Part of what historians know about the ceremony was confirmed with the finding in 1856 of the miniature golden raft depicting the ceremony. This piece was not found in Guatavita, but rather in a cave close to Bogotá. That raft, of course, is one of the main displays at the Museo del Oro.

From the European perspective, there must have been a profound sense of disappointment once they realized that the "city of gold" just didn't exist. It was the promise of wealth beyond their wildest dreams that had sustained them as they made their arduous trek through the swamps of the muggy Río Magdalena valley, swatting away mosquitoes night

Laguna de Guatavita

after night as they desperately tried to get some rest. When they arrived in Guatavita, they drained the lake, at least three times, to see what could be found at the bottom. A giant cut in the lake can be still seen today.

After years of neglect, today Laguna de Guatavita (9am-4pm Tues.-Sat., COP$13,600) is being given the respect it deserves. An environmental agency maintains the park and, in order to preserve it, has forbidden direct access to the lake. The lake is much better appreciated from above on the well-maintained path along the top of the crater. To reduce the impact on the fragile environment, the path does not go all the way around. On the weekends, you must join a tour group to see the lake. These leave every half hour. Guides are knowledgeable and passionate about their work. English tours are possible, especially for larger groups, but those should be reserved in advance. During the week you can amble along the path at your own pace.

While much of the brick path is flat, there is a fairly steep climb, making it difficult for those with physical limitations. The entire tour takes less than an hour. At the end of the walk, you can walk or hop on a minibus to the entrance of the park. When Monday is a holiday, the park is open Wednesday-Monday.

GETTING THERE

Getting to the Laguna de Guatavita via public transportation is a little tricky, but doable. At the TransMilenio Portal del Norte station, take a bus bound for the town of Sesquilé. On the main square in front of the church you can usually find taxis that will take you to the Laguna de Guatavita and back (one way around COP$25,000). One (and just one) *colectivo* (minivan) by Cootranscovadonga leaves at 8:45am on weekends and holidays for the park, returning at around 4pm, making for a very long day. In addition, several *colectivos* leave all day long from Sesquilé bound for El Hato/Ranchería/El Uval that can drop you off about a two-kilometer hike to the park.

Many visitors opt to hire a driver for the day to make the trip to Guatavita and back. This varies in price and it would be wise to check with a few drivers and bargain. Make sure to specify if there will be additional stops (for a coffee break or for a lakeside lunch). Hotels, hostels and travel agencies in Bogotá can also arrange this trip for you.

Another option is driving. Once you get out of Bogotá, it is fairly stress-free for Colombian standards, as the road is good (mostly four-lane) and with decent signage. Take the Autopista Norte towards Tunja and take the exit to Sesquilé. Past the town a dirt road leads up to the park. If you get lost, locals along the road will help you find your way. You can park right at the park entrance.

An excellent place on the way for a mid-morning coffee and arepa is Carajillo Restaurante (Km. 41).

Nueva Guatavita

The actual town of Guatavita no longer exists. Back in the 1960s, when this kind of thing could be done without cries from environmentalists or community activists, the town was flooded in order to build the Emblase de Tominé, a large reservoir. They moved the town a little bit inland, calling it Nueva Guatavita. All the buildings here are painted white, as if they were built in the colonial period, but the streets are California-wide. There are two small museums by the water. The Museo de Arte Religioso de Guatavita La Antigua (COP$1,000) displays some of the relics from the church salvaged before the great flood. There is a short presentation about the flood and some photos of the submerged town. You used to be able to see the top of an obelisk from the town cemetery, but either a boat ran over it or it just crumbled into the depths. Nearby is a small indigenous culture museum. A few restaurants in town serve fried trout and other local specialties.

Emblase de Tominé

Between Nueva Guatavita and the Laguna de Guatavita alongside the Tominé reservoir are a handful of restaurants, hotels, and marinas.

La Juanita (cell tel. 310/213-5793, felipes-path@gmail.com, www.lajuanitaguatavita.com/place) is wonderfully crunchy-granola, in a quiet place within walking distance of the reservoir and about halfway between the Laguna de Guatavita and Nueva Guatavita. They grow their own vegetables, have yoga classes, and offer pottery making and horseback-riding excursions. You can even walk from there to the Laguna de Guatavita.

Overlooking the water, family-run Los Pinos (Km. 11 Vía Sesquilé-Guatavita, cell tel. 310/777-6631, www.lospinos.com.co, weekends and holidays only) is a fine place for an afternoon lunch after a day at the lake. Grilled fish and barbecued pork ribs are their specialties, although they can accommodate vegetarians. You can rent a Sunfish sailboat for excursions on the water.

Literally next door to the restaurant, the Club Marina de Guatavita (cell tel. 312/592-7468) rents sailboats (Sunfish COP$60,000 per day). You can also rent windsurfing equipment and take classes. You can water-ski for about COP$40,000 for a half-hour trip (including wetsuit). Canoes can be rented for only COP$10,000 per hour. There is also camping available next to the water, which costs COP$25,000. There are five very basic cabins for rent.

PARQUE NACIONAL NATURAL CHINGAZA

The Parque Nacional Natural Chingaza extends over 76,000 hectares (188,000 acres) in Cundinamarca and Meta and makes for an excellent day trip of hiking among armies of *frailejones* plants through the melancholy and misty *páramo* (highland moor). One of the better hikes is a 3.5-hour one that takes you to the Lagunas de Siecha, which include the three mountain lakes: Suramérica, Siecha, and Guasca. Along with Laguna de Guatavita, these were also sacred Muisca lakes.

The park limits the number of visitors, so it is best to request an entry permit in advance. Hire an experienced guide (COP$50,000/day), as trails are often not obvious. The guides are generally very

frailejones at the Parque Nacional Natural Chingaza

knowledgeable and friendly. However, they may not speak English. To arrange a visit, call Parques Nacionales (tel. 1/353-2400, www.parquesnacionales.gov.co) and request permission to visit PNN Chingaza. They will ask you to send the names of the members of your group in an email and confirm the reservation. They will also provide contact information for the local association of guides. You can save a lot of money, and help the local economy, if you do it this way rather than through an organized private tour.

Packing rubber boots is a must, as you will be hiking along really muddy paths. Sneakers just won't do. A light raincoat or windbreaker and sweatshirt are essential, as well as a packed lunch, snacks, and water. The hike to the *lagunas* takes about 3.5 hours.

Other excursions within the Parque Nacional Natural Chingaza can be made from different entry points.

In the town of Guasca you can relax, eat, and stay at the Posada Café La Huerta (cell tel. 315/742-0999, www.cafelahuerta.com). They make great American cornbread. If you decide to stay with them for a weekend, they can arrange your transportation and visit to PNN Chingaza.

Down the road a ways from Posada Café La Huerta is the abandoned colonial-era Capilla de Siecha, a picturesque white chapel in the middle of farmland. It is guarded by many sheep and some tiny dogs, and you can buy a ticket for entrance from an elderly farmer.

From Bogotá, take a bus to Guasca and from there take a *buseta* (minivan) towards Paso Hondo. The *buseta* will leave you at the intersection of the road that leads to the park. It is about a 90-minute walk to the park entrance from there. These leave at 6:30am, 7:30am, and 9:30am and so forth. You should leave Bogotá by around 7am to make the 9:30am *buseta*. Buses to Guasca leave from the Portal del Norte bus terminal as well as from an informal bus pickup area between Calles 72 and 73 at Carrera 14. It may sound iffy, but if you go there, you can ask any taxi or bus driver where to find the right bus.

If you travel with private transportation, it is possible to drive closer to the park, but only if you have a four-wheel-drive vehicle.

SUESCA

It's all about rock climbing in Suesca. On the weekends, Bogotanos converge on this little Cundinamarca town and head to the *rocas*. Most climbing takes place along cliffs just behind the town—some up to 250 meters high—parallel to some old train tracks and the Río Bogotá. It's a beautiful setting, and the fresh smell of eucalyptus trees and mountain mist add to the feeling of the place.

Several outdoors shops in Suesca rent equipment and organize rock-climbing classes and excursions. Explora Suesca (cell tel. 311/249-3491 or 317/516-2414, www.explorasuesca.com) rents out bikes in addition to rock-climbing gear and classes. Monodedo (Cra. 16 No. 82-22, tel. 1/616-3467, cell tel. 316/266-9399, www.mondodo-edo.com) has an office in Bogotá. Expect to pay around COP$60,000 for a three-hour rock-climbing excursion with a guide.

Many folks like making Suesca a camping weekend. The most popular place for this is Campo Base (cell tel. 320/241-9976 or 321/415-3930), right across from the rocks. They've got hot water, a place for cooking, and they rent out tents.

At the other end—way other end—of the spectrum is Casa Lila (cell tel. 320/204-8262 or 300/835-9472, patriciavalenciaturismo@gmail.com, COP$220,000). This luxurious bed-and-breakfast with nine rooms is so cozy, with fireplaces all around and its own restaurant, that it may be hard to leave. It's right next to an old train station at kilometer 3. In between those two is El Hostal Vivac (cell tel. 312/539-5408, www.elvi-vachostal.com, shared room COP$25,000, private room COP$65,000).

After all that rock climbing, it's time for some Thai food. Check out Restaurante Vamonos Pa'l Monte for Phuket vegetables or pad Thai. It's right at the entrance of the *rocas*. The other really popular place is Rica Pizza (cell tel. 312/379-3610), on the main road, also near the entrance to the park. They serve more than pizza.

Buses from Bogotá regularly serve Suesca from the Portal del Norte station. You can also contact one of the tour companies based in Bogotá that specialize in rock climbing, who can arrange for transportation for a day trip.

SOUTH AND WEST OF BOGOTÁ
◖ Parque Natural Chicaque

It's hard to believe that such natural beauty is so close and accessible to Bogotá. You can basically take TransMilenio to this natural, private park and be walking amid the cloud forest within an hour.

Parque Natural Chicaque (tel. 1/368-3114/18, www.chicaque.com) is a little-known and underappreciated gem in Bogotá. This private park offers 18 kilometers of excellent paths that meander through virgin cloud forest. It's more than likely that it is only silence that you hear as you explore the park, save for the occasional bird or rustle of leaves. It's got a pretty good website with detailed information on prices and services (in English as well).

Horseback riding is possible, and you can climb a towering oak tree (and spend the night there for COP$110,000). There are two good restaurants, one at the entrance of the park and one below in the lodge. Rooms at the lodge are very simple, designed for families (one adult COP$86,000 including all meals). There are a few cabins with fireplaces for more privacy (COP$250,000 for two people and all meals), and camping (COP$50,000 including all meals) is also available.

Getting to the park is fairly easy. You can take the TransMilenio to the Portal del Sur station and take a park bus from there. This bus leaves at 8am, 10am, 1:30pm, and 4:30pm. There is a fee of COP$6,000 for this trip. The rendezvous point is the fast food Restaurante Choribroaster (Cra. 72D No. 57J-03). It is near a large Jumbo store.

© ANDREW DIER

vista from the Parque Natural Chicaque

Salto del Tequendama

West of Chicaque, on the road towards Mesitas del Colegio, is the Salto del Tequendama (Tequendama Waterfall). Back in the early part of the 20th century, this was a lovely place to visit, and the falls are certainly dramatic. What was once an elegant hotel overlooks the falls. It has very recently opened its doors once again, this time serving as an exhibition space. The problem with any visit to Tequendama is the horrible stench coming from the Río Bogotá, which you must drive along, into which much of the city's waste is poured. It is a shame.

Parque de Orquideas del Tequendama

The Parque de Orquideas del Tequendama (Km. 19 Vía Bogotá-Mesitas del Colegio, cell tel. 300/464-5960, www.orquideasdeltequendama. com, 10am-5pm Sat.-Sun., COP$7,000) has been described as *"un jardín de los dioses"* ("a garden of the gods"). Within minutes of chilly Salto de Tequendama, you descend toward the Río Magdalena valley and it is suddenly—and violently—hot. At this farm, Omar Chaparro has around 6,000 varieties of orchids on display, including delicate miniature orchids, fragrant orchids, and many orchids that are nearly extinct. You'll see the official orchids of Bogotá and Colombia there, too. A true expert and enthusiast on orchids, Omar has a seed bank with the ultimate goal of propagating orchid species and planting them in their natural habitats throughout Colombia so that they will survive for another generation. Guided tours, unfortunately only in Spanish, are interesting, as Omar and his staff educate guests on the flowers. There is a little open-air restaurant that serves lunch on Sundays, with, of course, colorful views. You can visit during the week if you make a reservation in advance.

Midway between the falls and the orchid farm is the Zoológico Santa Cruz, a zoo in which jaguars native to Colombia are sadly confined to small pens.

Parque de Orquídeas del Tequendama

Public transportation is available from the Portal del Sur bus station to both the Salto del Tequendama and the orchid farm.

Bogotá to Melgar

Heading from Bogotá towards the Río Magdalena valley, you'll pass several *tierra caliente* (hot country) resort towns, such as Anapoima, Girardot, and—just across the border into the Tolima department—Melgar and Carmen de Apicalá. Many wealthy Bogotano families have second homes in this part of Cundinamarca, while Melgar, the "city of swimming pools," caters to a more middle-class clientele. These towns are easily reached by bus from Bogotá.

Several websites (www.fincasenarriendo.com or www.alquilerdefincasenmelgar.net) rent houses in this part of the country. Searching under *alquilar* (to rent), *fincas* (farms), and *casas* (houses) will provide you with several options.

During World War II, Fusagasugá, between Bogotá and Melgar, had an internment facility for Germans, Japanese, and Italians at the Hotel La Sabaneta. Most of the more than 400 people there had moved to Colombia decades prior to the war and were forced to leave their families and stay in the hotel under the watchful eyes of the Colombian police. There is but a faint reminder of the facility, with just a part of the hotel facade still standing.

A landmark just before Melgar that is an obsession of Colombian kids is the Nariz del Diablo (Devil's Nose), a rock formation that juts out along that windy road.

Bogotá to Honda

Guaduas is home to one of the few heroines in the Colombian independence movement, Policarpa (endearingly known as La Pola) Salavarrieta. A thatched roof house, the Casa de la Pola, is now a small museum dedicated to her life and is located just off the main plaza. Near a statue of La Pola, vendors at a small outdoor market sell things like hammocks and goat's milk. The surrounding blocks of the town have several colonial buildings set along cobblestone streets.

Puente Navarro, Honda

A popular place for pastries is Nectar, right on the square, and La Pesebrera Gourmet restaurant, in a colonial house nearby the plaza, is a fun place for a hearty lunch; it doubles as a tourist information center.

There is not much in the way of tourist attractions in this hot country town; however, its plaza is a divine place for a cool beer under the shade of massive ceiba trees. In the town of Villeta, the old two-lane road (through Facatativá) and the newer road (which leads to Calle 80 in Bogotá) meet. Buses from Villeta to Bogotá are frequent and cost around COP$12,500.

In Sasaima, towards Facatativá, is a lovely old country farm/vacation home built by a Swiss architect in the 1940s that has been converted into a hotel/spa. It's called El Refugio (tel. 1/243-3620/25, www.elrefugiohotelspa.com), and a refuge in the lush Colombian countryside it certainly is. Rooms are comfortable and the restaurant serves nice meals. It's a popular place for city slickers to get away from the honking horns of Bogotá.

Honda

The steamy town of Honda, known as the City of Bridges, rests on the banks of the Río Magdalena, almost exactly halfway between Bogotá and Medellín. It was the country's first and most important interior port city. The Río Magdalena has shaped its history, and was the reason for its rise to importance. From the 16th century until the mid-20th century, the Río Magdalena was the main transportation route connecting Bogotá to the Caribbean coast and the rest of the world.

Honda was founded in 1539. As a port, Honda was a place where quinine, coffee, lumber, and slaves were loaded and unloaded along the banks of the river.

From this city of 29 bridges, steamships would ply the route toward the coast. In 1919, the Barranquilla-based SCADTA airlines became the very first airline of the Americas, bringing seaplane service to Honda. The river served as an airstrip. It must have been quite a sight to see these planes on the muddy Magdalena. SCADTA would later become Avianca Airlines.

The steamships and seaplanes no longer make their appearances in Honda today. But if you head down to the river's edge, you can ask a local angler to give you a quick jaunt along the river in his boat. Be sure to walk across the bright yellow Puente Navarro, a pedestrian bridge built by the San Francisco Bridge Company in 1898. Check out the Museo del Río Magdalena (Cl. 10 No. 9-01, tel. 8/251-0129) on the way.

Honda and its sleepy streets makes for a nice stopover en route between Bogotá and Medellín. A popular weekend destination for Bogotanos in need of *tierra caliente* (hot country) relaxation, the town has some good hotel options. For pampering try the Posada Las Trampas (Cra. 10A No. 11-05, tel. 8/251-7415, www.posadalas-trampas.com). For a friendly welcome, stay at the Casa Belle Epoque (Cl. 12 No. 12A-21, tel. 8/251-1176, www.casabelleepoque.com), a moderately priced hotel popular with international travelers.

Tobia

The one and only game in town in Tobia, about 2.5 hours from Bogotá, is adventure sports. Specifically that includes white-water rafting on the Río Negro, ziplines, rock climbing, and horseback riding. The scenery is quite beautiful as you enter town through a valley surrounded by cliffs. The town itself is nothing special.

It will not be hard to find tour companies to help you organize your adventures. Touts are everywhere selling packages. Here are some of the prices: rafting (COP$30,000), horseback riding (COP$30,000), and canopy tours (COP$40,000). EcoAndes (tel. 1/803-1130 or 1/252-6529, www.ecoandes.net) is a good option for a tour operator. Los Tobianos (cell tel. 314/397-0360, www.

lostobianos.com) and Dosis Verde (tel. 1/232-3735 or 1/492-9329, www.dosisverde.com) are others.

The largest of the basic hotels in town is La Gaitana (tel. 1/631-0461, cell tel. 313/466-9092, www.lagaitana.com). On the other side of the river is Hotel San Juanito.

Tobia is easily reached by public transportation, costing around COP$16,000 from the Terminal de Buses. It is also a pretty easy drive if you have your own car. There are some expensive tolls, however.

An excellent stop-off between El Vino and La Vega is La Vara restaurant, overlooking a verdant valley. You can enjoy an arepa (cornmeal cake) and chocolate or a heartier, meatier lunch.

Buses depart all day long for both of these "hot country" destinations. It takes 2.5-3 hours to get there from the Terminal de Transporte.

Boyacá and the Santanderes

Located north of Bogotá, the mountainous departments of Boyacá, Santander, and Norte de Santander (these last two are known collectively as the Santanderes) are rich in history, natural beauty, and outdoor activities. The countryside is dotted with historic colonial towns, including two of the most beautiful and well-preserved in Colombia: Villa de Leyva and Barichara.

© ANDREW DIER

The scenery of the region runs the gamut from the desert landscape near Villa de Leyva to the bucolic rolling hills and pastures of agriculturally rich Boyacá, and from the awe-inspiring Río Chicamocha canyon to the dramatic snow-capped peaks of the Sierra Nevada del Cocuy (Cocuy Range).

Outdoor activities are the draw here, like trekking in the Sierra Nevada del Cocuy and white-water rafting, caving, and paragliding near San Gil. Except for the frenetic and modern Bucaramanga, stoic Tunja, and the border city of Cúcuta, a refreshingly slow pace prevails. The pueblos of Boyacá are easily accessed from Bogotá and can even be visited on a long weekend. It will take a little more time to discover Santander, located between Bogotá and the Caribbean coast. Although most people only stop in the sultry city of Cúcuta on their way to Venezuela or on a visa run, it is a pleasant surprise. The historic pueblo of Pamplona is the most chilled-out place in all of Norte de Santander.

HISTORY

Before the Spanish conquest, Boyacá was part of the Muisca heartland. Hunza, where present day Tunja is located, was the seat of the Zaque, one of the Muisca leaders. The Sun Temple, one of the Muiscas' sacred sites, was in Sogamoso, northeast of Tunja.

Boyacá and the Santanderes played a major role in the struggle for independence. In 1811, Boyacá became the seat of the Provincias Unidas de la Nueva Granada (United Provinces of New Granada), the first republican independent government. It was in Boyacá in 1819 that the two decisive battles of independence were fought: the Batalla del Pantano de Vargas (Battle of the Vargas Swamp) and the Batalla del Puente de Boyacá (Battle of the Bridge of Boyacá). These battles marked the end of Spanish domination in Colombia.

Santander was one of the more dynamic regions in 19th-century Colombia, with an export economy based on the cultivation of quinine, coffee, cocoa, and tobacco. In the early 20th century, Norte de Santander became the first major coffee-producing region in Colombia.

The mid-20th-century fighting between Liberals and Conservatives was particularly acute in Santander and Norte de Santander. In 1960, the Ejercito de Liberación Nacional (National Liberation Army) or ELN guerrilla group was born in rural Santander.

The region has experienced steady economic growth since the early 2000s. Bucaramanga, the capital of Santander, has become a prosperous center of manufacturing and services. Cúcuta, in the neighboring Norte de Santander department, is a center of commerce whose fortunes are linked to Venezuela's.

While poverty is widespread in the Boyacá countryside, the area is an important agricultural center and supplies Bogotá with much of its food. The departmental capital of Tunja has also become a major center of learning: It is home to 10 universities.

PLANNING YOUR TIME

There are three main draws in Boyacá and Santander: the lovely colonial town of Villa de Leyva, the snowcapped wonderland of the Sierra Nevada del Cocuy, and, in Santander, the action-packed area around San Gil, including the nearby town of Barichara.

Villa de Leyva can be visited in a short two-day excursion from Bogotá, but you could easily spend a couple more relaxing days seeing all the sights, including a hike to Laguna Iguaque. Add on a day to visit the churches of Tunja, but be sure to confirm hours beforehand. To further explore Boyacá, extend your visit for a couple of days to the area around Sogamoso, particularly the postcard-perfect towns of Iza and Monguí and Lago de Tota. There are good public transportation links throughout Boyacá, but this is also a fairly easy place to drive.

Getting to the Sierra Nevada del Cocuy is a schlep (11 hours by bus from Bogotá), so a trip there requires a minimum of 4-5 days to make it worthwhile. To just do day hikes into the park, base yourself in either Güicán or El Cocuy, or nearer to the park in one of several lodges. To do the six-day circuit around the park, plan on 10 days so as to include a day or two of acclimatization before you embark. This is a

HIGHLIGHTS

LOOK FOR 【 TO FIND RECOMMENDED SIGHTS, ACTIVITIES, DINING, AND LODGING.

de Leyva is just a couple of hours away from Bogotá (page 74).

【 **Santuario Flora y Fauna Iguaque:** Hike through Andean forest and mysterious *páramo* to a sacred Muisca lake (page 82).

【 **Tunja's Historic Churches:** Glimpse the splendor of Tunja's colonial past in its beautiful churches (page 86).

【 **Parque Nacional Natural El Cocuy:** Stunning scenery greets you at every turn in this remote park of snowcapped peaks (page 100).

【 **Cañón del Chicamocha:** Experience the blue skies and deep canyons at this photogenic park not far from Bucaramanga and San Gil (page 111).

【 **Paragliding near San Gil:** Soar through the air with the greatest of ease in Colombia's recreational capital (page 114).

【 **Barichara:** Decompress and rejuvenate in one of the most beautiful pueblos in the country (page 117).

【 **Camino Real:** Follow in the footsteps of native Guane indigenous traders and Spanish colonists on this meandering path through the Santander countryside (page 119).

【 **Villa de Leyva:** One of Colombia's most visited and beloved colonial pueblos, relaxed Villa

remote area and there are fewer public transportation options. Buses depart for the area from Tunja. Roads are for the most part in good shape.

San Gil and Barichara have a lot to offer, so plan on spending at least three days. Barichara is a much more beautiful base for exploring the region, but San Gil is home to the main adventure sport tour operators.

There are good public transportation links between Bucaramanga and San Gil and between San Gil and Barichara. However, getting from Bucaramanga and San Gil to Tunja or Villa de Leyva is not fun, as the highway is often saturated

with big trucks and buses. On holidays it can be difficult to get a seat on a bus out of or to San Gil, an intermediary stop between Bucaramanga and Bogotá.

Between Villa de Leyva and San Gil it is 6-7 hours, with a change of bus in Barbosa and/or Tunja. Even though San Gil and the Sierra Nevada del Cocuy are only 75 kilometers as the crow flies, to get from one to the other, you must transfer buses in Tunja, requiring more than 15 hours on various buses.

There's frequent bus service between Bucaramanga and Pamplona/Cúcuta.

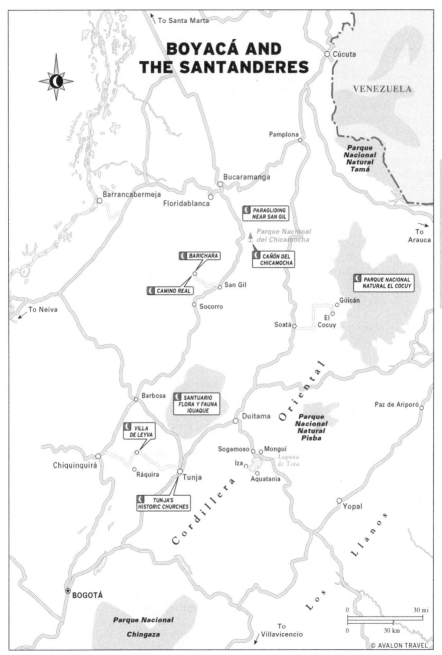

BOYACÁ AND THE SANTANDERES

To Santa Marta

Cúcuta

VENEZUELA

Pamplona

Parque
Nacional
Natural
Tamá

Bucaramanga

Barrancabermeja

Floridablanca

PARAGLIDING
NEAR SAN GIL

Parque Nacional
del Chicamocha

To
Arauca

BARICHARA

CAÑÓN DEL
CHICAMOCHA

PARQUE NACIONAL
NATURAL EL COCUY

CAMINO REAL

San Gil

Güicán

To Neiva

Socorro

El
Cocuy

Soatá

O r i e n t a l

Barbosa

SANTUARIO
FLORA Y FAUNA
IGUAQUE

Paz de Ariporó

VILLA
DE LEYVA

Duitama

Parque
Nacional
Natural
Pisba

Sogamoso   Monguí

Iza   Laguna
           de Tota

Chiquinquirá

Ráquira

Tunja

Aquatania

Yopal

TUNJA'S
HISTORIC CHURCHES

C o r d i l l e r a

L l a n o s

★ BOGOTÁ

L o s

Parque Nacional

Chingaza

To
Villavicencio

0   30 mi

0   30 km

© AVALON TRAVEL

BOYACÁ

Boyacá

To the northeast of Bogotá and the department of Cundinamarca, the Boyacá department is a mostly rural agriculture-oriented area of bucolic highlands, home to campesinos (peasants) often dressed in their warm woolen *ruanas* (capes) as they tend to their dairy cows and potato crops. Boyacá is also known for its role in Colombian history: The capital city of Tunja was effectively the runner-up to Bogotá when the Spaniards sought a capital city for their New World territory of Nueva Granada. Its colonial-era importance can be seen today in the number of impressive churches that stand in its historic center. Nearby, Villa de Leyva has the perfect combination of colonial charm, good hotels and restaurants, attractions, and fantastic weather. Boyacenses are known for their politeness, shyness, and honesty, and will often address you not with the formal *usted* but rather with the super-deferential *sumercé,* a term that is derived from the old Spanish *su merced* (literally, "your mercy").

◖ VILLA DE LEYVA

This enchanting colonial pueblo is set in an arid valley (Valle de Saquencipá) and has been a major tourist destination for decades. The population triples on weekends, when city folk from Bogotá converge on the town. The surrounding desert scenery, a palette of ever-changing pastels, is gorgeous, the typically sunny weather is never too hot nor too cool, and the town's architecture of preserved whitewashed houses along stone streets is charming.

The influx of visitors every weekend doesn't diminish the appeal of VDL, as it's known. A surprising number of activities and attractions are in reach, including paleontological and archaeological sites and outdoor activities such as biking and hiking. The nearby Santuario Flora y Fauna Iguaque is one of the most accessible national parks in the country, and you need only a decent pair of boots to hike to its sacred lakes. Villa de Leyva is also a good base from which to explore the Boyacá countryside and towns such as Ráquira.

Sights
PLAZA MAYOR

Villa de Leyva's Plaza Mayor is one of the most photographed locations in Colombia. The town's main square, the largest plaza in the country, is indeed photogenic, but it can be a frustrating task capturing it all in one take: At 14,000 square meters (3.5 acres), it's big. In the middle of the square is a Mudejar-style well, the Ara Sagrada, that was the source of water for the townspeople in colonial times. On the western side of the square is the Iglesia Parroquial (Cra. 9 No. 12-68, 8am-noon and 2pm-6pm Tues.-Sat., 8am-noon Sun.), made out of stone, adobe, and wood, which was built in the 17th century. It features a large golden *retablo* altar.

On the western side of the plaza is the quirky Casa Museo Luis Alberto Acuña (Cra. 10 No. 12-83, tel. 8/732-0422, www.museoacuna.com.co, 9am-6pm daily). In addition to cubist-influenced paintings of pre-Hispanic indigenous culture, rooms are filled with the artists' private art collection and antiques. The courtyard holds some wood sculptures of the artists. The museum also has a pint-sized gift shop. Acuña was instrumental in the restoration of and preservation of colonial architecture in Villa de Leyva.

One of the oldest houses in Villa de Leyva, and best preserved, is the Casa Juan de Castellanos (Cra. 9 No. 13-11) on the northeast corner of the Plaza Mayor. It is so well preserved, in fact, that it today serves as the main office of the city government. The house is not officially open to the public, but you can take a peek. The house belonged to Spaniard Juan de Castellanos, who came to the New World as a soldier. He was an important chronicler of the time.

Across from the Casa Juan de Castellanos is the historic Casa del Primer Congreso de las

© ANDREW DIER

a charming cobblestone street in Villa de Leyva

Provincias Unidas de la Nueva Granada (Cra. 9 No. 13-04). Restored by artist Luis Alberto Acuña in the 1950s, this is where the era of the Patria Boba, as it would later (and derisively) be known, was begun. The Casa Real Fábrica de Licores (Cl. 13 No. 8-03) was the first official distillery in Nueva Granada. After standing in ruins for decades, the house was restored in the 1950s.

The Museo El Carmen de Arte Religioso (Cl. 14 No. 10-04, 10am-1pm and 2pm-5pm Sat., Sun., and holidays, COP$2,500) presents paintings, crucifixes, manuscripts, and religious figures from the colonial era. The museum is on the southwest corner of the grassy Plazoleta de la Carmen. The complex (which dates to around 1850) also includes a monastery and convent.

The Casa Museo Antonio Nariño (Cra. 9 No. 10-25, 9am-noon and 2pm-5pm Thurs.-Tues., tel. 8/732-0342, free) is a house in which independence figure Antonio Nariño lived and died. It was built in the 17th century, and the museum displays some

of his manuscripts as well as items from everyday life in the 19th century, such as a giant mortar used to mill corn. The short and sweet museum often puts on temporary art exhibits, which may have a small admission charge.

OTHER SIGHTS

On the Plaza Ricaurte, the 19th-century Convento de San Agustín today houses the highly respected Instituto Humboldt (Cra. 8 No. 15-98, tel. 8/732-0791, www.humboldt.org.co, free), a research institute dedicated to conservation and environmental education. A small room on threatened animal species in Colombia is open to the public, and a tour is given on Fridays (3pm-5pm). The Humboldt occasionally hosts cultural events.

The Casa Museo Capitán Antonio Ricaurte (Cl. 15 No. 8-17, 9am-noon and 2pm-5pm Tues.-Sun., no phone, free) is in the small house where this independence figure was born in 1786. He is a hero of the Colombian air force, and one room is filled with uniforms and memorabilia of that military branch. He died heroically, sacrificing his life by blowing himself up with a cache of gunpowder so that it would not land in the hands of Spaniards.

Entertainment and Events

The most popular place to hang out in the evenings is on the Plaza Mayor, where the thing to do is buy a couple of beers and watch the world go by. But there are other watering holes in town. La Cava de Don Fernando (Cra. 10 No. 12-03, tel. 8/732-0073) is a spot for a cocktail where the music is generally, but not always, rock.

For a movie night, head to the Cine Club Casa Quintero (Casa Quintero, 2nd fl., tel. 8/732-1801, Thurs.-Sun. evenings).

The dark, crystal-clear skies above Villa de Leyva make for great stargazing. In February each year the town hosts the Festival de Astronómica de Villa de Leyva (www.astroasasac.com), during which all are invited to view the stars from powerful telescopes in the Plaza Mayor.

Shopping

In Villa de Leyva as in the rest of Boyacá, the special handicraft is woolen goods. But the town is home to many creative types, and small jewelers, galleries, and handicraft shops are found on every street.

Alieth Tejido Artesanal (Cl. 13 No. 7-89, tel. 8/732-1672, www.alieth.8m.com) is an association of about 35 women who weave woolen sweaters, *ruanas* (ponchos), *mochilas* (backpacks), gloves, scarves, and some colorful, slightly psychedelic bags. A tour, the "Ruta de la Lana," can be taken to nearby farms to learn about the process from sheep to sweater. It costs COP$48,000 per person, lasts for about five hours, and snacks and a souvenir are included. Alieth Ortíz, the head of this interesting program, requests reservations be made a few days in advance so that they can organize things with the artisans. Another excellent store to browse wool items is Creaciones Dora (Cra. 10 No. 10-02, 9am-7pm Mon.-Fri., 9am-9pm Sat.).

Boyacá is known for its woven woolen scarves and *ruanas*.

© ANDREW DIER

La Libelula (Cra. 9 No. 14-35, tel. 8/732-0040, 10am-7pm daily) specializes in leather: handbags, belts, and accessories. The mysterious shop Misterio (Cl. 14 No. 9-85, tel. 8/732-0418, 10am-8pm daily) sells colorful scarves, handmade jewelry, and semiprecious stones like quartz, amethyst, and emeralds. Coal mining is a major industry in rugged Boyacá; Arte al Carbón (Cl. 15 No. 9-46, www.artealcarbon.galeon.com, 9am-7pm Mon.-Sat.) sells jewelry made out of coal by women from mining communities.

Recreation

HIKING

Close to town, sporty locals regularly take a brisk morning hike up to the Santo, a statue on the eastern side of Villa de Leyva. The walk takes about an hour in total, and it is a steep climb. From the statue of the saint you can get a good view of the town and will better appreciate the scale of the fantastic Plaza Mayor. To get to the path, walk east along Calle 11 to the tennis court and track/soccer field. This is to the north of the Hotel Duruelo. The path entrance is marked and it practically leads straight up. The rocks are covered, unfortunately, with religious graffiti. It's best to make the climb early in the morning, before the midday heat envelops the valley. Although the view is nice, you'll be better off leaving your camera at your hotel, not necessarily due to safety reasons, but rather because you may not want to be loaded down with things as you climb. At parts you may be on all fours!

TOURS

Tour companies in Villa de Leyva mostly specialize in adventure activities nearby. The best outfit is Colombian Highlands (Renacer, Av. Cra. 10 No. 21, tel. 8/732-1201, www.colombianhighlands.com), the same folks running the Renacer hostel. Armonita Tours (Av. Perimetral No. 8-08, tel. 1/643-3883, www.amonitatour.com) can take you to the Santa Sofía area for waterfall rappelling (COP$85,000), caving (COP$75,000), and the Paso de Ángel hike (COP$75,000). They also can arrange horseback riding trips to the Pozos Azules, and they rent bikes. In addition, they have day-trip packages to places like Museo El Fósil de Monquirá and the Convento del Santo Ecce Homo. These cost about COP$60,000 and include transportation and entry to the attractions.

BIKE RENTAL

You'll need plenty of sunscreen and water, but renting a bike to see the sights in the valley near Villa de Leyva is a great way to spend a day and get some good exercise as you huff and puff up that hill to the Convento del Santo Ecce Homo.

Mountain bikes, not necessarily of the highest quality, are readily available for rent in Villa de Leyva. These usually all go for about COP$20,000 for a half day (until 1 or 2pm). Sentimiento Natura (Cl. 8 No. 9-47, cell tel. 321/217-2455) rents bikes, usually from a house that is conveniently located near the road through the valley. Bici Motos (Transversal 10 No. 7A-10, Barrio Los Olivos, cell tel. 321/225-5769) is also on the way, and the friendly owner lives above the bike shop. That means you can get there on the early side (6am-7am) if you want to pick up a bike. (He doesn't mind.) He charges only COP$10,000 for a five-hour rental.

Accommodations

Villa de Leyva gets hopping on weekends and on holidays, and hotel rates bump up accordingly. Rates are even higher during the Christmas holidays through the second week of January and during Holy Week. During the week you will have your choice of hotels and ought to try to negotiate a better price. Many will provide additional discounts if you pay in cash.

There aren't many midrange hotel options in town, as most hotels target the luxury hotel market. A number of hotels that call themselves boutique have sprung up in recent years just outside of the town or farther in the valley. They may be comfortable but they may lack in the charm department. Hostels in Villa de Leyva are reliably friendly options, and staff are chock full of knowledge and tips on where to go and what to do.

UNDER COP$70,000

Renacer (Av. Cra. 10 No. 21, tel. 8/732-1201, www.colombianhighlands.com, COP$35,000 shared room, COP$65,000 d) is the best-known hostel in town and is popular for good reasons. Its location is a hike away from town (about a 15-minute walk), but guests will be reimbursed for their taxi ride upon arrival. It is set amidst green at the foot of a mountain. Facilities are well kept and there is ample open-air common space. There are seven rooms and cabanas for varying numbers of guests, some with private bathrooms. There is also a place for those arriving in campers or vans. The on-site restaurant, Pekish, is excellent, with options to please anyone, such as falafels (COP$12,000) and Vietnamese spring rolls (COP$10,000). In addition to the hostel, Renacer, through Colombian Highlands (www.colombianhighlands.com), arranges outdoor expeditions to nearby attractions and can even assist in excursions outside of the Villa de Leyva area. They have very good information on how to hike or bike the area solo. This is an excellent place to swap travel tips with backpackers from around the world.

Run by an Austrian-Colombian couple, the Casa Viena Hostel (Cra. 10 No. 19-114, Sector de la Banadera, tel. 8/732-0711, www.hostelvilladeleyva.com, COP$17,000 s, COP$40,000 d) is a quiet and relaxed guesthouse on the same road as Renacer (just before it). It has just three rooms and the owners live in the same house. You may bump into them going to the shared bathrooms. They opened a new farmhouse in 2013 called Casa Puente Piedra (COP$25,000 pp) that is even more tranquil. It is within walking distance of the Santuario Flora y Fauna Iguaque. They have excellent mountain bikes for rental. These cost COP$25,000 for a half day.

A low-key and lesser-known hostel option is Hostal Rana (Cl. 10A No. 10-31, tel. 8/732-0330, www.hostalrana.com or www.learnspanishinvilladeleyva.com, COP$20,000 dorm,

COP$40,000 d). It opened in 2010 and has one dorm room and four private rooms. Rooms are clean and beds are firm. There is a small kitchen for use. One problem is that the tiny camping area in the courtyard area is sort of icky. They can arrange for Spanish lessons here.

The no-frills **Hospedaje Los Balcones de la Plaza** (Cl. 13 No. 9-94, cell tel. 314/360-8568, COP$45,000 pp w/shared bath) has about four rooms and occupies a corner of real estate overlooking the Plaza Mayor. The views from your balcony can't be beat. They don't provide wireless Internet, but the town government does on the Plaza Mayor. Here there is no common area, but the plaza is as common as it gets.

If you ask locals for a less expensive hotel option, many will tell you to check out **Hospedería Don Paulino** (Cl. 14 No. 7-46, tel. 8/732-1227, COP$35,000 s, COP$65,000 d). It's not a fancy place by any means, but the price can't be beat! The 16 rooms all have wireless Internet and TV, but the ones on the first floor are a little on the stuffy and small side. From the second floor balcony overlooking the outdoor patio you can enjoy the sunset. There's no breakfast included but each morning they do provide coffee.

COP$70,000-200,000

Family-run **Hospedería La Roca** (Cl. 13 No. 9-54, COP$160,000 d) has been a cheapie quietly overlooking the Plaza Mayor for years, but it's no longer a budget option. More than 20 rooms with high ceilings surround two interior courtyards that are filled with greenery. Try for one on the second floor with a squint of a view of the mountains. Around the corner is the welcoming **Posada de Los Ángeles** (Cra. 10 No. 13-94, tel. 8/732-0562, COP$110,000 d), a lovely option overlooking the Plazoleta de Carmen. Some rooms have balconies overlooking the church. Take your American-style breakfast in the cheerfully painted patio filled with potted plants and flowers. No wireless Internet.

Friendly and colorful **Sol de la Villa** (Cra. 8A No. 12-28, tel. 8/732-0224, COP$120,000) has 30-some

comfortable rooms and an excellent "in town" location. Walls are a little on the thin side, as are curtains. Rooms towards the back and upstairs are best. A nice service they provide, one that all environmentally aware hotels ought to offer, is free filtered water, so there's no need to buy plastic bottles of water each day. The inviting **（** **Hospedería El Marqués de San Jorge** (Cl. 14 No. 9-20, tel. 8/732-0240, www.hospederiaelmarquesdesanjorge.com, COP$130,000-200,000 d) is just a block from the Plaza Mayor, has two interior patios that are filled with greenery, and has clean and comfortable modern rooms (despite having been around since 1972). It's a bargain compared to other luxury hotels in town.

OVER COP$200,000

The location of the **（** **Hotel Plaza Mayor** (Cra. 10 No. 12-31, tel. 8/732-0425, www.hotelplazamayor.com.co, COP$306,000 d), with a bird's-eye view of the Plaza Mayor from its western side, is unrivaled. The hotel's terrace is a great place to watch goings-on in the plaza and to take a photo of the cathedral bathed in a golden light in late afternoon. Rooms are spacious, some have a fireplace, and all are tastefully decorated. Breakfast is served in the pleasant courtyard.

Two other upscale options face parks. On the cute Parque Nariño, the elegant **Hotel La Posada de San Antonio** (Cra. 8 No. 11-80, tel. 8/732-0538, www.hotellaposadadesananantonio.com, COP$295,000 d) is lavishly decorated and has a pleasant restaurant area, a cozy reading room, a pool, an art gallery, a billiards room, and even a small chapel. It was originally a wealthy family's home built in 1845. On the Plaza de Ricaurte, the **Hotel Plazuela de San Agustín** (Cl. 15 No. 8-65, Plaza de Ricaurte, tel. 8/732-2175, www.hotelplazuela.com, COP$300,000 d) is a cozy hotel with enormous (yet carpeted) rooms. Mornings get off to a nice start with breakfast in the courtyard, near a fountain. The hotel is two blocks from the Plaza Mayor. They have another hotel in the countryside towards Santa Sofía.

Food

CAFÉS, BAKERIES, AND QUICK BITES

The many cafés and bakeries in town have fiercely loyal clienteles. Bakery Pan Típica (Cl. 11 No. 11A-64) is an old local favorite and specializes in *mogolla batida* (whipped bread). Panadería San Francisco (Cl. 10, 8am-7pm) is famous for its *galletas de maiz* (corn cookies). The owners of Pastelería Francesa (Cl. 10 No. 6-05, 9am-7pm Thurs.-Mon.), a French bakery, often skip town, so don't be disappointed if it is closed, foiling your plan to sip a café au lait accompanied by a *pain au chocolat* (chocolate croissant). Panadería Doña Aleja (Cl. 14 No. 9-21, 8am-8pm Mon.-Sat., 9am-4pm Sun.) is known for its *mogollas* (rolls).

At Sybarita Caffe (Cra. 9 No. 11-88, cell tel. 316/481-1872, 8am-8pm daily) the owners are on a mission to bring coffee appreciation to the masses. Even if you are one of those "coffee is coffee" people, once you try one of their coffees (from the southern Colombian highland departments of Cauca or Nariño), you may just be jolted out of your slumber. That's some good coffee! If you want your coffee from the Coffee Region, Quindío to be specific, then Café Los Gallos (Cra. 8 No. 12-96, cell tel. 300/659-9511, 9am-8pm daily) is your place. This sweet place is filled with rooster paraphernalia; it's named after the family name.

Gelatería Pizzería Santa Lucia (Cra. 10 No. 10-27, cell tel. 314/305-8150, 11am-9:30pm) serves homemade ice cream and yogurts. It's all natural, and the pizza's not bad either. If you just want a thin crust pizza without a big production and expense try Crepes Pizza y Algo Más (Cra. 9 11-80, cell tel. 313/854-2051, www.crepespizza.blogspot.com, 6pm-10pm Mon.-Thurs., 1pm-10pm Fri.-Sun., COP$12,000).

Merengues y Besitos (Cra. 9 No. 11-84, cell tel. 312/394-3601, 10am-7pm daily) has very sweet sweets wrapped in colorful packaging.

COLOMBIAN

The Albahaca Restaurante-Bar Viejoteca (Cra. 8A No. 13-46, cell tel. 313/844-6613, 10am-9pm daily) is a favorite for visitors for two reasons: the lovely ambience, especially in the evening, and for its non-outrageous prices! Their top dishes include *cuchuco de trigo con espinazo de cerdo* (buckwheat soup with pork back, COP$17,000) and grilled trout in *uchuva* (Peruvian groundcherry) sauce (COP$18,000). Ask for a table in the garden or by the fireplace. The word *viejoteca* is in the name because the owners like oldies music.

MiCocina (Cl. 13 No. 8-45, tel. 8/732-1676, www.restaurantemicocina.com, noon-10pm daily, COP$25,000), where there is a cooking school within the restaurant, has earned a name for itself as an ever-so-slightly upscale restaurant serving the best of Colombian cuisine. After a *calentado bogotano,* a beloved hangover cure made with fried eggs and potatoes, save room for the cheese ice cream from Paipa. It's mostly Colombian meat-based dishes here, but they offer a few vegetarian plates.

Locals tend to steer clear of the overpriced restaurants on the Plaza Mayor. When it comes to *comida,* it's got to be *buena, mucha, y barrata* (good, plentiful, and cheap). Close to the Terminal de Transportes, but not too close, Los Kioscos de los Caciques (Cra. 9 No. 9-05, cell tel. 311/475-8681, noon-3pm and 6pm-8pm daily, COP$6,000) specializes in filling local dishes such as *mazamorra chiquita* (beef stew with potatoes, corn, and other vegetables) and *cuchuco con espinazo* (stew with a base of pork spine and potatoes). You can also order from the menu. It's an atmospheric place, where you dine in thatched kiosks. At the Saturday market, those in the know go to Donde Salvador (between Clls. 12-13 and Cras. 5-6, Plaza de Mercado) for *mute rostro de cordero,* a hearty corn-based soup with lamb. You can also, of course, pick up plenty of cheap and fresh fruit. La Parilla (Cra. 9 No. 9-17, 7am-9pm daily, set lunch COP$5,000) is an everyman kind of place. At the plaza, Estar de la Villa (Cl. 13 No. 8-58, tel. 8/732-0251, 10am-9pm daily, COP$8,000) is always packed, often with employees from some of the fancier restaurants nearby.

Traveling Taste Buds

© ANDREW DIER

Hot, sweet, and gooey—the arepas of Tinjacá are worth both the calories and the trip.

Forget about counting calories as you try these local specialties near Villa de Leyva.

WINE

Villa de Leyva is one of a handful of areas in Colombia where wine is produced. Take a tour of Viñedo Aim Karim (Km. 10 Vía Santa Sofía, cell tel. 317/518-2746, www.marquesvl.com, 10am-5pm, COP$5,000) and try their Marqués de la Villa wine. Their sauvignon blanc won an award in Brussels in 2011.

SAUSAGE

About 25 kilometers west of Villa de Leyva, the town of Sutamarchán is famous for its spicy *longaniza* sausage. The best place to sample this is at La Fogata (tel. 8/725-1249, www.longanizasutamarchan.com). It's on the main road on the left as you go toward Ráquira.

AREPAS

Most visitors to Colombia develop a love or hate relationship with arepas, corn-based pancakes that accompany just about every meal. Every region has their own distinct type of arepa, and every Colombian believes that theirs is superior to the rest. It would be hard to find anyone who could resist the famed *arepa quesuda* from the town of Tinjacá about 18 kilometers southwest of Villa de Leyva. Meaning "sweating arepa," *arepa quesudas* are two small arepas with sweet, melted cheese in the middle. They're a big mess to eat, but they're so good.

JAM

Tinjacá is also known for its delicious jams made by El Robledal (Vereda Santa Bárbara, cell tel. 310/226-5299, www.elrobledal.co). Check out their exotic fruit jams such as *uchuva, lulo,* and rhubarb. Their products can also be found in Villa de Leyva at the Savia restaurant in the Casa Quintero on the Plaza Mayor.

BROILED HEN

Sáchica is an orderly, quiet town just outside of Villa de Leyva on the way toward Tunja. Here, the local specialty is broiled hen. Try it at La Candelaria (Cl. 3 No. 2-48, cell tel. 311/845-7786).

INTERNATIONAL

Mercado Municipal (Cra. 8 No. 12-25, tel. 8/732-0229, noon-3pm Mon.-Thurs., noon-3pm and 8-midnight Fri.-Sun. and holidays, COP$22,000) has without a doubt one of the coolest settings in VDL. It is in a courtyard (which was once the third patio of a parsonage) filled with herb gardens in which a traditional Mexican barbecue wood-burning oven is built into the ground. In it they cook their famous barbecued goat. International dishes on the menu include pastas and several vegetarian offerings. It's open for breakfast on the weekends and there is a nice bakery in front. The set lunch special is a very good deal.

Authentic French food can be found in Villa de Leyva! That would be at **Chez Remy** (Cra. 9 No. 13-25, tel. 311/848-5000, noon-10pm Fri.-Sat., noon-4pm Sun., COP$24,000). The French-inspired dishes include a *quenelle de mar* (COP$28,000) that combines a myriad of tastes from the faraway sea: salmon, hake, shrimp, and lobster. But on chilly nights, the French onion soup (COP$9,000) really hits the spot.

The **Casa Quintero** on the corner of the Plaza Mayor has several restaurants in a sort of fancy food court setting. There is a little something for everyone here, including a Lebanese restaurant, a surprisingly filling arepa joint, and a pizza place. If you are in the mood for Mexican, try **La Bonita**, run by the same people as the Mercado Municipal, where you can sample delicious dishes such as *lomo a la tampiquena* (COP$33,000), which includes grilled baby beef, a chicken flauta, a quesadilla, and rice with beans. Or go for a barbecued pork taco (COP$26,000).

While you await your rosemary, veggie, *higo* (fig), or barbecue burger (COP$8,500) and refreshing basil lemonade at **Vastago** (Cl. 13 No. 8-43, 9am-8pm daily, COP$17,000), you can check out the little shops and stands in a sort of arcade that has several small shops (ceramics, jewelry) and vendors (old Colombian magazines, antiques). There's a cupcake café in back if you want something sweet afterwards.

La Ricotta (Cra. 10 No. 11-49, tel. 8/732-1042, noon-10pm Fri.-Sun., COP$16,000) makes its own pastas and is a reasonably priced Italian cuisine option.

VEGETARIAN

Casa Salud Natural (Cl. 12 No. 10-74, no phone, noon-9pm daily, COP$14,000) is a mostly lunch place where you get a set meal of a soup and a vegetable protein. A pricey vegetarian/organic restaurant, **Savia** (Casa Quintero, Plaza Mayor, tel. 8/732-1778, noon-9pm Thurs.-Mon., COP$25,000) has an extensive menu and also sells locally produced jams and other items for sale in their *tienda* (store).

Information and Services

The Villa de Leyva **tourist office** (corner Cra. 9 and Cl. 13, off of Plaza Mayor, tel. 8/732-0232, 8am-12:30pm and 2pm-6pm Mon.-Sat., 9am-1pm and 3pm-6pm Sun.) has free tourist maps and brochures. There are several ATMs in Villa de Leyva, particularly along the southern end of the Plaza Mayor. Internet cafés are also numerous.

An efficient and inexpensive laundry service in town near the bus terminal is **Lava Express** (Cra. 8 No. 8-21, cell tel. 320/856-1865, 8am-noon and 2pm-7pm Mon.-Fri., 8am-7pm Sat.). They can provide rush service and pick up and return your items to your hotel.

In case of an emergency contact the **Policía Nacional** (tel. 8/732-1412 or 8/732-0391) or the **Hospital San Francisco** (tel. 8/732-0516 or 8/732-0244).

Getting There and Around

With a recently expanded four-lane highway that bypasses Tunja, Villa de Leyva is easily accessible by private car or by public bus from Bogotá, as well as from Tunja. It isn't a crazy idea to rent a car in Bogotá and drive to Villa de Leyva. That gives you a lot of flexibility to be able to drive around the countryside and visit enchanting pueblos to your heart's content! Nearly all hotels have parking lots.

There are a few direct buses to Villa de Leyva from Bogotá (COP$20,000); however, often it is quicker and easier to take a bus from the Terminal Norte to Tunja and then transfer to a *buseta* (small bus) onward towards Villa de Leyva. These leave around every 15 minutes from the Terminal Villa de Leyva, not the main bus terminal. The last bus leaves Tunja at 7pm. This trip costs just COP$6,000.

Vice versa, the last bus bound for Tunja departs the Terminal de Transportes (Cra. 9 between Clls. 11-12) in Villa de Leyva at 6pm. It takes about 45 minutes.

Returning to Bogotá, several companies offer two daily buses that depart between 5 and 6am and again at around 1pm. There are many more options on Saturdays, Sundays, and Monday holidays. These tend to leave in the late afternoon at around 3pm.

To get to Villa de Leyva from Bucaramanga or San Gil in Santander, you'll have to hop on a bus to Tunja. This highway that extends from Bogotá to Venezuela is a busy one, and the journey can take five or six hours.

Once in Villa de Leyva, it is easy (and more importantly, a pleasure) to walk everywhere. A few streets around the Plaza Mayor, including the main drag, the Calle 13, are pedestrian only. Even on non-pedestrian streets it's hard for vehicles to zoom along.

Vicinity of Villa de Leyva
⑥ SANTUARIO FLORA Y FAUNA IGUAQUE

One of the country's most accessible national parks is about 13 kilometers from Villa de Leyva. The Santuario Flora y Fauna Iguaque (www.parquesnacionales.gov.co, COP$37,500 non-Colombians, COP$14,000 residents in Colombia, COP$7,500 children and students) is an excellent place to experience the unique landscape of the Andean *páramo* (highland moor) as well as dry tropical forest. The protected area extends for some 6,750 hectares. It is also a park of several *lagunas* (mountain lakes). The Laguna Iguaque in particular is known as a sacred lake for the Muisca Indians who predominated in the area. According to their beliefs, the goddess Bachué was born out of the blue-green waters of this lake, giving birth to humanity.

Most day-trippers based in Villa de Leyva visit the park to make the climb up to the Laguna Iguaque. The climb, which takes you through three ecosystems—Andean forest, sub-*páramo*, and *páramo*—begins at the Centro Administrativo Carrizal at an elevation of 2,800 meters (9,185 feet) and ends 4.6 kilometers (2.6 miles) later at the Laguna Iguaque (3,650 meters/11,975 feet). The enjoyable hike takes about 3-4 hours to make. Along the way you may be able to spot different species of birds and perhaps some deer or foxes. At the mist-shrouded Laguna Iguaque, you'll be surrounded by hundreds of *frailejones,* an unusual cactus-like plant found only in this special ecosystem.

It is best to make the hike during the week, as the trails get crowded on weekends. You do not need a guide for the hike to the Laguna Iguaque. During particularly dry spells the threat of forest fires forces the park to forbid entry to visitors. That is most likely to occur in January or August. Ask beforehand at your hostel or hotel to find out if the park is open to visitors.

If you are interested in exploring other paths in the park, consider overnighting at the Centro de Visitantes Furachiogua, the park's basic accommodations facilities (catering mostly to student groups). Seven rooms have 6-8 beds each (COP$38,000 pp), and the restaurant is open to day-trippers as well. This is about 700 meters beyond the Centro Administrativo Carrizal. There are camping facilities near the cabins (COP$10,000 pp). To inquire about accommodations or to make a reservation contact the community organization Naturar-Iguaque (cell tel. 312/585-9892 or 318/595-5643, naturariguaque@yahoo.es). A guided walk to the Laguna Iguaque costs COP$80,000 for a group of 1-6.

Buses serving the town of Arcabuco from the bus station in Villa de Leyva can stop at the Casa de Piedra (8 km from Villa de Leyva). The first bus leaves at 6am with another departing at 10am. From there it's about three kilometers/two miles (about an hour's walk) to the east to the Centro Administrativo Carrizal visitors center.

PALEONTOLOGICAL SITES

During the Cretaceous period (66-145 million years ago), the area around Villa de Leyva was submerged in an inland sea. Some of the marine species that lived in the area included the pliosaurus, plesiosaurus, and ichthyosaurus.

Towards the end of this period, many species became extinct. Simultaneously the Andes mountains were created when the earth shifted. As the waters gave way to mountains, the bones of these species became imbedded in rock, guaranteeing their preservation. Today there are a handful of paleontological sites worth visiting, where you can view fossils of parts of massive dinosaurs to small ammonites, of which there are thousands. Excavations continue throughout the valley.

In 1977, locals made a fantastic discovery: a distant relative of carnivorous marine reptiles from the pliosaurus family, to be classified as a *Kronosaurus boyacensis Hampe*. It roamed this part of the earth some 110 million years ago. The first ever find of this species in the world can be seen, imbedded in the earth extending for about 10 meters, in the location of its discovery at the Museo El Fósil de Monquirá (Km. 4 Vía Santa Sofía, Vereda Monquirá, www.museoelfosil.com, COP$6,000). Guides give a brief tour of the museum, which has hundreds of other animal and plant fossils on display. This is a major tourist sight, and there are souvenir shops and juice stands nearby.

Across the street from Museo El Fósil de Monquirá is the Centro de Investigaciones Paleontológicas (cell tel. 314/219-2904, www.centropaleo.com, 9am-noon and 2pm-5pm Mon., Wed., and Thurs., 8am-5pm Fri.-Sun., COP$8,000), which opened in late 2012. On view here are parts of a *Platypterygius boyacensis,* as well as a *Callawayasaurus colombiensis,* which were all found nearby. While the center is a museum as well, the main focus of this nonprofit organization is research. Technicians in lab coats and white gloves carefully work behind the glass preparing and preserving fossils (Fri.-Sun.). An informative 20-minute tour of the center in Spanish is included.

Gondava (Km. 6 Vía Santa Sofía, www.

granvalle.com, 9am-5pm Tues.-Sun., COP$13,000) is more about fun than paleontology. This park is geared toward kids, taking visitors back in time, around 100 million years ago, when Earth was the domain of giant dinosaurs. This park has to-scale replicas of dozens of terrestrial and aquatic dinosaurs. The largest is the *brachiosaurus,* which stands 14 meters (46 feet) high. Other park attractions include a playground, labyrinth, and a 3-D movie theater.

On the northeastern edge of town is the Museo Paleontológico de Villa de Leyva (Cra. 9 No. 11-42, tel. 8/732-0466, www.paleontologico.unal.edu.co, 9am-noon and 2pm-5pm Tues.-Sat., 9am-3pm Sun., COP$3,000). Run by the Universidad Nacional, this museum provides an introduction to the fossils that have been found in the area, which date back 110-130 millions of years ago. On display are ammonites, which have become a symbol for the area, and other prehistoric animals that roamed the area. In addition, the museum has an arboretum with gardens of palms, oaks, and an Andean forest. This is behind the museum. It is about a 15-minute walk from the Plaza Mayor to the museum. On weekday mornings it can be a zoo with school groups being herded through.

CONVENTO DEL SANTO ECCE HOMO

Set idyllically atop a hill overlooking the town, the Convento del Santo Ecce Homo monastery (Cra. 6A No. 51A-78, tel. 1/288-6373, 9am-5pm Tues. Sun., COP$5,000) was founded by the Dominicans on Palm Sunday in 1620. The monks were evicted on several occasions from this, their beautiful home. During the struggle for independence it was taken over by rebel troops under the command of a French general in 1816. In a matter of weeks the Spaniards seized it. Following definitive independence, President Santander, not a huge fan of the church, annexed the convent and ordered it to be used as a school. It was finally recuperated by the Dominicans in 1868.

The monastery is a delight to visit. Believers may find inspiration here; non-believers will appreciate the quiet beauty of its setting. In addition to the church, there are two striking small baroque chapels, plus a museum. Part of the museum is dedicated to indigenous cultures in the area. A monk's cell, library, and dining hall area provide a glimpse into monastery life. Surrounded by stone columns, the courtyard is awash in a rainbow of colors, with flowers always in bloom. Across the street from the monastery is a guesthouse and camping area open to the public.

For those feeling energetic, the trip up to the monastery makes for a great bike ride from Villa de Leyva. Be sure to get an early start and stop off at the Cabanita Roja (Vereda Barbilla, 1 km before the monastery, cell tel. 321/211-9653) for a pick-me-up snack to give you the stamina to conquer that last long hill.

HIKING

A popular hike for those seeking a thrill is the Paso de Ángel near the town of Santa Sofía. It's about six kilometers from town. The thrill comes when you walk along a narrow precipice between two canyons. You can take public transportation to Santa Sofía and walk to the Paso de Angel. Colombian Highlands (Renacer, Av. Cra. 10 No. 21, tel. 8/732-1201, cell tel. 311/308-3739, www.colombiahighlands.com) offers tours to the area and has maps if you'd like to do this on your own. You can take public transportation to Santa Sofía and walk to the Paso de Angel.

The popular La Periquera Waterfalls can be reached by taking a *colectivo* (small bus) bound for Gachantiva and getting off at El Uvalito. There are several falls, but the most impressive has a drop of 15 meters. The entrance to the falls is about 11 kilometers (7 miles) from town. This trip can be easily made on bike as well. A restaurant at the entrance serves snacks.

GETTING THERE AND AROUND

The environs of Villa de Leyva can be visited on bike, by taxi, or by public transportation. CoomultransVilla has hourly buses in the mornings, more or less, from the Terminal de Transportes in Villa de Leyva to Santa Sofía

(COP$2,500) departing at 6:45am, 8am, 9am, and 10am. They can let you off within easy walking distance of all the sights (Museo El Fósil de Monquirá, Convento del Santo Ecce Homo, etc.), as well as Santa Sofía if you are interested in the Paso de Ángel walk. Check the opening hours of the sights you'd like to visit so that you won't have to wait around to enter. There are also buses in the afternoon. The last bus departing Santa Sofía bound for Villa de Leyva leaves at around 4. You'll have to be on the lookout for it and flag it down. This company also can take you to the Periquera waterfalls (take the Gachantiva bus), fairly close to Iguaque (Arcabuco bus), and to Ráquira. It's easy and cheap. It's best to confirm all the bus schedules in advance.

RÁQUIRA

This town, 28 kilometers (17 miles) away from Villa de Leyva, is synonymous with *artesanías* (handicrafts). The main drag is lined with colorful shops, where in a one-stop shopping frenzy you can pick up handicrafts of every size and shape and from all across the country (and even from China): hammocks, *mochilas* (hats or handbags), and row after row of trinkets.

It's easy to be turned off by the trinket shopping scene, but there is some authenticity to be found in this little town. Ráquira is the capital of Colombian ceramics and has been since before the arrival of the Spaniards. In fact, it is said that the name Ráquira means "city of clay pots" in the Chibcha language of the Muiscas, who lived in the area. All of those reddish flower pots and planters you may have seen throughout the country most likely came from here.

Several shops in town specialize in pottery, and behind the shops you will often see trucks being carefully loaded up with pottery as they fulfill orders from across Colombia and beyond. One big shop within two blocks of the pleasant Parque Principal (Cras. 3-4 and Clls. 3-4) where you can peruse aisles upon aisles of the pottery is Todo Ráquira (Cra. 5 No. 3A-05, tel. 8/735-7000, www.todoraquira.com, 9am-6pm daily). The front of

© ANDREW DIER

Ráquira is Colombia's ceramics capital.

Convento de la Candelaria

One of the oldest monasteries in Latin America, and one that is still in use today, is the Convento de la Candelaria near Ráquira. A pair of Augustinian missionaries arrived in this desert area in 1588 with the mission of bringing Christianity to the native Muisca people. They lived in caves (which you can visit) until the monastery was constructed.

The complex includes two cloisters, which hold a chapel and a museum. The museum is a hodge-podge of religious art and objects, examples of technological advances through the years—from a *reloj borracho* (drunken clock) to an early Apple computer—and a display on the Colombian saint Ezequiel Moreno y Díaz, who is said to have healed cancer victims.

You may see a handful of young soon-to-be priests doing upkeep, often softly singing, in one of the colorful courtyards. They live in one part of the monastery with older monks in another.

Adjacent to the monastery is a modern hotel, Posada San Agustín (vocaciones@agustinosrecoletos.com.co, COP$168,000 d), which often hosts yoga and meditation retreats. Rooms are immaculately clean and completely free from clutter. Some even have hot tubs. At nighttime you can sit around a fire in the common area and sip hot, spiced wine. Meals are served in the restaurant, and they can also prepare vegetarian food. It's a quiet and peaceful place and there are some walks you can do nearby, one leading to a waterfall (a 1.5-hour walk).

Getting There

Buses from Villa de Leyva to Ráquira depart from the Terminal de Transportes, leaving between 7am and 8:30am. You may, however, prefer to hire a cab for the day, especially if you're traveling in a small group. Cab drivers typically charge COP$80,000 (for the car) to visit the Convento de la Candelaria and Ráquira, for example, with a couple of stops along the way. They will *esperar* (wait) for you to visit each stop. Be specific about where you want to go and the price at the beginning (put things in writing) to avoid unpleasant surprises later. If you

the store is filled with a variety of handicrafts, but if you meander to the back, you'll see their pottery factory and can check out bowls, flowerpots, and other items. Many designs are elegant in their simplicity, like the many square planters. It is said that some 500 families in the area make their living harvesting the clay in nearby areas or firing the pottery in their own workshops. A dwindling number of women in the area do things the old-fashioned way—with their hands. They make mostly decorative items like candlestick holders and clay hen piggybanks. These aren't perfect, but they have so much character.

If you'd like to observe the ceramic-making process you can visit the *taller* (workshop) of Isaias Valero (cell tel. 310/774-5287, COP$5,000 suggested donation). You can watch him at work, and he can show you the multi-day steps that go into to the process. If he is there, Isaias will gladly welcome your visit. To get to the workshop, walk up about 68 steps on the right just before the Casa de la Cultura.

BOYACÁ

are in a group you may want to upgrade to a mini-van. Contact Transportes G&J (cell tel. 313/259-0589 or 311/746-8434) for a minivan.

If you'd like to visit the monastery, you can rent a taxi from Ráquira, which will cost about COP$20,000-30,000 round-trip. The trip takes about 15 minutes each way to make. (The taxi driver will wait for you while you visit it.) You can also take public transportation from the Parque Principal, and the bus can leave you at the intersection with a dirt road that leads to the monastery. Buses (COP$2,000) are infrequent, however. You can also walk to the monastery from town. It's a pretty seven-kilometer (four-mile) walk through the hilly countryside to reach the monastery from there.

TUNJA

This university town (pop. 178,000), home to the Universidad de Boyacá, boasts some spectacular churches. Make sure you arrive during church visiting hours, as the city does not have much else to offer. As there are frequent bus connections with Bogotá and Santander, Tunja is a good base from which to explore Boyacá.

Sights

Everything you need to see in Tunja is located in its *centro histórico*.

◖ HISTORIC CHURCHES

Tunja is a city of churches, with over a dozen that date to colonial times. Hours of visitation can be irregular, but they are always open for mass, which is a good time to take a look. Most churches celebrate mass at about 7am and 6pm daily, with more frequent masses on Sundays. There tend to be more churches open for visitation in the mornings (8am-11:30am) than in the afternoons.

On the eastern side of the Plaza de Bolívar (Cl. 19 at Cra. 9), Catedral Santiago de Tunja (Cra. 9 at Cl. 19) is a 16th-century construction, originally built out of wood and earthen *tapia pisada,* which is an adobe technique. It was the first cathedral to be built in Nueva Granada. It has three naves, four side chapels, and two front chapels.

Santa Clara La Real (Cra. 7 No. 19-58, Cl. 21 No. 11-31, tel. 8/742-5659 or 8/742-3194, 8am-11:30am and 3pm-4:30pm Mon.-Fri., 8am-11:30am Sat., masses 7am and 5pm Mon.-Sat., 7am, 11am, and 5pm Sun.) was built between 1571 and 1574 and was the first Clarisa convent in Nueva Granada. It has one nave with spectacular gold decorations adoring its presbytery with golden garlands, grapes, pineapples (which were a sacred indigenous symbol), pelicans, an anthropomorphic sun, and other symbols of nature. Also look for the seal of Tunja, the double-headed eagle, modeled on the seal of Emperor Charles V, who gave the city its charter. In the choir is the tiny cell where Madre Josefa del Castillo lived for over 50 years in the late 17th and early 18th centuries. From there she wrote two books and several poems, with themes of sexual repression and mystical descriptions of heaven and hell. Near her cell are some frescoes made with coal, an abundant resource in the area. The adjacent Convento Santa Clara La Real was undergoing a painstakingly careful restoration at the time of writing.

The sky-blue interior of the Iglesia de Santa Bárbara (Cra. 11 No. 16-62, between Clls. 16-17, tel. 8/742-3021, 8:30am-12:30pm and 2pm-6pm daily, masses 5:30pm and 6pm Mon.-Fri., 7am, 9am, 10am, and 11am Sat., noon, 5pm, 6pm, and 7pm Sun.) and Mudejar ceiling designs make this one of the prettiest churches in Tunja. The single-nave structure, with two chapels making the form of a cross, was completed in 1599. When it was built, it was raised at the edge of Tunja, near an indigenous settlement.

Built in the 1570s, the Templo de Santo Domingo de Guzmán (Cra. 11 No. 19-55, tel. 8/742-4725, 8am-11:30am Mon.-Fri., 7am and 6pm masses Mon.-Fri., 7am and 6pm masses Sat., 7am, 10am, noon, and 6pm masses Sun.) is one of the most elaborately decorated churches in Colombia. Visitors have been known to audibly gasp at their first sight of the spectacular Capilla del Rosario, a chapel constructed of wood painted in red and gold-plated floral designs. It's often dubbed the Sistine Chapel of baroque art in Latin America. Figures of

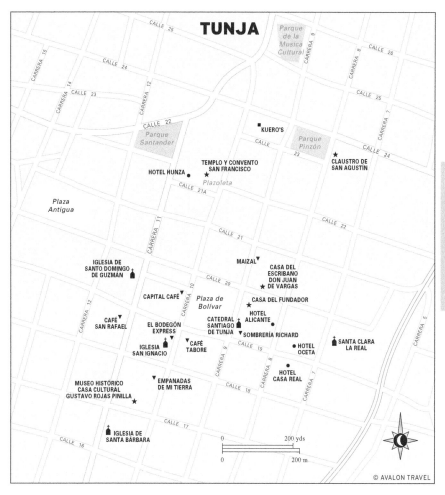

El Nazareno and El Judío Errante are part of the collection of paintings and woodcarvings in this church with several chapels. If you have time to visit just one church in Tunja, make it this one.

The **Claustro de San Agustín** (Cra. 8 No. 23-08, tel. 8/742-2311, ext. 8306, www.banrepcultural. org/tunja, 8:30am-6pm Mon.-Fri., 9am-1pm Sat., free) dates to the late 16th century. It served as an Augustinian convent until 1821, when it was taken over by the government. The friars were sent to another convent, and the building would become the home of the Colegio de Boyacá and later transferred to the Universidad de Boyacá. Adorning the corridors around the patio are several murals dating back to the colonial era. The *claustro* (cloister) is administered by the Banco de la República, and they often hold cultural events here. You can settle down with a book or work on your computer in the pleasant reading rooms.

Other religious sights worth visiting include the

© ANDREW DIER

a decorative church ceiling

17th-century Iglesia San Ignacio (Cra. 10 No. 18-41, tel. 8/742-6611, 8am-noon and 2pm-5pm Wed.-Sat.), which now serves as a theater, and the Templo y Convento San Francisco (Cra. 10 No. 22-32, tel. 8/742-3194, 10:30am-12:30pm and 3pm-5:30pm daily, 7am, 11am, noon, and 7pm mass Mon.-Fri., 11am, noon, 6pm, and 7pm mass Sat., 8am, 10am, 11am, noon, 5pm, 6pm, and 7pm mass Sun.), one of the oldest churches and monasteries in Tunja. It was an important base for evangelization of nearby indigenous communities.

MUSEUMS

The Mudejar-Andalusian style Casa del Fundador Gonzalo Suárez Rendón (Cra. 9 No. 19-68, Plaza de Bolívar, tel. 8/742-3272, 8am-noon and 2pm-6pm daily, COP$3,000) was built in the middle of the 16th century. The most remarkable aspects of the house are the frescoes of mythological creatures, human figures, exotic animals, and plants. These whimsical paintings date from the 17th century, although not much else is known about them.

Casa del Escribano del Rey Don Juan de Vargas (Cl. 20 No. 8-52, tel. 8/74-26611, 9am-noon and 2pm-5pm Tues.-Fri., 9am-noon and 2pm-4pm Sat.-Sun., COP$2,000) was owned by an important person in colonial Tunja, the scribe to the king. The scribe's jurisdiction covered all of present-day Boyacá, Santander, Norte de Santander, and parts of Venezuela and Cundinamarca. Student guides will give you a thorough tour of the museum. The house showcases furniture and other examples of colonial life, but the highlight of this Andalusian-style house has to be the unusual painted ceilings portraying exotic animals and mythological creatures, similar to the frescoes that can be found in the Casa del Fundador.

The childhood home of former president Gustavo Rojas Pinilla is now a museum: Museo Histórico Casa Cultural Gustavo Rojas Pinilla (Cl. 17 No. 10-63, tel. 8/742-6814, 8:30am-noon and 2pm-6pm Mon.-Fri.). Rojas, after seizing power in 1953, became the only dictator that Colombia has ever had. Upstairs are two exhibition spaces, one with memorabilia of Rojas and the other with portraits of 12 presidents that hailed from Boyacá. Despite his anti-democratic credentials, Rojas is revered in Tunja as the man who brought the mid-20th-century violence between Liberals and Conservatives to an end.

Shopping

Small 7 Kuero's (Cl. 23 No. 9-90, tel. 8/743-7328, josekueros@hotmail.com, 9am-5pm Mon.-Sat.) is a shop specializing in leather goods. Next to the cathedral, the Sombrería Richard (Cr. 9 No. 19-06, tel. 8/747-1276, daily) is an old-school hat shop selling hats that seem to be from the 1950s.

Unicentro (Av. Universitaria No. 39-77, tel. 8/745-4108, 8am-11pm daily) is Tunja's mall, holding a movie theater, food court, and a *plazoleta de cafés,* an area with many different cafés. It is located in the modern neighborhood of La Pradera, to the north of downtown.

Accommodations

Most overnight visitors to Tunja stay in the decent hotels in the *centro histórico* within easy walking distance of the Plaza de Bolívar and sights of interest.

Two blocks from the Plaza de Bolívar is ◖ Hotel Casa Real (Cl. 19 No. 7-65, tel. 8/743-1764, www.hotelcasarealtunja.com, COP$58,000 s, COP$72,000 d), which is a colonial-style house with 10 rooms surrounding a divine courtyard. That's where a very nice breakfast is served for an additional cost in the morning. You can order your breakfast the night before and even request it to be delivered to your room. Rooms are tastefully decorated and comfortable. Prices here are astoundingly low. The courtyard walls are decorated with lovely tile paintings depicting Boyacá country scenes. The artist, Adriano Guio (cell tel. 314/319-0822, aguio1@hotmail.com), has a studio near the town of Nobsa.

Across the street from Hotel Casa Real is the Hotel Ocetá (Cl. 19 No. 7-64, tel. 8/742-2886, www.hotelocetatunja.com, COP$90,000 d). It opened in 2012 and is clean and functional; beds are firm.

With the same owners as Hotel Casa Real, Hotel Alicante (Cra. 8 No. 19-15, tel. 8/744-9967, www.hotelalicantetunja.com, COP$72,000 d) caters to business clientele. This small hotel may not have the charm of Casa Real, but it is clean and matter of fact.

The fancy hotel in town is, as it has been for decades, the Hotel Hunza (Cl. 21A No. 10-66, tel. 8/742-4111, www.hotelhunza.com, COP$228,000 d). It's got luxurious king-size beds and card keys to get in. Amenities include a decent sized indoor pool and a steam room. Its neighbor is the Iglesia Santo Domingo, which makes for a strange view. The hotel is a popular place for wedding banquets. There is a lively bar near the entrance, but it shouldn't keep you up at night.

Food

Comida típica (Colombian fare) rules the day in this city lacking in restaurant options. For a really local, greasy-spoon-type experience, try Restaurante Maizal (Cra. 9 No. 20-30, tel. 8/742-5876, 7am-8:45pm Mon.-Sat., 9am-4:45pm Sun., COP$12,000). It has been serving *sancocho* (beef stews), *mondongo* (tripe stew), and *ajiaco* (chicken and potato soup) to Tunja for over 50 years. Another old-timer is El Bodegón Express (Cra. 10 No. 18-45, cell tel. 321/221-4460, 8am-4pm Mon.-Sat., COP$10,000). It's next to the Iglesia San Ignacio. It specializes in trout dishes and *cocido boyacense* (COP$6,000), which has a variety of meats and some of the unusual tubers from the area, such as *cubios, ibias,* and *rubas.*

◖ Empanadas de Mi Tierra (Cra. 10 No. 17-67, cell tel. 320/414-0857, 10am-7pm daily) is a fast food joint that has 15 types of empanadas, with varieties such as Mexican, Asian, vegetarian, and cheese with quail's eggs. And you can douse them with many types of sauces. The empanadas go down well with a cool *avena cubana,* a creamy and cold oatmeal drink.

Pizza Nostra (Cl. 19 No. 10-63, tel. 8/740-2040, 11am-8pm daily, COP$18,000) has a few locations in and around town. The most famous one is at the Pozo de Donado (tel. 8/740-4200,

11am-11pm daily), a small park and Muisca archaeological site surrounding a lake.

It's a tradition in Tunja to while away the hours in cafés. It must be the chilly weather. While the actual coffee around town may disappoint, the atmosphere, with groups of retirees dressed in suits brushing shoulders with bevies of college students, does not. Put some *aguardiente* (anise-flavored liquor) in your coffee and enjoy the great view from the second floor of Café Tabore (Cl. 19 No. 9-57, tel. 8/742-2048, 7am-8pm daily), overlooking the Plaza de Bolívar. The lively Pasaje Vargas on the west side of the plaza is lined with several cafés. Try Capital Café (7am-7pm daily), which is at the entrance of the *pasaje* (passage) close to the Plaza de Bolívar. Café San Rafael (Cra. 11 No. 18-35, no phone, 8:30am-8pm Mon.-Sat.) is a tad more elegant than the rest.

Getting There and Around

Situated 150 kilometers northeast of Bogotá and 21 kilometers southeast of Villa de Leyva, Tunja is easy to get to by car or by bus. Buses to Bogotá, other towns in Boyacá, and to all major cities in Colombia depart from the Terminal de Transportes (Cra. 7 No. 16-40). Buses from Bogotá cost about COP$18,000 and from Villa de Leyva are COP$6,000. The best way to get around the *centro histórico* is on foot.

Puente de Boyacá

This war memorial on the road between Bogotá and Tunja celebrates a decisive battle, the Batalla del Puente de Boyacá, that effectively ended Spanish control of Nueva Granada. At this site today there are several memorials and statues, including the Plaza de Banderas, where flags from all the departments of Colombia fly. There is also a sculpture of Gen. Francisco Paula de Santander and a large sculpture of Gen. Simón Bolívar surrounded by angels representing the South American countries that he liberated (Bolivia, Colombia, Ecuador, Peru, and Venezuela). There is a small bridge on the memorial grounds, but this is from the 1930s; the original Puente de Boyacá long gone.

Santander and Bolívar achieved immortality as heroes of Colombian independence for their victory here. After defeating the Spaniards at the Batalla del Pantano de Vargas on July 25, 1819, revolutionary troops under their command marched toward Bogotá. South of Tunja, they engaged with the main Spanish army, defeating it decisively on August 7 at the Batalla del Puente de Boyacá. The engagement was a small affair with fewer than 3,000 men on each side, with about 100 royalists and only 13 rebels losing their lives. Bolívar marched onward to Bogotá, which he took without a fight, ushering in independence.

At 6pm every day there is a short flag-lowering ceremony. You can have your picture taken with Colombian soldiers. Buses passing through between Bogotá and Tunja can drop you off here, or you can contract a taxi from Tunja.

TUNJA TO LAGO TOTA
Paipa

The town of Paipa (pop. 32,000) is known for two things: its thermal baths and the Lanceros monument.

COMPLEJO TERMAL

The Complejo Termal (Km. 4 Vía Pantano de Vargas, tel. 8/785-0068, www.termalespaipa. co, 6am-10pm daily), the hot springs, is the biggest attraction in town. There are two parts to the hot springs complex; the Parque Acuático (COP$13,000) has three thermal water pools and pools for kids, and the Centro de Hidroterapia (COP$41,000) offers six activities for 20 minutes each, including hydro-massage, saunas, and mudbaths. On the weekends the park is packed, especially the Parque Acuático, which teems with families, so it's highly recommended to go on a much calmer weekday. To do the Centro de Hidroterapia circuit, call in advance to make a reservation. Slots are available daily at 7am, 10am, 1pm, 4pm, and 7pm. A limited number of people, around 16, are allowed during each session.

Between Paipa and the Complejo Termal is the manmade Lago Sochagota. The pedestrian path around the lake attracts locals and visitors alike, especially in the late afternoon. This is a nice thing to do after a good soak at the baths.

LOS LANCEROS

On the site of the Batalla del Pantano de Vargas (Battle of the Vargas Swamp) stands Colombia's largest sculpture, *Los Lanceros* (9 km south of Paipa on Paipa-Pantano de Vargas road, free). The massive monument was designed by Colombian sculptor Rodrigo Arenas Betancourt and built in commemoration of 150 years of Colombian independence. Bronze sculptures show the 14 *lanceros* (lancers on horseback) charging into battle, fists clenched in the air, with fear and defiance depicted on their faces. Above them is an odd triangular concrete slab that points into the heavens. It is 36 steps up to the platform of the monument, the age of Simón Bolívar on that fateful day. The monument generates strong opinions, and there is little gray area: You either love it or detest it.

The Batalla del Pantano de Vargas was a decisive battle during Simón Bolívar's independence march on Bogotá in 1819. After crossing the Llanos from Venezuela and climbing up the Andes via the Páramo de Pisba, the revolutionary army under Bolívar engaged with a contingent of Spanish troops at the Pantano de Vargas on July 25, 1819. Exhausted after their long slog over the Cordillera Oriental mountains, the revolutionary troops were nearly defeated. However, a charge by 14 armed horsemen led by Juan José Rendón saved the day. Soldiers from the British Foreign Legion, under the command of Irishman James Rooke, also played a decisive role in this battle. The royalists lost 500 men in the battle, while 350 revolutionaries perished.

Across from the monument is the Casa Museo Comunitario Juan Vargas (COP$1,000), a small museum mostly about the military campaigns of Simón Bolívar. It was in this house that Juan Vargas, his wife, and their 12 children were executed by the Spaniards for supporting the rebel troops. Oddly, there is not much information on

© ANDREW DIER

the memorial of the Batalla del Pantano de Vargas, *Los Lanceros*

the battle that occurred in the swamp across the street, but it's worth a quick look anyhow.

ACCOMMODATIONS AND FOOD
While there are some inexpensive hotels in town, it's much more pleasant to stay outside of town near the Complejo Termal, even if it means splurging somewhat. Midweek rates at these fancy hotels drop substantially.

The █ Hacienda El Salitre (Km. 3 Vía Paipa-Toca, tel. 8/785-1510, www.haciendadelsalitre.com, COP$350,000 d) is set in the countryside under towering eucalyptus trees, and you'll pass grazing cows to get there. At the hotel, go for one of the rooms with a thermal bathtub. Each day you'll be treated to a thermal bath three times (staff come in and change the water each time). Rooms are cozy, warm, and spacious, but not quite luxurious. The hotel has a very nice restaurant with outdoor seating, plus a café and a bar. Even if you are just passing through, the restaurant, with its lovely setting, is the best around. Here you can get a massage, and can take a horse out for a trot to a nearby lake. From Sunday to Friday there is a 30 percent discount. It's a big wedding banquet and honeymoon location on the weekends. The hacienda served as a barracks during the Pantano de Vargas battle in 1819.

Overlooking Lago Sochagota is the Estelar Paipa Hotel y Centro de Convenciones (tel. 8/785-0944, www.hotelesestelar.com, COP$286,000 d). This upmarket chain hotel is modern, service oriented, and well maintained. On site is a spa with thermal baths, the main attraction, and there are other activities on-site to keep you busy, such as a pool, tennis court, golf course, and horseback riding. With over 100 rooms, it is a popular place for large groups. Rates here don't substantially drop during the week, but it may be worth asking.

GETTING THERE AND AROUND
Paipa is 40 kilometers (25 miles) northeast of Tunja, and frequent buses make this route. The half-hour journey from Tunja costs COP$5,000.

From Paipa, taxis to the Complejo Termal area cost about COP$7,500. Buses from Sogamoso depart from the intersection of Carrera 14 and Calle 16 and cost about COP$4,000. The trip takes about 45 minutes.

Sogamoso
This city of over 100,000 habitants is about 75 kilometers (46 miles) east of Tunja and is known for being an important pre-Hispanic Muisca center. It was known as Suamoxi. It's a city of little charm; however, the Museo Arqueológico de Sogamoso is worth a stop.

SIGHTS
Run by the Universidad Pedagógica y Tecnológica de Colombia (UPTC) university in Tunja, the Museo Arqueológico de Sogamoso (Cl. 9A No. 6-45, tel. 8/770-3122, 9am-noon and 2pm-5pm Mon.-Sat., 9am-3pm Sun. and holidays, COP$5,000) has an extensive collection of artifacts of the Muisca civilization, the main indigenous group of Colombia. Muiscas lived in the area that is today the departments Boyacá, Santander, and Cundinamarca. Suamoxi was the seat of power for a confederation led by the Iraca. The Bacatá confederation (near Bogotá) and the Hunza (Tunja) confederation, led by the Zaque, were the most powerful of the Muisca confederations. The most memorable sight on the museum grounds is the fantastic Templo del Sol, a re-creation of a Muisca temple that was burnt to the ground by the Spaniards in the late 16th century. The museum is worth visiting, even though the exhibition spaces are drab and the sequence of exhibits does not flow very lucidly. That is a shame because there is an interesting history to tell and the collection is impressive. If you have the time and speak Spanish, hire a guide. Inquire at the ticket office. Look for the exhibit on *ocarinas*, which are whistles, usually ceramic, that are often zoomorphic in form. Also see the stunning black-and-white geometric designs of *torteros*, which are spindles used in spinning yarn, as well as remarkably well-preserved red-and-white ceramic vessels and urns.

ACCOMMODATIONS AND FOOD

The **Hotel Finca San Pedro** (Km. 2 Vía Aquitania, tel. 8/770-4222, www.fincasanpedro. galeon.com, COP$25,000 dorm, COP$80,000 d) is a lush hostel set among lovely gardens with fruit trees, vegetables, and flowers. (It's odd that there's no fruit at breakfast!) It's a popular place with international backpackers visiting Boyacá. The owner's son gives yoga classes on occasion. This friendly spot, a five-minute cab ride from Sogamoso (COP$4,000), is the best option in the area.

It is said that Bolívar stayed at the **Hacienda Suescun** (Km. 4 Vía Sogamoso-Tibasosa, tel. 8/779-3333, cell tel. 312/596-4506, www.haciendasuescunhotel.com, COP$164,000 d) before he headed off to face the Spaniards at the decisive Batalla del Puente de Boyacá. This *hacienda,* surrounded by tall trees covered with Spanish moss dangling towards the ground, has 18 rooms. It's north of Sogamoso. They have horses that can be taken out for a ride in the countryside.

GETTING THERE

There are easy bus connections between both Bogotá (3 hrs., COP$23,000) and Tunja to Sogamoso (1 hr., COP$15,000). The **Terminal de Transportes** (Cra. 17 between Clls. 11-11A, tel. 8/770-330) is downtown. Many buses connect Sogamoso with Paipa, Iza, Monguí, and Aquitania. Sogamoso is also a gateway to Los Llanos, with frequent bus service between Sogamoso and Yopal. This is a good, less expensive option for traveling to the Hacienda La Aurora south of Yopal. The trip between Sogamoso and Yopal takes about four hours to make and costs about COP$25,000.

Monguí

The chilly (average temperature is 13°C/55°F) highland colonial town of Monguí was founded in 1601 and was a strategic town for the Spaniards, as it was located between Tunja and the vast Llanos, the eastern plains. It has been designated as one of the most beautiful towns in Boyacá. Its narrow cobblestone streets are lined with white and green houses, many well over a couple of centuries old. It's in a valley below the highland moor of **Páramo de Ocetá,** dubbed the most beautiful *páramo* in the world. You can decide for yourself by hiking among its armies of *frailejón* plants, mountain lakes, and enormous boulders. Hotel staff can contact a knowledgeable local guide (around COP$50,000) to accompany you through this unusual landscape.

SIGHTS

Three colonial constructions in Monguí have been declared national monuments. The stone **Basílica y Convento de Nuestra Señora de Monguí** stand on the Plaza de Bolívar. The Franciscan convent today houses a Museo de Arte Religioso highlighting the work of the famous 17th-century Colombian baroque painter Gregorio Vásquez de Arce y Ceballos. Other historic buildings are the **Capilla de San Antonio de Padua,** which was the town's first church, and the photogenic stone bridge, the **Puente de Calicanto.**

Today Monguí is almost as famous for its soccer ball-making industry as for its colonial beauty. Around 70 percent of the town works in about 20 small factories in this industry, which has been around since the 1950s. They churn out some 30,000 balls each month. (More balls are produced during World Cup years as demand tends to spike.) You can pick up a "Made in Monguí" soccer ball at the shop **Balones Hurtado** (Cl. 7 No. 3-60, tel. 8/778-2021, www.baloneshurtado.com). Their slogan is "more than a ball...inspiration for your feet!"

ACCOMMODATIONS AND FOOD

There are not many accommodations options in and around town, but one of the best is **La Casona de San Francisco de Asis** (Cra. 4A No. 3-41, tel. 8/778-2498, COP$40,000 pp d). Rooms have a view over the Río Morro canyon, and the hotel is quite tidy. The restaurant, which has been in service for over two decades, is also one of the best in town. The restaurant specializes in *cocido boyacense,* which has a variety of meats and some of the unusual tubers from the area, such as *cubios, ibias,* and *rubas.*

The Calicanto Real (cell tel. 311/811-1519, juliosaenz66@hotmail.com, COP$25,000 pp) is an old house with five rooms located on the other side of the Puente de Calicanto. It was once owned by a wealthy emerald miner, was abandoned for several years, and now it is has been refurbished as a hotel. Rooms are spacious with nice views and have a lot of character, but the beds are soft. Adjacent to the hotel is a tavern filled with decorations like cowboy hats, animal heads, and an homage to Monguí's most famous poet: Mora Sáenz Rómulo, also known as "El Indio Romulo." Born in the 1930s, the charismatic poet became famous nationwide for defining a genre of campesino poetry, commenting on social ills using the language of rural folk. He recorded several albums of poetry, was awarded dozens of medals for his contributions to cultural life, and even served as mayor of his hometown.

The Hospedaje el Rincón de Duzgua (Vereda Duzgua, tel. 8/778-2130) is a cabin outside of town, and it's a good place for exploring the Páramo de Ocetá.

GETTING THERE

There are two roads between Sogamoso and Monguí. The old but scenic route is partly unpaved and winds through eucalyptus forests and the pueblo of Morca. It's about 20 kilometers (12 miles) and makes an excellent bike ride. On the new road, a bus ride to Monguí costs about COP$4,000 and takes about 45 minutes. The bus leaves from the intersection of Carrera 14 and Calle 16.

Iza

Serene and sleepy Iza (pop. 2,081), 14 kilometers (9 miles) southwest of Sogamoso on the way to Lago Tota, is a charming pueblo. There are not heaps of activities to do here, and there is no huge attraction except for possibly the nearby hot springs. This well-preserved town, originally a Muisca settlement before the conquest, is nestled in a valley of green pastures and is surrounded by low mountains. Iza's a good place to walk about, take in some fresh air, exchange pleasantries with locals (and cows) surprised by your presence, and escape from the tourist trail.

© ANDREW DIER

traffic in Iza

The thermal baths are just outside of town (you can even walk there) at Termales Erika (Vereda Aguacaliente, tel. 8/779-0038, 7am-6pm daily, COP$8,000). They are closed on Mondays for cleaning, thus Tuesday is the best day for a soak!

In Iza, the local specialty is cakes, pies, and other sugary sweets. Bakers constantly swat away bees at their stands on the shady Parque Principal as they await customers on the weekends. A good place to eat something other than sweets is La Casona Parrilla Bar (cell tel. 320/222-6293, 1pm-10pm Sat.-Sun., COP$12,000). It specializes in grilled meats.

To get to Iza from Sogamoso, take a bus (COP$3,000) that leaves from the intersection of Carrera 11 with Calle 8. This is known as the Puente de Pesca.

Lago Tota

One of the most popular destinations in Boyacá is the Lago Tota, Colombia's largest lake. The views are spectacular here with mountains, valleys, and fields surrounding the lake. It measures 47 kilometers (29 miles) in perimeter. The main town on the lake is Aquitania; however, most visitors choose to stay at one of the cozy lakeside lodges nearby. A day trip from Sogamoso to Playa Blanca, a chilly lakeside beach, can also be arranged. But to truly relax, plan to stay the night so that you can enjoy watching the sun slowly slip away in the distance at sunset and relax by the fireplace with a glass of wine (bring your own) as the night wears on. Biking, walks, and boat rides to one of the handful of uninhabited islands on the lake are other activities you may enjoy. If you have a mountain bike, a nice ride is along the western side of the lake, along a mostly dirt road.

The lake and surrounding countryside, a patchwork of fields of green onions and potatoes, is beautiful, without a doubt. However, the lake is in peril. The dumping of fertilizers and pesticides from lakeside farms has been the primary reason that the Lago de Tota, a lake that provides drinking water for hundreds of thousands of people, has been declared one of the top five most threatened wetlands in the world by the World Wetlands Network. There are other culprits as well: large caged trout farms, the use of lake water at a nearby steel plant, and the most recent threat, oil exploration in the area by a large French oil company.

RECREATION

Playa Blanca (COP$3,500 entry) is the lake's beach, and a strange scene often awaits you there. Boys playing soccer on the white sand, university students from Bogotá hanging out drinking beer, and teenage boys in swimsuits alongside *abuelas* (grandmothers) bundled up in their wool *ruanas* (ponchos) watching the proceedings. Besides sampling one of 16 fresh trout dishes on offer at the restaurant (open 8am-5pm daily), other activities at the beach include taking a tour of the lake (COP$6,000) and horseback riding.

ACCOMMODATIONS

A handful of inviting lodge-type hotels are around the lake to the north and west of the lakeside town of Aquitania. Bargains can be had during the week, when you will have the lodge (if not the lake) blissfully to yourself. The area caters to weekenders from Bogotá.

The Decameron all-inclusive hotel chain has agreements with three hotels in the area. The Decameron Refugio Santa Inés (Km. 29 Vía Sogamoso-Aquitania, tel. 8/772-8860, cell tel. 313/261-2429, santaineshotel@gmail.com, COP$99,000 pp d) is a comfortable lodge-type hotel with 13 rooms and two cabins. Wood ceilings and floors add to the atmosphere. Set on the eastern side of the lake, the hotel's terrace is an ideal vantage point to watch the sunset. Beds are very comfortable, there is wireless Internet access, and breakfast is included. The restaurant offers other meals as well. Hotel staff can arrange for walks to a *páramo,* and horseback riding and taking a boat around the lake are other activities on offer. This is the nicest Decameron option. Hotel El Camino Real (Km. 20 Vía Sogamoso-Aquitania, tel. 8/770-0684, mauriciofigueroa@yahoo.com,

serene countryside around Colombia's largest lake, Lago Tota

© ANDREW DIER

www.decameron.com, COP$84,000 pp d) and Refugio Rancho Tota (Km. 21 Vía Sogamoso-Aquitania, tel. 8/770-8083, www.hotelranchotota.com, COP$80,000 pp d) are the other two. These have similar pricing and similar facilities, and both have small spas.

For charm, and a room with a view, there are two longstanding stone lodge options. Rocas Lindas (cell tel. 310/349-1107, www.hotelrocaslindas.wordpress.com, COP$85,000 pp d) is a cozy lodge with 10 rooms and one cabin. There's no wireless Internet here, and this hotel could use some upgrading. C Pozo Azul (Bogotá tel. 1/620-6257, cell tel. 320/384-1000, www.hotelrefugiopozoazul.com, COP$196,000 d) was one of the first nice hotels on the lake, and it still oozes charm. When you walk in you'll often see guests gathered by a circular fireplace in the lobby area. The hotel has 15 rooms and two *cabañas*. It is on an inlet of the lake. Some beds are on the soft side, and you have to descend 80 steep steps to get from the parking lot to the lodge. That could be difficult for those with physical limitations, and it will leave all but

Olympic athletes out of breath when they finally reach the hotel.

Getting There

Buses that go directly to Playa Blanca, via Iza, depart Sogamoso from the intersection of Carrera 11 with Calle 8 (Puente de Pesca). Otherwise, take any bus bound for the town of Aquitania (Plaza Principal). From the market, four blocks away, take another bus to Playa Blanca. It takes about an hour to get to the lake, and the bus costs about COP$4,000. Taxis are also available.

SIERRA NEVADA DEL COCUY

The Sierra Nevada del Cocuy, the highest mountains within the Cordillera Oriental (Eastern Range) of the Andes mountain chain, is 260 kilometers (162 miles) northeast of Bogotá in northern Boyacá. The entire mountain range is contained within and protected by the Parque Nacional Natural El Cocuy, the country's fifth largest national park. With its 11 jagged snowcapped peaks, massive glacier-formed

© ANDREW DIER

the beach at Playa Blanca on Lago Tota

valleys, extensive *páramos* (highland moors) studded with exotic *frailejón* plants, and stunning crystalline mountain lakes, streams, and waterfalls, it is one of the most beautiful places in Colombia. The sierra appeals to serious mountaineers and rock climbers, but it is also a place that nature-lovers with little experience and no gear can explore by doing easily organized day hikes.

PLANNING YOUR TIME

Getting to the Sierra Nevada del Cocuy entails a long, grueling trip, albeit through the beautiful, verdant countryside of Boyacá. Ideally you would want to spend at least four days there, taking in the spectacular mountain landscapes.

The park has three sectors: the Northern, Central and Southern Sectors, each with many options for day hikes, more strenuous ascents to the snow-capped peaks, or highly technical rock-climbing expeditions. There is also a spectacular six-day trek along a valley between the two main ridges of the sierra. It is not a highly technical trek but requires

good high-altitude conditioning. For many visitors, this is the main reason to visit the sierra.

The towns of El Cocuy and Güicán are convenient arrival and departure points to visit the area. In both you can find basic tourist services, tour operators and guides, and stores to stock up on food, though not trekking equipment (though this can be rented from local tour operators). Both have a few interesting sights and are departure points for day hikes. El Cocuy is better located to access the Southern Sector of the park and Güicán the Northern Sector. However, since both of these towns are around 20 kilometers (12 miles) from the park and there is limited public transportation, a good option is to base yourself nearer to the park edge in one of several pleasant lodges or campsites. You could easily spend a few days in each one of the three sectors, setting off on beautiful day hikes.

The only way to do the six-day hike around the park is with an organized tour, as the trails are not marked. If you are planning to do this trek, you may want to arrive a few days earlier to do some high altitude acclimatization hikes. Many peaks are above 5,000 meters (16,000 feet) high.

The only dependable time to visit the Sierra Nevada del Cocuy is from December to March, during the *verano* (main dry season) in the Cordillera Oriental. At other times, there may be permanent cloud cover and much rain. High season, when Colombian visitors flock to the mountains, is from mid-December to mid-January, and again in Holy Week (late March or April). So, if you have the flexibility, visit in early December or from late January through early March.

The best available topographical maps of the Sierra Nevada de Cocuy, which might be helpful in planning your visit, can be viewed and downloaded online (www.nevados.org).

El Cocuy

El Cocuy is a charming colonial town nestled in the lower folds of the Sierra Nevada del Cocuy at an altitude of 2,750 meters. The town is meticulously kept up, with whitewashed houses painted with a band of aquamarine blue. The only real sight to check out is in the Parque Principal, where there is a large diorama of the Sierra Nevada del Cocuy. This will allow you to understand the broken mountain geography, with its multitude of snowcapped peaks, lakes, and valleys. In the town there are decent accommodations, a few tour operators, and some stores to stock up for a visit to the park, though no specialized mountaineering stores.

RECREATION

For a spectacular panoramic view of the entire sierra, take a hike to Cerro Mahoma (Mahoma Hill), to the west of the town of El Cocuy. It is a strenuous six- to seven-hour excursion often used by people who are acclimatizing to high altitude before trekking in the Sierra Nevada del Cocuy. The trailhead is outside of town on the road that leads to the town of Chita. As the trail is not marked and splits several times, it is better to go with a guide. For an experienced local guide, contact the local guide association,

ASEGUICOC (Asociación de Prestadores de Servicios Ecoturísticos de Güicán y El Cocuy, cell tel. 311/557-7893, aseguicoc@gmail.com).

ACCOMMODATIONS AND FOOD

Hotel la Posada del Molino (Cra. 3 No. 7-51, tel. 8/789-0377, www.elcocuycasamuseo.blogspot.com, COP$20,000 pp d) is a friendly guesthouse. Rooms in this old house are set around two colorful interior patios. The house has a little history to it, as well. Apparently during the deadly feuds between Güicán and El Cocuy (Güicán was conservative and El Cocuy was liberal), the famous Virgen Morenita image was taken from its shrine in Güicán and hidden away in the house where the hotel is located. You can see the room that hid this secret.

Casa Muñoz (Cra. 5 No. 7-28, tel. 8/789-0328, www.hotelcasamunoz.com, COP$20,000 pp d) has a great location overlooking the main plaza in town. It offers a restaurant in the patio on the main floor. Rooms are fine, though somewhat small, with firm beds and wooden floors.

Hotels, like the Casa Muñoz, generally offer the best food, but don't expect to be gobsmacked come dinnertime. Vegetarians may want to travel with a can of emergency lentils to hand over to kitchen staff to warm up for you.

INFORMATION AND SERVICES

At the offices of the Parque Nacional Natural El Cocuy (Cl. 5 No. 4-22, tel. 8/789-0359, 7am-noon and 1pm-4:45pm daily, cocuy@parquesnacionales.gov.co, COP$37,500 non-Colombians, COP$14,000 residents, COP$7,500 children/students), you can obtain a park entry permit and general information.

There is an ATM at the Banco Agrario at Carrera 4 and Calle 8.

GETTING THERE

The towns of El Cocuy and Güicán are served from Bogotá by three bus companies. The trip takes 11 hours, stops at El Cocuy, and terminates at Güicán. The most comfortable option is with the bus company Libertadores (COP$50,000), which operates a big bus, leaving Bogotá at 8:30pm. The return trip departs El Cocuy at 7:30pm. Bus line Fundadores (COP$45,000) has two buses, leaving Bogotá at 5am and 4:30pm, returning from El Cocuy at 7:30am and 8:30pm. Concord (COP$45,000) also has two services, leaving Bogotá at 3am and 5pm and leaving El Cocuy for Bogotá at 5:30am and 7:30pm.

Güicán

Long before its foundation in 1822, Güicán was a place of significance for the U'wa indigenous people. The U'wa fiercely resisted the Spanish conquest, and, rather than submit to domination, their chief Güicány led the people to mass suicide off a nearby cliff known as El Peñón de los Muertos. This little-known act of defiance is the New World's equivalent of the Masada mass suicide in ancient Judea.

The town, damaged by fires and civil war, is a mix of modern and old buildings, without much charm. However, it is a convenient starting point to visit the Northern Sector of the park. It has good accommodations, several tour operators, and some interesting sights and is the starting point for numerous beautiful day hikes.

Folks in Güicán resent that the national park carries the "El Cocuy" name. They feel that this natural wonder is just as much theirs as it is their rivals in the town of El Cocuy. You can score points with them by referring to the park as Parque Nacional Natural El Güicán.

SIGHTS

The main sight in town is the image of the Virgen Morenita de Güicán, located in the Iglesia de Nuestra Señora de la Candelaria (Parque Principal). This image of the virgin, with strong indigenous traits, appeared to the survivors of the U'wa mass suicide and ushered in their conversion to Christianity.

At the entrance to the town on the road from El Cocuy is the Monumento a la Dignidad de la Raza U'wa (Monument to U'Wa Dignity), a large statue that depicts the culture and history of the U'Wa people. It was designed by a local artist with input from the community.

RECREATION

There are several pleasant day hikes to be done from Güicán. A mildly strenuous three-kilometer (two-mile), two-hour round-trip hike takes you to the base of the Peñón de los Muertos (3,800 meters/12,500 feet), site of the U'wa mass suicide. The 300-meter cliff is imposing, and the thought of hundreds of people jumping off in defiance will send shivers through your body. From the Parque Principal, follow the road east towards the Vereda San Juan. Several signs indicate the way, so you will not need a guide.

A longer and more strenuous 11-kilometer (7-mile), six-hour hike leads northeast along the Sendero del Mosco (Mosco Trail) up the Río Cardenillo, passing sheer cliffs to a spot called Parada de Romero, which is the initial (or ending, depending on which way you go) segment of the six-day circuit around the Sierra Nevada del Cocuy. The hike ends at an altitude of 3,800 meters and is a good acclimatization walk. The trailhead is off the road that leads from El Güicán to the Parque Nacional Natural El Cocuy. As the trail is not marked, it is better to take a guide. Contact the association of local guides, ASEGUICOC (Asociación de Prestadores de Servicios Ecoturísticos de Güicán y El Cocuy, cell tel. 311/557-7893, aseguicoc@gmail.com).

ACCOMMODATIONS

The Brisas del Nevado (Cra. 5 No. 4-57, cell tel. 310/629-9001, http://brisasdelnevado.com, COP$35,000 pp) has the best accommodations and restaurant in town. Four rooms in the original house sleep 2-4 persons each. Outside is a nicer cabin with two rooms. The only problem is it is located next to a *tejo* bar. *Tejo* is a Colombian sport heavily associated with drinking.

El Eden (Tr. 2 No. 9-58 Urbanización Villa Nevada, cell tel. 311/808-8334, luishernandonc@hotmail.com, COP$30,000 pp) is in a residential neighborhood about 10 minutes up from the main plaza. It's a friendly place with lots of rooms, and you can use their kitchen. Rabbits and parakeets are caged in the garden below.

Hotel Guaicani (Cl. 5 No. 6-20, cell tel. 312/524-3449, guaicany@hotmail.com, COP$20,000 pp d) is not wonderful, but it does offer trekking services and equipment rental.

Just outside of town is the Hotel Ecológico El Nevado (road to El Cocuy, cell tel. 320/808-5256 or 310/806-2149, www.hoteleconevado.jimdo.com, COP$60,000 d), in a spacious and green setting. There are two parts to the hotel: the original quaint farmhouse with an interior patio and a modern wing. The farmhouse has loads more character, but the modern wing is, well, modern.

INFORMATION AND SERVICES

At the offices of the Parque Natural Nacional El Cocuy (Tr. 4 No. 6-60, 7am-noon and 1pm-4:45pm daily) you can obtain a park entry permit and general information.

GETTING THERE

Güicán is served from Bogotá by three bus companies. The trip takes 11 hours and terminates at Güicán, with a stop at El Cocuy. The most comfortable option is with company Libertadores (COP$50,000), which operates a big bus, leaving Bogotá at 8:30pm and returning from Güicán at 7pm. Fundadores (COP$45,000) has two buses, leaving Bogotá at 5am and 4:30pm and departing Güicán at 7am and 8pm. Concord (COP$45,000) also has two services, leaving Bogotá at 3am and 5pm and returning to Bogotá from Güicán at 5am and 7pm. If you are in a hurry, you can take Cootransdatil to Soatá (COP$15,000) at 7am, 11am, or 2pm. From Soatá there are frequent departures for Duitama and Bogotá.

◖ PARQUE NACIONAL NATURAL EL COCUY

Located about 20 kilometers (12 miles) east of the towns of El Cocuy and Güicán, the Parque Nacional Natural El Cocuy (tel. 8/789-0359, cocuy@parquesnacionales.gov.co, COP$37,500 for non-Colombian visitors, COP$14,000 Colombians and residents, COP$7,500 children/students) covers an area of 306,000 hectares (760,000 acres) spanning the departments of Boyacá, Arauca, and Casanare.

The Sierra Nevada del Cocuy, consisting of two parallel ranges 30 kilometers long with 11 peaks higher than 5,000 meters, is the centerpiece of the park. However, the park extends far north and east from the sierra and includes extensive tracts of temperate and tropical forests. It also includes 92,000 hectares (230,000 acres) of U'wa indigenous *resguardos* (reservations), which are not open to tourism.

The Sierra Nevada del Cocuy is home to the largest expanse of glaciers in Colombia, extending 16 square kilometers (6 square miles). What are usually referred to as *nevados* (snowcapped mountains) are in fact glacier-capped mountains. The highest peak is Ritacuba Blanco (5,380 meters/17,650 feet). Other notable glacier-capped peaks are Ritacuba Negro (5,350 meters, 17,550 feet), San Pablín Norte (5,200 meters, 17,060 feet), Cóncavo (5,200 meters/17,060 feet), and Pan de Azúcar (5,100 meters, 16,730 feet). One of the most striking peaks in the Sierra Nevada del Cocuy is the Púlpito del Diablo or Devil's Pulpit (5,100 meters, 16,730 feet), a massive rectangular flat-top rock formation. (A side note: Be sure to refer to it as the Púlpito del Diablo (Devil's Pulpit) and not Pulpíto del Diablo, which means the Devil's Little Octopus.) Of these, Ritacuba Blanco, Cóncavo, and Pan de Azúcar can be ascended by anyone in good physical shape and do not require mountain climbing skills.

Unfortunately, all the glaciers in Colombia, including those of the Sierra Nevada del Cocuy, are rapidly melting due to global warming. A 2013 report by the Colombian Hydrological, Meteorological, and Environmental Studies Institute (IDEAM) forecasts that, by 2030, all the glaciers in Colombia will have disappeared.

At the base of the peaks are numerous glacier-formed valleys supporting *páramos,* unique tropical high altitude ecosystems of the Andes. The *páramos* are covered with beautiful *frailejones,* plants that have imposing tall trunks and thick yellow-greenish leaves. Other *páramo*

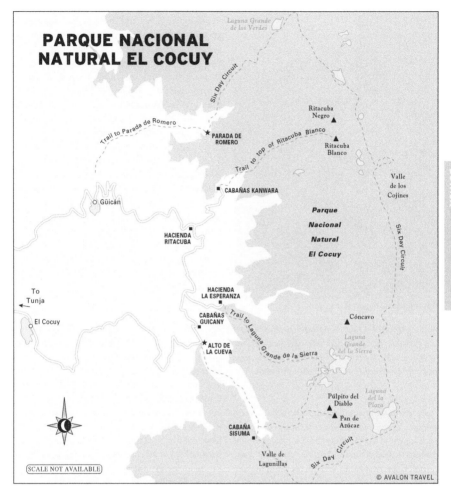

PARQUE NACIONAL NATURAL EL COCUY

Laguna Grande de los Verdes

Six Day Circuit

Trail to Parada de Romero

★ PARADA DE ROMERO

Ritacuba Negro ▲

Trail to top of Ritacuba Blanco

▲ Ritacuba Blanco

■ CABAÑAS KANWARA

Valle de los Cojines

O Güicán

Parque Nacional Natural El Cocuy

Six Day Circuit

■ HACIENDA RITACUBA

To Tunja ←

■ HACIENDA LA ESPERANZA

O El Cocuy

■ CABAÑAS GUICANY

Trail to Laguna Grande de la Sierra

▲ Cóncavo

★ ALTO DE LA CUEVA

Laguna Grande de la Sierra

Púlpito del Diablo ▲

Laguna del la Plaza

▲ Pan de Azúcar

■ CABAÑA SISUMA

Six Day Circuit

Valle de Lagunillas

SCALE NOT AVAILABLE

© AVALON TRAVEL

BOYACÁ

vegetation includes shrubs, grasses and *cojines* (cushion plants).

Erwin Krauss, a Colombian of German descent was the first modern explorer of the sierra in the 1930s. In the 1960s and 1970s, Colombian and European expeditions climbed most of the peaks. During the 1980s and 1990s, there was significant ELN and FARC presence and tourism all but disappeared.

In the past decade, the army has reestablished control of the area around the Sierra Nevada de Cocuy, and tourists have started to come back. In the 2012-2013 season, there were an estimated 9,000 visitors. The Colombian Park Service has been scrambling to deal with the influx of visitors.

Entry permits (which include entry fees) are required and can be easily obtained at the park offices in El Cocuy or Güicán. In peak season from mid-December to mid-January and during Easter week, it is better to obtain the permit several weeks in advance through the Park Service in Bogotá. Call (tel. 1/353-2400) or email (ecoturismo@

Parque Nacional Natural El Cocuy

parquesnacionales.gov.co) with the names of visitors, passport numbers, and expected dates of your arrival. The Park Service will provide instructions for paying and will send the permit by email.

Hiking

There are three separate sectors where you can do spectacular one- to two-day hikes into the park. Each of these sectors has lodges and camping grounds that serve food and make convenient starting points for these hikes. You can get to any of these lodges on the morning *lechero* (milk truck). Every morning the milk man collects fresh milk from family dairy farms throughout the countryside.

SOUTHERN SECTOR

This sector is accessed by a road from the Alto de la Cueva, a stop on the *lechero* route. There are two good lodging options in this area, and they serve as points of reference: Cabañas Guicany, a lodge at Alto de la Cueva outside the park, and Cabaña Sisuma, a lodge 10 kilometers (6 miles) from Alto de la Cueva inside the park.

One popular day hike in the Southern Sector is up to Lagunillas through a wide glacier-formed valley strewn with different types of *frailejones* and passing four large lakes. From Alto de la Cueva it is a six- to seven-hour round-trip hike to an altitude of 4,300 meters (14,100 feet). From the Cabaña Sisuma lodge within the park, it is a four- to five-hour round-trip hike. You do not need a guide to do this excursion.

A strenuous hike takes you to the Pan de Azúcar. From the Cabaña Sisuma lodge it is a six-hour round trip hike to the border of the glacier that covers Pan de Azúcar or 10 hours round-trip to the top of the glacier. Along the way you will pass the Púlpito del Diablo (Devil's Pulpit), a stunning, huge rectangular flat-topped rock formation. From the top of Pan de Azúcar there are spectacular views of the Laguna Grande de la Sierra, Púlpito del Diablo, and Cóncavo peaks. A guide is required for this hike.

CENTRAL SECTOR

The starting point for visits to the Central Sector is Hacienda La Esperanza, which is a stop on the daily *lechero*. From there, it is a strenuous six-hour round-trip hike to the Laguna Grande de la Sierra, a beautiful lake nestled between the Cóncavo and Púlpito del Diablo peaks. A guide is not necessary for this hike. By camping at the lake, it is possible to ascend to the Cóncavo (5,200 meters/17,060 feet), Concavito (5,100 meters, 16,730 feet), or Toti (4,900 meters/16,075 feet) peak. Each ascent involves a strenuous four- to five-hour round-trip hike and should be done with a guide. From the Laguna Grande de la Sierra, it is also possible to reach Cabaña Sisuma, in the Southern Sector, in nine hours. A guide is necessary as this trail is not well marked.

NORTHERN SECTOR

The starting point for hikes in the Northern Sector is Cabañas Kanwara. A short and mildly strenuous three- to four-hour round-trip hike takes you to the Alto Cimiento del Padre, a mountain pass at 4,200 meters (13,800 feet). This hike offers spectacular views of Ritacuba Negro peak. This hike does not require a guide.

Cabañas Kanwara is also the starting point for hikes to the gently sloping Ritacuba Blanco, the highest peak in the Sierra Nevada del Cocuy. The ascent to the top can be done in one grueling 9- to 10-hour excursion, leaving at 2am or 3am in order to reach the peak in the morning when conditions are best for climbing on the glacier. Most people, however, split the trek into two, camping at the Playitas camp spot halfway up. A guide is necessary for this trek.

SIX-DAY CIRCUIT

An unforgettable experience is to do the six-day trek through the glacier-formed valleys lying between the two north-south ranges of mountains. Along the whole trip you will have glacier-capped mountains on both sides. There are a few mountain passes, but generally the altitude is 4,000-4,500 meters (13,100-14,800 feet). You do not need to be an expert mountaineer, but in addition to being in good physical condition, you need to be acclimatized to the altitude. A few days of day treks before doing the circuit may be required. Do not attempt this trek without a knowledgeable guide, as it's easy to get lost in this treacherous landscape. The basic tour, which involves carrying all your own gear, will cost on average COP$700,000 per person. Don't pay less than that because it means the operator is skimping on the guide's salary. High-end tours, with porters and a cook, will cost COP$1,500,000 per person.

TOUR OPERATORS AND GUIDES

Whether you decide to do a couple of day hikes or the six-day trek, securing a reliable, professional guide will greatly increase your enjoyment. For day hikes, contact the local guide association Asociación de Prestadores de Servicios Ecoturísticos de Güicán y El Cocuy (ASEGUICOC, cell tel. 311/557-7893, aseguicoc@gmail.com). For day hikes, expect to pay about COP$80,000-100,000. If you ascend to the top of a glacier, the daily rate goes up to COP$130,000-150,000 and includes necessary gear. One highly knowledgeable guide is Julio Suárez (cell tel. 311/509-4413, ucumary13@gmail.com).

One of the leading trekking operators in the Sierra Nevada del Cocuy is Colombia Trek (Cra. 4 No. 6-50, Güicán, cell tel. 320/339-3839, www.colombiatrek.com), run by knowledgeable veteran Rodrigo Arias. It is one of the few operators offering English-speaking guides, and it is highly recommended.

Another tour company based in El Cocuy is Servicios Ecoturísticos Güicány (Cra. 5 at Cl. 9, El Cocuy, cell tel. 310/566-7554), run by Juan Carlos Carreño, son of the owner of Cabañas Güicány.

Avoid horseback rides through the park. Horses and cattle have caused significant damage to the flora of the park, and both are officially illegal. Unfortunately, many lodge owners do not agree with this environmental policy and refuse to adhere to it.

Accommodations

While not luxurious by any means, the lodging options in and around the park are just what you'd expect and want in this mountain environment. And the owners are all quite attentive and extremely friendly. Plan to spend some time hanging out in and around your hotel. It's nice to explore the countryside and meet locals.

SOUTHERN SECTOR

The best located accommodation in the Southern Sector is (Cabaña Sisuma (cell tel. 311/236-4275 or 311/255-1034, aseguicoc@gmail.com, COP$35,000 pp), a cozy cabin inside the park in the Lagunillas sector run by the local tour guide association ASEGUICOC. It has six rooms, good food, and fireplaces to keep one warm. It is a two-hour hike into the park from the Alto de la Cueva, a stop on the daily *lechero*.

Another pleasant and comfortable option is (Cabañas Güicány (Alto de la Cueva, cell tel. 310/566-7554, cab_guaicany@yahoo.es or guaicany@hotmail.com, COP$50,000 pp with meals, COP$30,000 without meals, COP$10,000 pp camping), owned by old timer Eudoro Carreño. The *lechero* can drop you off at the lodge. It's rustic and the owner is a delight to chat with over a hot *tinto* in his rustic kitchen.

CENTRAL SECTOR

C Hacienda La Esperanza (cell tel. 310/209-9812, haciendalaesperanza@gmail.com, COP$50,000 d), a working farm on the edge of the park, provides accommodations in a rustic farmhouse oozing with character. The family running the hotel is very hospitable, and the host is a trained chef who enjoys pampering his guests. Nothing beats hanging out by the fireplace in the late afternoon drinking something hot after a day of mountain climbing. The *lechero* makes a stop at this hacienda.

NORTHERN SECTOR

The most conveniently located place to stay in this sector is C Cabañas Kanwara (cell tel. 311/231-6004 or 311/237-2260, infokanwara@gmail.com, COP$35,000 pp). This lodge of cute wooden A-frame houses has a great location and

serves good food, too. To get there, you must get off the *lechero* at Hacienda Ritacuba and walk 90 minutes towards the park.

Getting There and Around

From El Cocuy and Güicán to the three park sectors there are three transportation possibilities: hiking 4-5 hours uphill from these towns to the park, taking an express service costing COP$80,000-100,000 (ouch!), or riding an early morning *lechero* (milk truck). This is a working truck that picks up milk along a predetermined route. Merchandise and passengers share the back of the truck, which is covered with canvas. Don't expect any comforts, but expect to have some good tales to tell. The *lechero* leaves Güicán from Carrera 5 and Calle 6 every morning at 5:30am and stops at El Cocuy around 6am. Around 7:30am it arrives at Alto de la Cueva, where you can get off to visit the Southern Sector. Around 9am it pulls right up to Hacienda La Esperanza in the Central Sector. Around 10:30am it reaches Hacienda Ritacuba, from where you can walk up to Cabañas Kanwara in the Northern Sector.

Santander

Beautiful, lush scenery, a delightful climate, well-preserved colonial pueblos, and friendly, outgoing people—this is the Santander department. Located in northeast Colombia, Santander lies to the north of Boyacá and southwest of Norte de Santander. Bucaramanga is the modern capital city, but you'll probably be drawn to the countryside. San Gil and the Cañón del Chicamocha will keep you busy with a smorgasbord of outdoor adventures, while nearby Barichara will seduce you with its tranquil ambiance.

BUCARAMANGA

The Ciudad Bonita (Beautiful City) is the capital of the department of Santander. Bucaramanga is a busy and growing city with a young and vibrant

population and an agreeable climate where the flowers are always in bloom. Its central location makes for a strategic launching point for visits to the Santander countryside and is a midway point between Bogotá and Santa Marta on the Caribbean coast as well as Cúcuta in the far east. Including neighborhoods that are an extension of Bucaramanga (Floridablanca, Girón, and Piedecuesta), the population exceeds a million.

ORIENTATION

Most of your time will probably be spent in Cabecera (the upscale shopping and residential area), in the city center (between Cras. 9-17 and Cl. 45 and Av. Quebrada Seca), and in nearby municipalities such as Girón and Floridablanca.

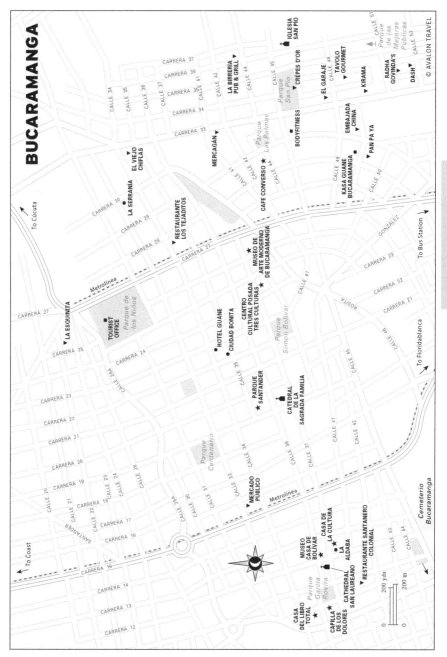

BUCARAMANGA

© AVALON TRAVEL

Carreras (avenues) run north to south, increasing in number from west to east. The main *carreras* are 15, 27, and 33. *Calles* (streets) run east to west and increase in number from north to south.

Sights

Bucaramanga's main sights are contained within the walkable city center. If you're staying in the Cabecera neighborhood it's a long, hot walk to the city center, so you're better off taking a cab.

Bucaramanga prides itself on its parks, and one of the most famous is the Parque García Rovira (Cras. 10-11 and Clls. 36-37). Filled with towering palms, it doesn't provide much shade, but with the pale yellow and white 19th-century Catedral San Laureano (Cra. 12 No. 36-08) standing prominently on the park's eastern side, it is rather photogenic. On the west side of the park is Bucaramanga's oldest church, the Capilla de los Dolores (Cra. 10 No. 36-08). This unassuming, white-washed structure dates back to 1748 and no longer has a religious mission. It's generally not open to the public. Across from it is La Casa del Libro Total (Cl. 35 No. 9-81, tel. 7/630-3389, www.lacasadellibrotal.com, 8am-10pm Mon.-Fri.), a newish cultural center that (oddly) has a number of bank offices and at the same time exhibition spaces (air-conditioned) for interesting art exhibits. There is also a small library, and a café serves free coffee.

The Libertador, Simón Bolívar, stayed in his friend Juan Eloy Valenzuela's house, now known as the Museo Casa de Bolívar (Cl. 37 No. 12-15, tel. 7/630-4258, 8am-noon and 2pm-6pm Mon.-Fri., 8am-noon Sat., COP$2,000) for about 70 days in 1828 while he awaited news from the Convención de Ocaña. (Things went badly at that convention, with a rift between Bolívar and Santander growing wider, and the end result was Bolívar's self-declaration as dictator.) The museum has personal belongs of the Liberator, an original diary from the first Expedición Botánica led by José Celestino Mutis, an original shield of the Estados Unidos de Colombia, and an exhibit on the Guane indigenous people from the area.

Across the street from the Museo Casa de Bolívar, the Casa de la Cultura (Cl. 37 No. 12-46, hours vary) hosts occasional art exhibitions and other events. The restaurant on the first floor is packed at lunchtime.

Five or six blocks to the east is the Parque Santander (Cras. 19-20 and Clls. 35-36). It's a lively park in the middle of the hustle and bustle of modern Bucaramanga. Hare Krishnas beat drums, unimpressed skateboarders show off, and dozens others look on. The Romanesque Revival Catedral de la Sagrada Familia (Cl. 36 No. 19-56) took over a hundred years to complete. It was finished in 1865. Some of the most striking features inside include the many stained glass windows. The church, with twin towers and statues of the Virgin Mary, the baby Jesus, and Joseph in between, looks particularly grandiose at night when it is lit.

The Museo de Arte Moderno de Bucaramanga (Cl. 37 No. 26-16, tel. 7/645-0483, www.museodeartemodernodebucaramanga.blogspot.com, 8:30am-noon and 2pm-5:30pm Mon.-Fri., 8am-noon Sat., COP$2,000) is worth checking out, but it's only open when there is an exhibit. The Centro Cultural Posada Tres Culturas (Cl. 37 No. 24-62, tel. 7/683-9142, www.librostresculturas.com, 9am-noon and 2pm-7pm Mon.-Sat.) is near the museum and often has events going on. It has a nice art bookstore.

The Parque San Pío (between Cras. 33-35 and Clls. 45-46) is a vibrant greenspace near the Cabecera neighborhood. At the western end stands the Fernando Botero sculpture *Mujer de Pies Desnuda*. On the opposite end is the modern Iglesia San Pío (Cra. 36 No. 45-51), where there are paintings on permanent display by local artist Oscar Rodríguez Naranjo. Farther up is the Museo Guane at the Universidad Autónoma de Bucaramanga (UNAB, Av. 42 No. 48-11, tel. 7/643-6111), which has a collection of over 600 ceramic pieces (figures, ceremonial and daily vessels, shell necklaces, stone utensils, and ceramic spindle whorls) found near Bucaramanga. Some 90 pieces are on display in a small lobby area. Nobody seems to know where the exhibition space is, and you'll have to ask around. You may have to climb around lounging students to even get a look at the collection.

Nightlife

The nightlife scene in Bucaramanga? Maybe exuberant is the right word to describe it. Most bars and clubs are open Thursday through Saturday, closing at 2am or 3am.

Café Con Verso (Cl. 44 No. 28-63, tel. 7/647-1486, 4:30pm-late Mon.-Sat.) is a pleasant café with occasional live music and film nights. La Birrería Pub & Grill (Cra. 36 No. 43-46, tel. 7/657-7675, noon-midnight Sun.-Thurs., Fri.-Sat. noon-2am) serves sports bar-type food (although there are some healthy selections) and beer. It's open-air and waitstaff are very attentive. This is the place to watch big *fútbol* matches. El Garaje (Cl. 48 No. 33-39, tel. 7/657-4768) is more about burgers and beer.

La Esquinita de los Recuerdos (Cl. 22 No. 25-55, tel. 7/632-0640 or 7/645-6861, hours vary Tues.-Sat.) is a beloved bar and a good place to have a beer while listening to old (Latino style) favorites. The bar itself is an oldie, more or less, having been around since 1965. Cali Son (Cl. 33 No. 31-33, no phone) is one of the top salsa bars in Bucaramanga.

As you might imagine from its name, Dash (Cl. 52 No. 34-27, cell tel. 315/624-6905) is a high-energy club popular with the college crowd.

Shopping

Bucaramanga is well known in Colombia for its leather shoes, handbags, and wallets. Nora Lozza First Class (Centro Comercial El Cacique, Tr. 93 No. 34-99, Local 113, 10am-8pm daily) is a well-known designer of leather bags and accessories made in Bucaramanga. There are stores in El Cacique and several other shopping malls.

Latin Lover (Cra. 35 No. 44-41, tel. 7/695-1369, 9am-noon and 2pm-8pm Mon.-Sat.), created by a pair of Bucaramanga hipsters, sells groovy and original Latino-chic T-shirts. They cost around COP$60,000.

For handicrafts, check out the woven items, including handicrafts made from leaves of the *fique* palm tree, and other accessories at Luz y Vida (Centro Comercial Cuarta Etapa, 4th floor, Local 402/9, tel. 7/673-0680, cell tel. 317/316-4487, www.artesaniasluzyvida.webnode.com.co, 10am-8pm Mon.-Sat., 10am-5pm Sun.). This is an association of women heads of household who have been forcibly displaced from their homes.

Accommodations

UNDER COP$70,000

It's not just backpackers who flock to the ◖ Kasa Guane (Cl. 49 No. 28-1, tel. 7/657-6960, www.kasaguane.com, COP$25,000 dorm, COP$80,000 d). This busy yet friendly place with both dorms and private rooms hosts activities, provides tons of insider information and tips, and is in a great location in Cabecera. The guys here will get you hooked up with paragliding and give you expert insider tips on all the Bucaramanga party spots. On weekends the top floor bar gets lively.

Nest Fly Site Hostel (Km. 2 Vía Mesa de Ruitoque, cell tel. 312/0432-6266, www.colombiaparagliding.com, COP$25,000 dorm, COP$60,000 d) is the place to stay if you're interested in paragliding. It's right next door to the fly site. It's a quiet and cute place, 20 minutes away from the bustle of Buca. Nest is run by the same people as Colombia Paragliding and the Kasa Guane hostel. It is near the Ruitoque town next to the Las Águilas launching pad for most paragliding flights near Bucaramanga.

COP$70,000-200,000

Antigua Belén Bed and Breakfast (Cra. 31 No. 17-22, tel. 7/634-9860, www.hotelantiquabelen.com, COP$133,000 d with a/c) has 13 rooms in a modern house full of antiques. It's located in a rather dull part of town not terribly close to nor too far from anything. Breakfast is served in a pleasant patio in the back.

The Hostal UNAB (Av. 42 No. 48-160, tel. 7/643-6111, ext. 652, COP$154,000 d) has just four comfortable rooms and a restaurant on-site. Right

BOYACÁ

across the street from the university, it might be an odd place to be for a visit to Buca. But it is extremely low-key. It's about a 15-minute walk down to the Parque San Pío from here.

OVER COP$200,000

Hotel Guane (Cl. 34 No. 22-72, tel. 7/634-7014, www.hotelguane.com, COP$206,000 d) is a mid-sized hotel with 40 air-conditioned rooms, a pool, and two restaurants. Cheesy decor. La Serranía (Cl. 33 No. 30-26, tel. 7/691-7535, www.laserrania-hotel.com, COP$250,000 d) has about 50 new and minimalist-style rooms along with a rooftop pool and restaurant. It's overpriced. Ciudad Bonita (Cl. 35 No. 22-01, tel. 7/635-0101, www.hotelciu-dadbonita.com.co, COP$260,000 d) is the fancy hotel in town. It has 70 rooms, two restaurants, a café, a pool, gym, sauna, and there's live music Thursday, Friday, and Saturday evenings. The area it's in is not a pleasant place to walk around day or night.

Food

Want to eat like a local? Look for these Santanderean specialties: *cabrito con pepitoria* (goat fricassee), *carne oreada* (dried meat), and *mute santandereano* (a corn-based meaty stew). And don't forget the ants: fried big bottom ants or *hormigas culonas*. These queen ants are harvested throughout Santander, typically after Semana Santa. After months of hibernation, on one prickly hot day, the queens leave their colony. That's when they are caught. They are later toasted. Eating ants has always been popular and dates back hundreds of years to the Guane culture. Wealthy Santandereanos used to be embarrassed to admit any fondness for the creepy-crawlers, but that's changed, and in fact the ants are showing up more and more on the plates of diners on a quest for the exotic.

◖ Santanero Colonial (Cl. 41 No. 10-54, tel. 7/696-0538, 7:30am-4pm Mon.-Thurs., 7:30am-late Fri., COP$15,000) is one of the top choices for government bureaucrats on lunch break. There is always a set lunch menu (plus à la carte), and frequently you'll have to wait a bit to be seated. Tables are set up around a pleasant sunny patio. It is behind the Gobernación building. La Aldaba (Cl. 37 No. 12-32, tel. 7/642-4062, noon-3pm Mon.-Sat.) is a popular place for an inexpensive lunch. They always have a lunch special that features trout, chicken, or beef for under COP$12,000.

One of Bucaramanga's favorite restaurants is ◖ El Viejo Chiflas (Cra. 33 No. 34-10, tel. 7/632-0640, 9am-midnight Mon.-Wed., Thurs.-Sun. 24 hours, COP$23,000). The atmosphere here is cowboy style with wooden tables and interiors, and the menu features local specialties, such as goat and the Santander classic *carne oreada*. And there's always an arepa (cornmeal cake) with your meal. Portions can be huge. Los Tejaditos (Cl. 34 No. 27-82, tel. 7/634-6028, www.restaurantelostejadi-tos.com, 11am-10pm Tues.-Sat., 11am-5pm Sun., COP$23,000) is an old-style restaurant with a popular special menu at lunchtime. Mercagán (Cra. 33 No. 42-12, tel. 7/632-4949, www.merca-ganparrilla.com, 11am-6pm Mon. and Thurs., 11am-11pm Tues.-Wed. and Fri.-Sat., 11am-4pm Sun., COP$25,000) is a legendary steakhouse in Bucaramanga that has multiple locations, including in many shopping malls.

For a break from the *comida típica* (Colombian fare) thing, there are a few options in Buca. Radha Govinda's (Cra. 34 No. 51-95, tel. 7/643-3382, lunch Mon.-Sat.) is a vegetarian option. It's Hare Krishna-run and is on a quiet street in Cabecera. The Embajada China (Cl. 49 No. 32-27, tel. 7/647-1931, 10am-10pm daily, COP$15,000) is run by a Chinese family, and they serve generous portions. It's in Cabecera near the Kasa Guane. Stir-fries, salads, and pastas are on the menu at Tavolo Gourmet (Cra. 35 No. 48-84, tel. 7/643-7461, www.tavologourmet.com, 11am-10pm Tues.-Sun., COP$18,000). It's a bright and airy place in a fancy neighborhood. The wildly popular Colombian chain Crepes & Waffles (Centro Comercial La Florida, Cl. 31 No. 26A-19, 3rd floor, Local 3090, tel. 7/632-1345, 11:45am-9:30pm Mon.-Sat.,

11:45am-8:30pm Sun., COP$17,000) is a welcome sight.

We'll admit that the crêpes at **C** Crêpes D'Or (Cl. 46 No. 34-28, tel. 7/657-4770, 3:30pm-10pm Mon.-Sat., COP$13,000) are nothing to write home about, although they're fine and fairly priced. What makes this unpretentious family-run spot a delight is its setting overlooking the Parque San Pío. Imagine an outdoor terrace where you look out onto park goers, dogwalkers, and joggers and not onto a steady stream of traffic!

Kirama (Cl. 49 No. 33-37, tel. 7/657-6989, 6am-9pm daily) is a wildly popular spot for breakfast on the run, like an *arepa boyacense* (cornmeal cake stuffed with cheese). Do not be confused by Karima, which is immediately next to it. Kirama says Karima came later. Pan Pa Ya (Cl. 49 No. 28-38, tel. 7/685-2001, 8am-10pm Mon.-Sat, 9am-noon and 5pm-8pm Sun.) is in all the major cities of Colombia, and it's always a reliable place for a decent cup of coffee, pastries, and inexpensive breakfasts (eggs, fresh fruit).

The Mercado Público (between Cras. 15-16 and Clls. 33-34, daily) downtown is a great place to wander about. On multiple floors, you can do some cheap shopping, walking swiftly past the meat section, get a cheap meal on the fourth floor, and enjoy some pretty nice views of the city as well. On the top floor they sell loads of Piedecuesta cigars for cheap as well as baskets, herbs, and *artesanías* (handicrafts). Several stands sell juices and lunches. Some stalls even sell bull's eyes, if you're feeling adventurous.

Information and Services

The tourist office (Cl. 30 No. 26-117, tel. 7/634-1132) is parkside at the Parque de los Niños. Police can be reached by dialing 123, the Hospital Universitario González Valencia (Cra. 33 No. 28-126) by calling tel. 7/634-6110.

Getting There and Around

The Aeropuerto Internacional de Palo Negro (Vía Lebrija), Bucaramanga's airport, is 25 kilometers (15 miles) west of town. Avianca (Cl. 52 No.

35A-10, tel. 7/657-3888, www.avianca.com, 8am-6pm Mon.-Fri., 8am-1pm Sat.), EasyFly (tel. 7/697-0333, www.easyfly.com.co), VivaColombia (tel. 1/489-7989, www.vivacolombia.com.co), and LAN (Col. toll-free tel. 01/800-094-9490, www.lan.com) all serve the city. Taxis to and from the airport to Bucaramanga cost COP$32,000.

Frequent bus service is offered between Bucaramanga and all major cities nationwide as well as small locales in Santander. The Terminal de Transportes (Km. 2 Tr. Metropolitana, tel. 7/637-1000, www.terminalbucaramanga.com) is modern, clean, and open-air. It is off of Calle 70 on the way towards Girón.

The MetroLinea (www.metrolinea.gov.co) is the Bucaramanga version of the Bogotá TransMilenio. These green buses are clean and efficient, and the system covers just about the entire city, although it can be difficult to figure out. Maps of the system are hard to come by, obligating you to ask fellow travelers for information. You can purchase cards for the regular buses (ones that do not have dedicated lanes) at kiosks on the streets.

Taxis are plentiful in Bucaramanga. To order one call Radio Taxis Libres (tel. 7/634-8888) or Taxmovil (tel. 7/633-9090).

The city center area is easily visited on foot, although there is a lot of traffic. The Cabecera area is also more or less walkable, especially in the evenings when traffic calms down.

Mesa de Ruitoque

A surprisingly quiet and rural area to the southeast of Bucaramanga and Floridablanca, Mesa de Ruitoque sits on a plateau and is perfect for paragliding.

PARAGLIDING

The Bucaramanga area is a great place to get over that fear and fly your first tandem paragliding flight, or to take a 10-day course, and the plateau of Mesa de Ruitoque, just 10 minutes from downtown, is where to go.

The area is blessed with 350 flyable days per year, meaning more air time and less waiting around. Colombia Paragliding (www.co-lombiaparagliding.com) offers tandem flights of different durations from the Voladero Las Águilas (Km. 2 Vía Ruitoque, tel. 7/678-6257, www.voladerolasaguilas.com.co) launch point just outside of town near Ruitoque. The Kasa Guane hostel can arrange transportation for you in their van. Instructors are all certified.

A 10-minute flight costs COP$50,000, 20 minutes is $90,000, and a 30-minute flight costs $120,000. Winds are best at this fly site in the afternoon, from noon until 4pm, and the site itself opens each day at 10am. A 10-day certification course is offered by Colombia Paragliding at the Águilas site with additional flight time in Chicamocha. It costs COP$2,300,000 including transportation, meals, and lodging.

The views are quite spectacular from above Bucaramanga. (Bring your camera!) The best way for pilots to judge the winds is by observing the *chulos* (black vultures) as they fly and glide high above. At the fly site there is also a snack bar. The place gets crazy crowded on weekends and on holidays. For a fee of COP$25,000 you can get a DVD of your flight.

a resident yellow-footed tortoise at the Jardín Botánico Eloy Valenzuela

Floridablanca

There aren't loads of reasons to make a special trip to Floridablanca, which has evolved to become essentially a southeastern suburb of Bucaramanga, five kilometers away, but a good one is to take a bite out of one of their famous *obleas,* crisp paper-thin wafers filled with gooey and delicious *arequipe* (caramel spread). Obleas Floridablanca (Cra. 7 No. 5-54, tel. 7/648-5819, 10am-8pm daily) is the most famous *oblea* factory of them all. They've been around since 1949 and as you can imagine have their share of loyal customers. There are around 30 types of *obleas* you can order, although there really is no need to go beyond the classic *oblea* with just *arequipe*. The names of the *obleas* are whimsical. Two of the more popular ones are the *amor eterno* (eternal love), which has *arequipe,* cheese, and

blackberry jam, and the *noviazgo* (courtship), which has *arequipe* and cheese. They also have do-it-yourself *oblea* kits that you can take back home with you.

The Museo Arqueológico Regional Guane (Casa de la Cultura, Cra. 7 No. 4-35, tel. 7/619-8181, 8am-noon and 2pm-6pm Mon.-Fri., COP$1,000) is in need of some love, but the collection of ceramics on display is impressive and extensive. In the courtyard are some pre-Hispanic designs that were found on a large boulder.

Along the manicured lawns of the Jardín Botánico Eloy Valenzuela (tel. 7/634-6100, 8am-5pm daily, COP$4,000) you can wander along paths (sharing them with turtles) and view enormous ceibas and other trees. If you look closely in the tops of trees you might even see some sloths. The Río Frío (it's a stream, really) flows through the gardens. The gardens were revamped and reloaded in 2012. Security is present in the park, and there are always visitors, but be on your guard at some of the far reaches of the gardens. It's not terribly easy, but you can get to the gardens by way of MetroLínea from Bucaramanga.

Girón

While Bucaramanga is a pulsating tribute to the economic growth of modern Colombia, nearby Girón, under 15 minutes and 12 kilometers (7 miles) away to the west, is a living reminder of the colonial past, at least in the town's historic center: The population of Girón is around 150,000 today! It's somewhat surprising to see, in this age of television, Internet, and shopping malls, how the plaza is still the main meeting place in Girón, as it has been since the 17th century. Locals take pride in their town, and winners of the best facades, doors, and windows contest proudly display their plaques in front of their whitewashed *tapia pisada* (adobe) homes.

While it is easy to visit at any time, on weekends Girón has a festive air to it as city folk from Bucaramanga and other day-trip visitors stroll the town's cobblestone streets. There isn't much in the way of tourist sights here, but be sure to visit Basílica Menor San Juan Bautista and the Parque las Nieves, and walk along the *malecón* (wharf).

You might want to consider making Girón your base, instead of Bucaramanga. It's got charm, it's quiet, and traveling back and forth to the metropolis is not an issue. The trip takes under 15 minutes, and taxis will cost only around COP$10,000. You can also get to Girón on the MetroLínea system.

 Girón Chill Out Hotel Boutique (Cra. 25 No. 32-06, tel. 7/646-1119, www.gironnchillout. com, COP$144,000 d) is run by an Italian couple (hence the Italian flag), and while the name suggests an Ibiza atmosphere, the hotel is in a remodeled colonial house. It's quiet, cute, and homey, and they serve authentic Italian food. Las Nieves (Cl. 30 No. 25-71, tel. 7/681-2951, www.hotellasnieves-giron.com, COP$116,000 d with a/c, COP$82,000 d with fan) is right on the plaza, and the best rooms, although at the same time the most used rooms, are the six that have a balcony overlooking the plaza. The interior of the hotel is full of palm trees and greenery, and the owner's dog will let you pet him/her. There are about 30 rooms, many full of twin beds. It's OK.

La Casona (Cl. 28 No. 28-09, tel. 7/646-7195, www.lacasona-restaurante.com, noon-8pm Tues.-Sun., COP$16,000) is a spiffy old place, and they have a fun *onces* (tea time) menu for late afternoon tea, Colombian style: You get a *tamal* (tamale), cheese, breads, and hot chocolate.

CAÑÓN DEL CHICAMOCHA

With an absolutely spectacular location above the Cañón del Chicamocha, the privately run Parque Nacional del Chicamocha (PANACHI, 54 km/34 mi south of Bucaramanga, tel. 7/639-4444, www.parquenacionaldelchicamocha.com, 9am-6pm Tues. and Thurs., 9am-7pm Fri.-Sun., COP$40,000 admission plus round-trip gondola ride) is a mostly cheesy amusement park geared towards Colombian families, but the views? Insert your favorite superlative here. This privately run park has several

a gondola ride across the Cañón del Chicamocha

© ANDREW DIER

attractions, like an ostrich farm, areas that celebrate Santander culture and traditions, extreme sports, and soon a water park, but most people opt for the cable car ride (6.3 kilometers/3.9 miles) across the canyon over the Río Chicamocha. For locals and for tourists who are opposed to backtracking, this is not just a nice excursion, it's a means of transportation. On weekends, holidays, and during the Christmas and Easter holidays, from Bucaramanga you can take a PANACHI bus (cell tel. 316/696-3780) to the park, as a day trip. To get there using public transportation, buses leaving from the Bucaramanga bus terminal bound for San Gil can drop you off at the park. (There are always buses passing the park between San Gil and Bucaramanga, and you can flag them down and hop on.) If you happen to be in that part of town, buses also depart for San Gil from the Papi Quiero Piña store in Floridablanca. By the way, the vistas from the road that hugs the canyon high above the Río Chicamocha make that right-hand side window seat from Bucaramanga worth fighting for.

Mesa de los Santos

The village of Los Santos is on the other side of the canyon from the PANACHI. In this area, known as Mesa de los Santos, there are a number of country homes for weekenders from Bogotá, a few places to stay, and numerous outdoorsy things to do, like visit El Duende waterfall. It ranks second in the world for annual number of tremors at 390 per month (a rate of about one every two hours).

The **Refugio La Roca** (Km. 22 in La Mojarra, cell tel. 312/333-1480, www.refugiolaroca.blogspot.com, COP$60,000 d shared bath) is a kind of hippy-ish pad for "rock climbers, walkers, artists, and other dreamers." Their specialty is rock climbing and it's got quite a jaw-dropping view, overlooking the Chicamocha canyon. Here you can camp for COP$10,000 per night (they also have tents and sleeping bags for rent). There is also one dorm room with four beds for COP$80,000.

At the other end of the spectrum is **El Roble** hotel (after La Mesa toll booth, Mesa de los Santos,

tel. 1/232-8595, www.cafemesa.com, COP$398,000 d). The rate includes a tour of the on-site coffee plantation. This lovely getaway is on a large certified organic coffee farm, set underneath towering oak trees, and teeming with over 100 species of birds. **Ecoposada Vina de Aldana** (cell tel. 317/270-5077 or 300/438-5522, ecoposada.dealdana@gmail.com, COP$80,000 d) is a guesthouse with 20 rooms at a vineyard, where you can take walks, view birds, and take a tour of the vineyard.

SAN GIL

Rafting, paragliding, caving, mountain biking, canyoning, hiking, birding, and rappelling are all within reach in San Gil, Colombia's outdoor adventure capital. This spry city (pop. 43,000) on the steep banks of the Río Fonce is 95 kilometers (59 miles) southwest of Bucaramanga. It caters to international tourists. Even if your idea of "adventurous" is merely being in Colombia, the breathtaking Santander scenery of canyons, rivers, waterfalls, and mountains is more than enough reason to warrant a visit.

During the late 19th and early 20th centuries, San Gil and nearby towns built their prosperity on quinine, coffee, cocoa, and tobacco cultivation. Today, old tile-roofed hangars to dry tobacco, known as *caneys,* still dot the landscape. Today it is a peaceful place to visit and a top tourist destination. San Gil can feel claustrophobic, but accommodations in San Gil are plentiful, comfortable, and inexpensive, and it's got Gringo Mike's.

There's no need to stay in bustling San Gil in order to enjoy the many outdoor activities that the area offers. You can easily organize rafting trips or paragliding adventures from quieter and more charming towns such as Barichara (20 kilometers/12 miles north).

Sights

On the Río Fonce about a 15-minute walk from town is the **Jardín Botánico El Gallineral** (8am-5pm daily, COP$8,000). This used to be just a park, but it has been given a fussy makeover to apparently make it more appealing to tourists, and now

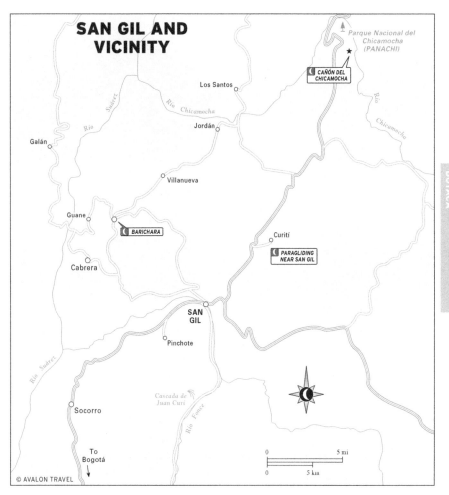

SAN GIL AND VICINITY

Parque Nacional del
Chicamocha
(PANACHI)

CAÑÓN DEL
CHICAMOCHA

Los Santos

Río Chicamocha

Río Chicamocha

Jordán

Río Suárez

Galán

Río

Villanueva

Guane

BARICHARA

Curití

PARAGLIDING
NEAR SAN GIL

Cabrera

SAN
GIL

Pinchote

Río Suárez

Cascada de
Juan Curí

Río Fonce

Socorro

To
Bogotá

0   5 mi

0   5 km

© AVALON TRAVEL

it is a botanical garden. There are cute stalls selling handicrafts, sweets, and coffee along the park's orderly paths. It is a pretty place, and a late-afternoon walk among the towering trees is a nice plan. A restaurant on-site is open for lunch.

Shopping

The best place in San Gil to browse handicrafts is at Corporación Patrimonio Guane, Agata y Yarigui (Cra. 10 No. 9-67, cell tel. 313/892-9681).

Recreation
RAFTING AND KAYAKING

Three rivers near San Gil offer some excellent rafting adventures. The Río Fonce, whose banks the town stands on, is the closest and one of the best suited for rafting. It's a category II-III. It's fine year-round, although in March and April the water level is higher. A rafting trip on the Fonce costs about COP$30,000 for a 90-minute trip. The Río Suárez is a category III-V river. The

BOYACÁ

The Río Fonce flows through San Gil.

© ANDREW DIER

starting point is about an hour's drive towards Bogotá. You'll definitely get wet on this one. The trip leaves at 10am, returning at 4pm, and costs COP$125,000. You're on the water for about 2.5 hours. The third river is the Río Chicamocha, but many consider the previous rivers to be the best.

Colombia Rafting Expeditions (Cra. 10 No. 7-83, tel. 7/724-5800, www.colombiarafting.com) is considered the best rafting company in town. They focus exclusively on river activities. The walls of their small office are covered with diplomas and certificates earned by their team of experienced guides. They can organize trips down all the rivers, determining which one is right for you based upon on skill level, your sense of adventure, and water levels. They also do kayak trips. This company takes safety concerns very seriously and conducts safety training exercises in English.

Three-day kayaking courses (four hours per day starting at 8am) are offered by Colombia Rafting. These cost COP$400,000 and take place on the Río Fonce. They can also arrange for kayaking on the Río Chicamocha. They also rent out kayaks to those who can demonstrate their level of experience. You can also try your hydrospeeding (riverboarding) skills on the Río Fonce. That costs COP$45,000.

PARAGLIDING

There are two main paragliding areas near San Gil. One is the spectacular Cañón del Chicamocha and the other is 16 kilometers (10 miles) away at Las Vueltas in Curití. Tandem paragliding trips over the Chicamocha, of about a 45-minute duration, cost around COP$170,000. That price includes transportation to and from the landing and pickup sites. Chicamocha paragliding flights take place in the mornings. At the windy Las Vueltas location, it will cost you about COP$60,000. Those flights are held in the afternoon. As far as courses go, Colombian Paragliding (cell tel. 312/432-6266, www.colombiaparagliding.com) has the best reputation. They are based near Bucaramanga.

WATERFALLS AND RAPPELLING

The Cascadas de Juan Curí (road to Charalá, COP$7,000) are quite close to San Gil and easily reached on public transportation or by bike. These falls, about 18 meters high, are privately owned by two neighbors who are fierce rivals! For a more rustic climb through the jungle to reach your refreshing goal, go to the second entrance (Donde Efigenia). It's about a 15-minute hike, and it can be treacherous at points. Wear some shoes you don't mind getting muddy and wet. And bring a bathing suit to cool off in one of the pools. You can camp there as well. It's a nice excursion. If you don't want to sweat and struggle at all, take the first entrance. To test your rappelling skills here, contact Páramo Extremo (Cra. 4 No. 4-57, tel. 7/725-8944, www.paramosantanderextremo.com). They can organize an excursion, with all the safety equipment and an experienced guide, for COP$45,000.

CAVING

Several caves around San Gil make for good exploring. The Cueva Indio is one of the most popular. It's filled with bats, and you don't really have to do much bending over to explore. It is near the town of Páramo, just beyond the Cascadas de Juan Curí. An excursion including equipment and a guide costs COP$25,000, but that doesn't include transportation. Contact Páramo Extremo (Cra. 4 No. 4-57, tel. 7/725-8944, www.paramosantanderextremo.com) in the town of Páramo.

The Cueva Vaca, near Curití, is the most challenging of the caves in the area. You will be in water and mud the entire time you are underground, and at one point you'll have to swim underwater to get through to the next cave. It's action packed and there are some tight squeezes as well, but the adventure is worth it. There are lots of stalactites and stalagmites and bats to see. It costs COP$25,000 plus about COP$3,000 in bus transportation. Colombia Rafting (Cra. 10 No. 7-83, cell tel. 311/283-8647, www.colombiarafting.com) or other outfitters can organize a trip here.

The La Antigua cave is on the road towards

The Cascadas de Juan Curí are a great day trip from San Gil.

Barichara. El Dorado Hostel (Cl. 2 No. 8-55, tel. 7/723-7588, www.eldoradohostel.com) organizes an extreme trip that includes the cave plus canyoning, rappelling, and two waterfall descents. All that adventure during just five hours! This trip costs COP$80,000 including transportation.

The Medellín-based outfit Expedición Adventure (cell tel. 314/258-9499, www.expedicionadventure.blogspot.com, expedicionadventure@gmail.com) specializes in unique 3- to 20-day caving trips to mostly unexplored and unspoiled areas in Santander. The starting point is usually in Barbosa, a town between Tunja and Barichara.

BIKING

Colombian Bike Junkies (Cl. 12, No. 8-35, cell tel. 316/327-6101 or 313/411-5332, www.colombianbikejunkies.com), run by a pair from Seattle, Washington, and the United Kingdom, organizes downhill day-trip rides, crazy canyon adventures, multi-activity combos, and multi-day adventures. One day trip starts at 2,000 meters on the top of the Cañón del Chicamocha, going, down, down, down through beautiful countryside to the ghost town of Jordan. After a swim and lunch, there is yet one more downhill trip near Curití. Some 50 kilometers (30 miles) of downhill riding! All on top-of-the-line mountain bikes. If you want to rent a cheap-o bike for the day, go to Bicicletería El Ring (Cl. 7 No. 10-14, tel. 7/724-3189).

SWIMMING

On weekends and on holidays, families head to swimming holes to splash about. The atmosphere is joyous, and there's usually music and plenty of food and drink as well. (A little trash, too, unfortunately.) Pozo Azul is about five minutes by bus or taxi from San Gil (or a 20-minute walk). Pescaderito is in Curití, about a 40-minute bus ride away, and there are five swimming holes in which to cool off. During the week it's quieter.

TOURS

Your hostel or hotel can organize any activity you are interested in doing, but in case you'd like to shop around, contact the following companies. Planeta Azul (Parque El Gallineral, tel. 7/724-0000, www.planetaazulcolombia.com) is an agency that organizes rafting trips as well as a whole host of other activities, like bungee jumping (COP$46,000), caving (COP$40,000), rappelling (COP$40,000), paragliding (COP$60,000), and horseback riding (COP$95,000) to keep you stimulated. Aventura Total (Cl. 7 No. 10-27, tel. 7/723-8888, www.aventuratotal.com.co) has a good reputation as well. They offer all-inclusive packages that include rafting, caving, and other activities as well as hotel accommodations. Aventura Total often organizes activities for large school groups. Nativox (Cra. 11 No. 7-14 Malecón, tel. 7/723-9999, www.nativoxsangil. com) is similar to the previous two.

Accommodations

Good and affordable lodging options are plentiful in San Gil. However, for more space, fresh air, or for more luxury, consider staying in Barichara, Mesa de los Santos, or Pinchote, all close by.

One of the first hostels in town catering to international backpackers, Macondo Hostal (Cra. 8 No. 10-35, tel. 7/724-8001, www.macondohostel. com, COP$18,000 dorm, COP$55,000 d w/bath) remains an excellent choice. Clean dorm rooms, popular with backpackers, and private rooms, popular with older travelers, quickly fill up—make a reservation in advance! They have a hot tub, small garden, and hammocks for post-adventure relaxing. Staff are extremely knowledgeable, helpful, and great at organizing rafting, paragliding, and all other outdoor activities in the region. On the corner next door is the Hostal Colombo Inglés (Cra. 8 No. 9-133, tel. 7/724-3787, www.hostelcolomboingles.com, COP$18,000 dorm, COP$70,000 d), which opened in late 2013. It's small and the staff are friendly. There is no English connection here; it's just a name.

Welcome to *Sam* Gil. Native entrepreneur Sam has two lodging options in the center of town. Super-clean Sam's VIP Hotel (Cr. 10 No. 12-33, tel. 7/724-2746, www.samshostel.com, COP$17,000 dorm, COP$70,000 d) has a great location overlooking the plaza. The terrace is a great place for hanging out in the evenings. Plus there's a teeny pool and a sauna. His second place, with 11 rooms, is La Mansion de Sam Hotel Boutique (Cl. 12 No. 8-71, tel. 7/724-6044, http://hotelmansionsangil.com, COP$70,000-100,000 d) which is set in an old house just a block from the main plaza. Sam has an inviting pub that specializes in steaks, ribs, and beer. Colorful artwork by local artist "Rosenkranz" adorns the walls of the rooms. La Mansion has a lot of character, cool decoration, and big rooms, some with balconies. The only drawback is that cars sometimes park in the interior patio.

The multi-story Hostel Santander Alemán (Cra. 10 No. 15-07, tel. 7/724-0329, www.hostelsantanderalemantv.com, COP$20,000 dorm,

COP$60,000 d) is half a block from the local bus station. It's very clean. Friendly folks, but there's nothing German about it.

If you'd like to get away from the backpacker scene but still pay close to backpacker prices, there are three clean cheapies that may fit the bill. If you stay at the Hotel Capri (Cl. 10 No. 9-31, tel. 7/724-4218, hotelcaprisangil@yahoo.es, COP$40,000), get a room on the third floor overlooking the street. The Hotel Abril (Cl. 8 at Cra. 10, tel. 7/724-8795, hotelabrilsangilss@yahoo.es, COP$45,000 pp) has 28 rooms, good fans, wireless Internet, and hot water. With just six rooms, (Posada Familiar (Cra. 10 No. 8-55, tel. 7/724-8136, COP$45,000 pp high season) makes you feel at home. The patio is filled with flowers and plants, you can cook in the kitchen, and the owner is extremely nice.

To enjoy the peace of the countryside and charm of a colonial town but still be within easy striking distance of San Gil restaurants and activities, consider staying in the hamlet of Pinchote. (Hotel Boutique Wassiki (Km. 3 Vía San Gil-Bogotá, tel. 7/724-8386, www.wassiki.com, COP$164,000-227,000 d) is an excellent upscale hotel and offers well-appointed and airy rooms, comfortable common areas, a beautiful dining room, lots of hammocks, and a pool. It's got a fine view of the valley below and is within walking distance of the idyllic Plaza Principal of Pinchote.

Food

Mostly Tex-Mex (Gringo Mike's (Cl. 12 No. 8-35, tel. 7/724-1695, 8am-11:45am and 5pm-10pm daily, COP$18,000) is paradise for Americans who have been on the road a while. Guac and chips, barbecue burgers, black bean burgers, Philly cheese steak sandwiches, burritos, and even breakfast burritos. It's a bummer it isn't open for lunch, though. Wait staff are on the nonchalant side, and the place is full of tourists, but who cares? The margaritas are perfect!

To brush elbows with the locals try Rogelia (Cra. 10 No. 8-09, tel. 7/724-0823, 7am-7:30pm daily, COP$12,000) or Maná (Cra. 10 No. 9-42,

lunch daily, COP$12,000), which is a popular place for lunch, and inexpensive, too. Try the grilled chicken stuffed with ham and cheese, but don't expect gourmet nor charm.

The best aspect about the Gallineral Restaurante (Parque Gallineral, cell tel. 300/565-2653, 8am-5pm daily, COP$20,000) is its lush setting.

On a second-floor open-air terrace, La Terraza de Sevilla Video-Bar (Cl. 10 No. 9-09, tel. 7/724-3422, 8am-2am Mon.-Sat., COP$12,000) specializes in grilled hamburgers and hot dogs. It's the place to drink beer and watch soccer. For a coffee or drink and a friendly atmosphere, La Habana (Cra. 9 No. 11-68, tel. 7/724-6279, 9am-midnight Mon.-Thurs., 9am-2am Fri.-Sat., 4pm-midnight Sun.) is a good choice.

The market is small, and the atmosphere is peaceful. As you walk through the stalls, you may only hear the hushed tones of the vendors. For a huge fresh fruit juice or just plain fruit in the morning, this is the place to go.

Getting There and Around

The main Terminal de Transportes (Vía al Socorro, tel. 7/724-5858) for buses to the major cities, such as Bucaramanga, Tunja, and Bogotá, is five minutes out of town, on the other side of the river. The journey to Bucaramanga by bus takes 2.5 hours and costs COP$15,000. Traveling to Tunja by bus will take 3-5 hours, to Bogotá 7, and to Santa Marta or Medellín about 12 (vía Bucaramanga). Taxis to and from the main bus terminal to the town center cost COP$3,200.

A smaller bus terminal for nearby towns is on Carrera 15 at Calle 11. It serves towns such as Barichara, Charalá, Curití, and Pescadero. It doesn't have an official name, but some refer to it as the Mini Terminal. Buses to Barichara depart every half hour 6am-6:30pm and cost COP$3,800.

(BARICHARA

In 1975, when it was declared a national monument, Barichara (pop. 8,000) was named the most beautiful pueblo in Colombia. Despite its

BOYACÁ

© ANDREW DIER

Barichara is one of the country's most beautiful pueblos.

popularity with weekenders and a steady stream of international visitors, it hasn't lost its charm. This old tobacco town of sloping cobblestoned streets and white-washed colonial-era homes is permanently blessed with bright blue skies and warm temperatures. Located 20 kilometers (12 miles) northwest of San Gil, the town is on a plateau that overlooks the Río Suárez. Don't skimp on your time here.

Sights

On the serene Parque Principal is the Templo de la Inmaculada Concepción, with two grandiose towers that soar 22 meters into the air. When lit up at night, the sandstone church is particularly striking. The church was completed around 1780. On the west side of the park is the mayor's office. Next to it is the Casa de Cultura.

Up the picturesque Calle 6, at the top of the hill is the Capilla de Santa Bárbara, a Romanesque-style church that is a popular place for weddings. There is a cheesy sculpture garden, Parque de las Artes, at the edge of the Río Suárez canyon.

There are two other colonial churches to see, the Capilla de Jesús (Cra. 7 at Cl. 3), next to the cemetery, and the Capilla de San Antonio (Cra. 4 at Cl. 5). All around town you'll see houses and walls that utilize the *tapia pisada* adobe technique, and often, on these brilliantly white walls you'll see a small patch of the mud interior left exposed on purpose, to show passersby that it's not just a modern brick construction but real *tapia pisada*.

Barichara is the birthplace of Pres. Aquileo Parra Gómez, who was the 11th president of the Estados Unidos de Colombia. His childhood home, Casa Aquileo Parra Gómez (Cl. 6 at Cra. 2), has been extremely well preserved and is an excellent example of typical 19th-century Barichara architecture. The site is also a handicraft workshop for the elderly, who make woven bags and other items out of the natural fiber *fique*, which are sold for a pittance. It is an excellent social program, and they seem to have a good time. They are there Monday through Thursday.

BOYACÁ

© ANDREW DIER

the Camino Real between Barichara and Guane

CAMINO REAL

A must-do activity in Barichara is to take the 5.3-kilometer (3.3-mile) Camino Real path to the pueblo of Guane. It's a lovely path that zigzags down from the plateau of Barichara through farmland, affording nice views of the countryside and an excellent opportunity to burn off a few vacation calories. Parts of the path are lined with stone walls that have been there for centuries.

Before the conquest, indigenous tribes throughout what is now Colombia traded crops and goods with each other utilizing an extensive network of footpaths. These trails meandered through the countryside of present-day Santander, Boyacá, Norte de Santander, Cundinamarca, and beyond. During Spanish rule, the paths continued to be a major means of communication between colonial towns, and the networks became known as Caminos Reales.

In the late 19th century, a German, Geo von Legerke, restored the Barichara-Guane Camino Real and built a stone bridge across the Río Suárez

in order to improve transportation to the mighty Río Magdalena.

The hike down takes two hours, and you don't need a guide: It's well marked, well trodden, and safe. To get to the trailhead, walk east along Carrera 10 to the Piedra de Bolívar, where you'll see the stone path leading down towards the valley.

In Guane you can check out the small Museo Isaias Ardila Díaz (Parque Principal, hours vary), which has three rooms, one on paleontology (fossils), the next on archaeology (mummy), and a third on colonial life in rural Santander. *Sabajón,* which is the Colombian version of eggnog, is the sweet specialty in Guane, and it is sold in various shops around the park.

If you are not up for the hike a (cute) bus departs the Parque Principal in Barichara at 6am, 9:30am, 11:30am, 2:30pm, and 5:30pm (it returns 30 minutes later from Guane).

Festivals and Events

Little Barichara proudly hosts two annual film

BOYACÁ

© SOPHIE TRAEN/123RF

Cobblestone streets in the colonial village of Guane

festivals. The Festival Internacional de Cine de Barichara (www.ficba.com.co) takes place in June, and the Festival de Cine Verde (www.festiver.org), an environmentally themed festival, is held every September.

Shopping

Barichara has always been a magnet for artists and craftspeople, and many have shops in town.

The Fundación Escuela Taller Barichara (Cra. 5 No. 4-26, tel. 7/726-7577, www.tallerdeoficiosbarichara.com, 8am-7pm Mon.-Thurs., 8am-10pm Fri.-Sat., 8am-4pm Sun.) is a gallery, museum, school, shop, and restaurant, all wrapped up in one. Occasional photography and painting exhibitions are held at this lovely cultural center, decorative objectives traditional from the area are always on display, ceramics and other items made by students are for sale, and anyone can take a month-long or longer course here. They offer dozens for free, and the Cruces restaurant is the best restaurant in town (it's open on weekends and holidays).

An interesting stop to make is at the Taller de Papel de Fique (Cl. 6 No. 2-68, no phone, 8am-3pm Mon.-Thurs.). At this workshop, craftspeople make beautiful paper out of the natural fiber of *fique*. On sale in their small store are cards, stationery, and handicrafts, all produced using that natural fiber. They are also now experimenting with other paper made from pineapple leaves. Short tours explaining the paper-making process are given, and for this there is a small charge.

One of the best-known ceramic artists in town is Jimena Rueda (Cra. 5 No. 2-01, cell tel. 314/400-5071). In addition to browsing her work, ask about the famous rustic handmade pottery of the Guane people. There is only one person who knows and uses this technique: Ana Felisa Alquichire. Doña Ana Felisa has been declared a living national cultural treasure by the Colombian presidency.

Galería Anil (Cl. 6 No. 10-46, cell tel. 311/470-1175) is the studio for local artists Jasmín and Carlos.

Accommodations

With its growth in popularity, accommodations

options to fit all budgets and styles have popped up in Barichara.

Backpackers and budget travelers have several options in Barichara. The ((Color de Hormiga Hostel (Cl. 6 No. 5-35, cell tel. 315/297-1621, http://colordehormiga.com/hostel.html, COP$45,000 d) used to house teachers from a neighboring school. It's decorated with institutional furniture that was left behind and kept the groovy tiled floors as they are. Funky! There are seven small rooms for one or two people, each with its own private bath. The kitchen is open for use by guests. The ((Reserva Natural (Vereda San José Alto, cell tel. 315/297-1621, COP$70,000 pp d), from the same owner as the Color de Hormiga Hostel, is a step up, with more luxury, more solitude, and a crazy bird show every morning while you have a healthy breakfast. Birds representing all colors of the rainbow appear like clockwork every morning to munch on pieces of banana and papaya to the delight of guests enjoying their breakfasts. This is about a 10-minute walk from town. The staff is incredibly friendly.

The Tinto Hostel (Cl. 6 No. 2-61, Bloque E Casa 1, tel. 7/726-7725, www.hosteltintobarichara.com) is a friendly hostel. It's in a weird, mostly residential cul de sac, about a 10-minute downhill walk from town. It seems farther away than it actually is. They are helpful with organizing outdoor adventures in the San Gil area. The funky hostel award in Barichara goes to Casa Bakú (Cl. 5 No. 9-69, cell tel. 301/419-2136, bakuhostal@hotmail.com). Baku, as in the capital of Azerbaijan. Like it or not, it's a social place. It's tiny. The common area, with a little homage to Bob Marley, is basically a garden with a bar and chairs. That's where they serve breakfast, which is included.

On the edge of town past the hospital, Artepolis (Cra. 2 at Cl. 2, cell tel. 300/203-4531) was getting going when we arrived. It is a Frenchman's idea of creating a space for creative people to come and find creative inspiration in the marvelous setting of Barichara. Its formal and serious sounding name is the Centro Internacional de Encuentro y Formación para el Arte y Cultura.

Ahh, the boutique hotel. Barichara didn't have them before; now it does! La Nube (Cl. 7 No. 7-39, tel. 7/726-7161, www.lanubeposada.com, COP$330,000 d) was boutique before that word entered the Colombian hotel lexicon. It's still a comfortable choice. It has seven rooms and a good restaurant (breakfast not included), and the patio is a nice place for relaxing to the soothing sound of a fountain. Achiotte Hotel Boutique (Cl. 5 No. 3-52, tel. 7/726-7512, COP$220,000 d) is a well-done, quiet hotel, with large rooms and common spaces filled with bamboo, flowers, and trees. You can shower here in the open air (nobody will see you!). At present the hotel has about nine rooms, which makes it really feel boutique. Along with a pool, there are plans to add several more rooms, which may change the feeling.

((El Cogollo (Cra. 11 No. 7-37, cell tel. 311/202-4391, www.baricharacogollo.com, COP$280,000) is a very comfortable boutique-type hotel with eight rooms. The hotel uses construction materials and techniques from the earth, such as *tapia pisada, bahreque, adobe,* and stone. They operate the travel agency Barichara Travel (www.baricharaguanecito.com).

Finally, there is the peaceful Posada Sueños de Antonio (Cra. 9 No. 4-25, tel. 7/726-7793, www.suenosdeantonio.com, COP$120,000 d), with five spacious rooms surrounding an interior patio.

Food

The Restaurante y Café Las Cruces (Cra. 5 No. 4-26, tel. 7/726-7577, www.tallerdeoficiosbarichara.com, Fri.-Sun. and daily during high season, COP$28,000) is considered the top restaurant in Barichara. It's in the patio of the Fundación Escuela Taller Barichara. Plenilunio Café (Cl. 6 No. 7-74, tel. 7/726-7485, 6:30pm-10pm daily, COP$22,000) serves mostly Italian food but also has backpacker favorites like veggie burgers. There are just a handful of tables in this cozy spot, and most all of them are occupied by content foreign visitors on balmy Barichara evenings.

BOYACÁ

La Puerta (Cl. 6 No. 8-51, tel. 7/726-7649, www.baricharalapuerta.com, lunch and dinner daily high season, COP$22,000) is a beautiful place, candlelit at night. They serve tasty pastas and use local, organic ingredients when possible. Castañetos (Cl. 6 No. 10-43, tel. 7/726-7765, 6:30pm-10pm daily high season, COP$24,000) is the best pizzeria in town.

At the other end of town, near the canyon, is Al Cuoco (Cra. 4 No. 3B-15, cell tel. 312/527-3628, noon-9pm or 10pm daily, COP$22,000), an Italian place run by a Roman. They make their own pasta.

Locals throng to El Balcón de Mi Pueblo (Cl. 7 No. 5-62, cell tel. 318/280-2980, noon-5pm daily, COP$12,000) because they serve good, meaty Colombian food (*cabro, carne oreada, churrasco*) without serving up Bogotá prices! It's a cute place, up on the second floor. Another favorite is the lunch-only option Misifú (Cra. 6 No. 6 31, tel. 7/726-7321, noon-6pm daily, COP$12,000). Their specialty is the local specialty *carne oreada,* a dry and toothsome steak, reminiscent of beef jerky.

For a coffee or some of their world-famous (or at least pueblo-famous) *galletas de cuajada* (cheese cookies), head to Panadería Barichara (Cl. 5 No. 5-33, tel. 7/726-7688, 7am-1pm and 2pm-8pm daily). They've been around since 1954.

The best nightlife in town? Head to the Mirador bar on the west side of town overlooking the Río Suárez at around 5:30pm. Free sunsets are included with the price of your Águila beer!

Getting There

Most visitors arrive either in their own transportation or by bus to Barichara. Buses from Bogotá depart from the Autopista Norte Station. The journey to San Gil takes six hours or more, and you'll have to transfer in San Gil. It costs COP$30,000. From Bucaramanga, from the Piedecuesta terminal, a bus leaves at 4:45pm Monday-Friday. On Saturday the bus departs at 9am and on Sunday at 7:30pm. It takes three hours and costs COP$15,000. *Busetas* leave San Gil every half hour from the Terminal de Transportes Monday-Sunday starting at 6:10am, with the last bus departing at 8:15pm. The 20-kilometer (12-mile) journey takes 45 minutes.

Norte de Santander

This department in the northeast of the country borders Venezuela to the east and Santander to the south. The two main places of interest are Pamplona and Cúcuta, two very different cities. Pamplona is a charming and cool highland town that was important during the colonial era, though much of its colonial architecture has disappeared due to earthquakes and the march toward progress. To the north, the departmental capital of Cúcuta is a large, boiling hot commercial city and gateway to Venezuela. Both cities are easily accessed by road from Bucaramanga. The southernmost area of Norte de Santander and the northernmost area of Catatumbo have been plagued with guerrilla and paramilitary activity in recent years and are best avoided.

PAMPLONA

This historic and charming colonial town is a refreshing change from the *calor* (heat) of Cúcuta and Bucaramanga, set in a lush, agriculturally rich valley at 2,300 meters (7,500 feet). In addition to colonial remnants like the Casa de las Tres Marías (now Museo de Arte Moderno Eduardo Ramírez Villamizar), Pamplona is known for being the home of abstract expressionist artist Eduardo Ramírez, and for being a surprisingly lively college town, home to the Universidad de Pamplona and thousands of students.

Sights

Pamplona has its share of museums, and they are all easily visited in a day on foot. The best museum here is the Museo de Arte Moderno Eduardo Ramírez Villamizar (Cl. 5 No. 5-75, tel. 7/568-2999, www.mamramirezvillamizar.com, 9am-noon and 2pm-5pm Tues.-Sun., COP$3,000), prominently located on the Parque Agueda Gallardo. This museum, in a lovingly restored 16th-century house, features the work of this modernist sculptor and painter and also puts on temporary shows of modern and contemporary Colombian artists. In the courtyard, surrounding a magnolia tree, are many Ramírez sculptures. Born in Pamplona in 1922, Ramírez passed away in Bogotá in 2004.

Around the corner is the Museo Arquidiocesano de Arte Religioso (Cra. 5 No. 4-87, tel. 7/568-2816, 10am-noon and 3pm-5pm Wed.-Mon., COP$2,000). It houses oil paintings from masters such as Gregorio Arce y Ceballos and others, wood carvings dating back to the 17th century, and silver and gold ceremonial items.

The most interesting churches to check out include the imposing Catedral Santa Clara (Cl. 6 between Cras. 5-6), which dates back to 1584, and the Ermita del Señor del Humilladero (Cl. 2 between Cras. 7-8), which is next to the cemetery, filled with above-ground tombs. It is famous for its realistic carving Cristo del Humilladero.

The Casa Mercado (Cl. 6 between Cras. 4-5) stands on the previous location of a Jesuit college; this covered market was built in 1920. The Museo Casa Colonial (Cl. 6 No. 2-56, tel. 7/568-2043, www.casacolonialpamplona.com, 8am-noon and 2pm-6pm Mon.-Fri., free) packs quite a punch in its 17th-century abode. It includes exhibits on some of the native cultures from the area, touches on the independence movement and struggles of the early Colombian republic, and takes the visitor through to the 20th century.

Finally, the small Museo Casa Anzoátegui (Cra. 6 No. 7-48, 9am-noon and 2pm-5:30pm Mon.-Sat., COP$1,000) examines the life of General José Antonio Anzoátgui and the fight for independence from Spain. It was in this house that this war hero died in 1819. He was the head of Bolívar's honor guard and was promoted to general following the Batalla del Puente de Boyacá.

Accommodations and Food

Hostal 1549 (Cl. 8B No. 8-64, Calle los Miserables, tel. 7/568-0451, www.1549hostal.com, COP$130,000) has a big problem: Your room is so cozy that it will take an effort to get out and explore the town. Seven spacious rooms have big, comfortable beds, and many have fireplaces. The hotel has an adjacent restaurant where breakfast is served. At night locals gather to drink, but they are usually shown the door by 11pm.

Somewhat quirky, the Hotel Ursua (Cl. 5 No. 5-67, tel. 7/568-2470, COP$40,000 d) has a fantastic location right on the main park, and rooms, with beds that will do, come in all shapes and sizes. The restaurant serves inexpensive breakfasts and lunches.

Once home to a scribe to the Spanish authorities in the 18th century, El Solar (Cl. 5 No. 8-10, tel. 7/568-2010, www.elsolarhotel.com, COP$110,000 d) is one of the most popular accommodation and restaurant options in Pamplona. It has 10 rooms, and 21 beds. Breakfast at their restaurant is included, as is wireless Internet.

Pierro's Pizza (Cra. 5 No. 8B-67, tel. 7/568-0160, 5pm-11pm daily, COP$20,000) is the most popular place for pizza (as well as a whole host of other favorites), and it's run by an Italian. Other favorites include Sal y Pimienta (Cra. 5A No. 8B-66, cell tel. 301/196 2464, 5pm 10pm daily, COP$18,000), and Restaurante Pioko (Cl. 5 No. 5-49 tel. 7/568-3031, 7am-9pm, COP$18,000) specializes in trout dishes.

Vegetarians will want to hunt for the hard-to-find Hare Krishna-run Majesvara (Cra. 3B No. 1C-26, cell 310/267-9307, 11am-2pm and 6pm-9pm Mon.-Sat., COP$8,000). If you find it try their set lunch or dinner menu.

Every town should have a place like Stanco La Rokola (Cl. 9 No. 5-23 Plazuela Almeida). It's a tiny nook on the Plazuela Almeida, where for about COP$2,000 you can order a shot of tequila, vodka, or rum, and then be on your merry way.

Getting There

Pamplona is reached by bus from Cúcuta. These leave on an hourly basis, and the two-hour trip costs about COP$10,000. You can also take a bus to Pamplona from Bucaramanga. It costs about COP$28,000 and takes under five hours. Pamplona's bus station is the spic and span Terminal de Transportes (Barrio El Camellón), about a 10-minute walk from the town center.

CÚCUTA

Midway between Bogotá and Caracas, the sizzling capital (pop. 637,000) of the Norte de Santander department straddles the border with Venezuela. Streets are lined with vendors selling cheap Venezuelan gasoline. A favorite and cheap beer served in restaurants and bars is Polar, straight from Venezuela. There is a constant stream of traffic crossing the border on the Puente Internacional in both directions. Venezuelans used to come to Cúcuta for shopping, but now it is the Colombians who are going east to load up on goods. Nonetheless, there is always a Venezuelan presence in Cúcuta, especially on weekends and holidays.

In recent years, the city has seen a large influx of persons fleeing violence in other parts of Norte de Santander and Arauca. During the 1990s, there was a bloody turf war between paramilitaries and leftist guerrillas. In 2008, in response to months of simmering tension, pop singer Juanes organized *Paz sin Fronteras* (Peace Without Borders), a concert on the border between Colombia and Venezuela, to the delight of nearly 300,000 fans. Today the city is considered a safe place to visit.

Many foreign travelers in Cúcuta are there either to cross over into Venezuela so that they can extend their visit in Colombia on their tourist visa, or they are on their way to Caracas. Despite its reputation as a hot, uninteresting city, Cúcuta is a pleasant place to explore for a couple of days.

The downtown area of the City of Trees is quite walkable, with trees lining its broad streets. There are a handful of republican period churches and buildings worth a look. And at night, particularly on weekends, restaurants, cafés, and bars in the Caobos district are pleasant gathering places for Cucuteños of all ages.

The main tourist attraction is just outside of the city in Villa del Rosario, on the way toward Venezuela. That's where Colombia's Thomas Jefferson, General Francisco de Paula Santander was born, and also is where the first constitution for Gran Colombia was drafted. Simón Bolívar officially became the country's president here.

ORIENTATION

The western boundary of Cúcuta is basically the parched Río Pamplonita and, before that, the Avenida Libertadores. A lot of the big restaurants and nightlife spots are located here, and this is where the Ciclovía is held on Sundays. The Diagonal Santander represents the boundary of the downtown towards the north. It links the Terminal de Transportes in the northwest of the city to the stadium and finally merges into the Autopista Internacional (the road that leads to San Antonio, Venezuela) in the east. All the decent hotels and most sights of interest in Cúcuta are located in the downtown area between Avenida 0 to the east and Avenida 6 to the west and Calle 8 to the north and Calle 13 to the south. Ventura Plaza Centro Comercial is a good landmark to remember. It is between Avenida 0 and the Diagonal Santander. The Aeropuerto Camilo Daza is in the northwest of the city.

Sights

CITY CENTER

All the sights in downtown Cúcuta can easily be visited on foot. There is not a tourism culture here, so obtaining basic information such as opening hours and telephone numbers is not always easy. At the beautifully restored Biblioteca Pública Julio Pérez Ferrero (Av. 1 No. 12-35, Barrio La Playa, tel. 7/595-5384, www.bibliocucuta.org, 8am-noon and 2pm-6pm Mon.-Fri., 9am-noon Sat.) there is always something going on: photography exhibits on old Cúcuta, classes and workshops, concerts. The library building,

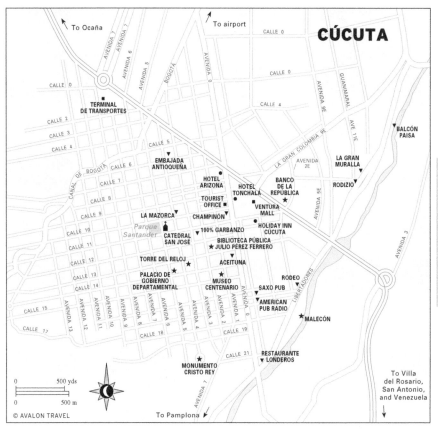

declared a national monument, originally served as a hospital in the late 18th century. The library also operates the Museo Centenario (Cl. 14 No. 1-03, tel. 7/595-5384, www.museocentenario.com, 8am-noon and 2pm-6pm Mon.-Fri., 9am-noon Sat.), which is often the host of art exhibitions and events. It is a newish addition to the cultural scene. It is open only when there is something going on.

The Palacio de Gobierno Departamental (Clls. 13-14 and Avs. 4-5, not open to the public) is noteworthy for its republican, neoclassical architecture. Torre del Reloj (Cl. 13 and Avs. 3-4) houses a clock that plays the national anthem on its bells at noon each day. The bells came from

Italy in the early 19th century. You can ask to check it out. From the top, if you can squeeze past the bells you can get a nice view of the city with the Monumento Cristo Rey (Av. 4 at Cl. 19) in the distance. The Torre del Reloj is part of the Casa de la Cultura complex. It also hosts art exhibitions. The neoclassical Catedral San José (Av. 5 No. 10-53) faces the shady Parque Santander (Avs. 5-6 and Clls. 10-11). Finally, be sure to walk along Calle 10 or Calle 11. Canned music blares from loudspeakers on the streets all day long.

The Banco de la República (Diagonal Santander No. 3E-38, tel. 7/575-0131, www.banrepcultural.org/cucuta, 8am-11:30am, 2pm-6pm

Parque Gran Colombiano

Mon.-Fri.) always has an art exhibition on view, usually featuring a Colombian artist. Concerts are also held at their theater. It is just outside of the city center.

PARQUE GRAN COLOMBIANO

The major historical site in Cúcuta is actually seven kilometers away in Villa del Rosario on the road towards San Antonio del Táchira, Venezuela. The Parque Gran Colombiano is in the middle of the busy highway that leads to the Venezuelan border. Although much of the park is green space where couples kiss under palm trees and others jog or walk their dogs, the most important historical sites within the park are the Casa Natal del General Santander (Km. 6 Autopista Internacional, tel. 7/570-0265, 8am-11am and 2pm-5pm Tues.-Sat., 9am-5pm Sun. and holidays, free) and the ruins of the Templo del Congreso. The museum tells the story of General Francisco de Paula Santander and is set in his childhood home. The Templo del Congreso is where Gran Colombia's Constitution of 1821 was drafted and where Simón Bolívar was sworn in as president (and Santander as vice president). The church was badly damaged in the Cúcuta Earthquake of 1875, and only the dome, in a different style altogether, was rebuilt. It's unavoidable that there is a bronze statue of Bolívar inside the ruins. The congress met for over a month to draft the constitution, and on their breaks, they would rest under the shade of a huge tamarind tree. It's still there, right in front of the church.

Across the highway is the Casa de la Bagatela, which was the seat of the executive branch of Gran Colombia. It was named La Bagatela in honor of independence figure Antonio Nariño, who penned a revolutionary paper in Bogotá by that same name. Don't bother scurrying across the highway to the Casa de la Bagatela, as there's nothing much to see.

You can take a shared taxi or a *buseta* (small bus) bound for San Antonio del Táchira at the Ventura Plaza mall. These cost around COP$2,500. Ask to be dropped off at the Parque Gran Colombiano. Private taxis cost about COP$7,500 from downtown Cúcuta.

Nightlife

There are three trendy nightlife areas: the lovely and leafy Caobos neighborhood, the *malecón* (wharf) along the Río Pamplonita, and in the Centro Comercial Bolívar.

In Caobos, in the newly branded Zona E (because many spots are along the Avenida 1E) there are dozens of pub-like places where you can have a bite and/or have a brew outside on the terrace. It's not a bad atmosphere. Pubs are all more or less the same, but be on the lookout for these popular spots: American Pub Radio (Av. 1E No. 16-20, tel. 7/594-8398, www.americanpubradio.com); Saxo Pub (Cl. 16 No. 1E-13 tel. 7/571-4270, www.saxo-pub.com, 4pm-2am daily); and British Pub (Cl. 17 No. 1E-05, 5:30pm-2am Tues.-Thurs., 5:30pm-3am Fri. and Sat.).

To the east and along the banks of the Río Pamplonita, many of the restaurants in town evolve into party places as the night wears on. Another very Cúcuteño way to party is to grab your friends and pick up some booze, drive down to the Avenida de los Libertadores and park, and pump up the *vallenatos* (ballads accompanied by accordions) or, occasionally, electronica. To the north the nearby Centro Comercial Bolívar has a number of bars, including a couple of gay clubs, as well as clubs catering to salsa aficionados.

Recreation

On Sunday morning, head to the Avenida de los Libertadores/Paseo de los Proceres/*malecón* along the Río Pamplonita. You can work up a sweat with the locals here as they ride their bikes and jog during their mini Ciclovía (7am-1pm). Bike rentals aren't available, but you can always jog or people-watch.

To arrange an organized tour of points of interest in Norte de Santander contact Crischarol Tours (Cl. 13 No. 5-60, tel. 7/572-0407, www.crischaroltours.blogspot.com). They offer day-trip tours to Pamplona.

Accommodations

Astonishingly, Cúcuta, the sixth largest city in Colombia, did not have any international or even national chain hotels until Holiday Inn announced its arrival in late 2014. With 98 rooms, and located across from the Ventura Plaza mall, it is a much needed addition. Most downtown hotels have seemingly been around forever, the kind where you are handed the remote control in its plastic cover when you check in, and staff are dressed in outdated uniforms.

Outside of town, in Villa del Rosario, there are other hotel options. These are popular places on the weekends. Continuing onward into San Antonio, hotel options are abysmal. They are cheap, but abysmal.

It once probably seemed very flashy, but retro Hotel Tonchalá (Av. 0 at Cl. 10, tel. 7/575-6444, www.hoteltonchala.com, COP$209,0900 d) has kept up with the times by updating the rooms (there are about 100 of them). The hotel has a pool, gym, and sauna. It's within easy walking distance of Ventura Plaza Centro Comercial.

Staff dressed in bright pink uniforms at the Hotel Arizona Suites (Av. 0 No. 7-62, tel. 7/573-1884, www.hotelarizonasuites.com, COP$245,000) are so exceptionally friendly, even the most persnickety of guests will find it hard to lodge any complaint. Rooms are fine, a little on the small side, and definitely overpriced. The restaurant overlooks a small pool, and the spa area was renovated in 2012. The location is OK, not great, near two busy streets and about a 10-minute walk to sights downtown.

If you would rather be surrounded by greencry than concrete you might want to consider the Hotel Villa Antigua (Autopista San Antonio-Villa del Rosario, tel. 7/570-0399, www.hotelvillantigua.amawebs.com, COP$120,000 d). It is geared mostly towards Colombian families and groups as a weekend place to kick back and drink by the large pool. During the week you'll likely have the place to yourself. They have cabanas of several sizes and then spacious regular hotel rooms. Breakfast is served in an outdoor restaurant overlooking the pool, but it smells like either gas or strong floor wax. Wireless Internet is available in the lobby. The Parque Gran Colombiano is just across the street, but you must be very careful crossing the street. This is the main drag to San Antonio, and cars and buses absolutely zoom by. At the park you can go for a morning or late afternoon walk. If you want to go into town during the day or at night, it is not an issue: Taxis are cheap and it takes about 15 minutes.

Food

The most typical food from Cúcuta includes *hayacas cucutenas,* similar to tamales; *mute,* a meaty stew; and *pastel de garbanzo* (a fried garbanzo bean pastry).

The **Embajada Antioqueña** (Cl. 6 No. 3-48, tel. 7/571-7673, 8am-10pm daily, COP$20,000) has hearty breakfasts (meaty *caldos* or broths), lunches, and dinners. It's been around for about 40 years, and the atmosphere, with tango music and Colombian classics, is quite nice. Try the baby beef or their *típica* plate with ground beef chorizo, *chicharón* (sausage), rice, and arepa, or at lunchtime the COP$8,000 set lunch. **La Mazorca** (Av. 4 No. 9-23, tel. 7/571-1800, 7am-8pm daily, COP$18,000) is a popular chain restaurant serving the gamut of Colombian fare.

For a welcome break from meat eating, try **Champiñon** (Cl. 10 No. 0-05, tel. 7/571-1561, 8am-8:30pm Mon.-Sat., COP$12,000). This, Cúcuta's best and biggest vegetarian restaurant, opens in the morning for coffee and pastries, then offers a generous set lunch. Off the menu you can order veggie burgers, salads, and pastas. **Aceituna** (Av. 0 No. 13-135, tel. 7/583-7464, 10:30am-10pm Mon.-Sat., COP$18,000) is a long-standing Lebanese food restaurant run by a Lebanese-Colombian family.

Vegetarians, almost always prohibited from the joys of Colombian street food delights, will rejoice at the sight of *pasteles de garbanzo* purveyor **100% Garbanzo** (Cl. 11 No. 2-83, cell tel. 313/498-1712, 8am-noon and 2pm-6pm Mon.-Fri.). This snack bar is a great place to sample the bean pastry.

When darkness falls in Cúcuta, especially on the weekends, the energy shifts to the *malecón* area, about a 10-minute cab ride from downtown.

That's where many of the big restaurants are located. **Londeros Sur** (Av. Libertadores No. 0E-60B, tel. 7/583-3335, www.restaurantelonderos.com, COP$25,000) is famous around town for its Argentinian steaks; **Rodizio** (Av. Libertadores No. 10-121, tel. 7/575-1719, www.rodizio.com.co, COP$30,000) for its Brazilian-style grilled meats; and **Rodeo** (Av. Libertadores No. 16-38, www.rodeogourmet.com, COP$25,000) is another very popular carnivorous option. **Balcón Paisa** (Av. Los Libertadores No. 6-40, tel. 7/575-0244, COP$22,000) is one of the most popular restaurants on the *malecón* and is huge. In addition to a vast menu of Colombian dishes, they often feature live shows. Late at night it becomes more rumba than restaurant. And for a departure, **La Gran Muralla** (Av. Libertadores No. 10-84, tel. 7/575-3946, COP$18,000) is one of the best-known Chinese places in town.

The mall, the **Ventura Plaza Centro Comercial** (between Clls. 10 and 11 at Diagonal Santander, www.venturaplaza.com.co) is usually a safe bet for a bite of fast food, if you have run out of ideas. The food court area is open until 10:30pm.

Information and Services

The **tourist office** (Cl. 10 No. 0-30, no phone, 8am-noon and 2pm-6pm Mon.-Fri., 8am-noon Sat.) has lots of brochures and maps for not only Cúcuta but also the rest of the Norte de Santander department. Staff can provide some good tips on visiting natural attractions in the area.

In case of an emergency, contact the **Policia Nacional** (tel. 7/576-0622, or 123). A major hospital in town is the **Hospital Erasmo Meoz** (Av. 11E with Cl. 4N Guaimaral, tel. 7/574-6888).

Getting There and Around

The **Terminal de Transportes** (Avs. 7-8 between Clls. 1-2) in Cúcuta is dirty, chaotic, and generally unpleasant, and is probably the main reason so many arrive in Cúcuta with a poor impression of the city. Try to get your ticket in advance or at least find out the schedule so you don't have to be there longer than necessary. If you are waiting for a bus, it's best to wait outside on the curb, far from the claustrophobic station. There are numerous buses to Pamplona and other towns near Cúcuta. The bus to Bogotá costs around COP$70,000 and the trip takes 14 hours. To Bucaramanga it costs COP$30,000 and takes six hours, and to San Gil it costs about COP$45,000 and takes eight hours.

The airport, Aeropuerto Camilo Daza (Km. 5 Autopista Panamericana), is a 15-minute cab ride from downtown. Avianca (Cl. 13 No. 5-22, tel. 7/571-3877, www.avianca.com, 8am-noon and 2pm-6pm Mon.-Fri., 8am-noon Sat.) flies nonstop between Cúcuta and Bogotá and Medellín; EasyFly (tel. 7/595-5005, www.easyfly.com.co) connects Cúcuta with Bucaramanga and Medellín; and LAN (Col. toll-free tel. 01/800-094-9490, www.lan.com.co) flies to Bogotá.

If you are staying downtown, all attractions are within relatively easy walking distance. It's always a good policy to call a cab beforehand, and always after dark. Two reputable services are Taxis Radio Taxi Cone (tel. 7/582-1666) and Radio Taxi Radio (tel. 7/583-6828).

CROSSING INTO VENEZUELA

Crossing the border from Cúcuta into San Antonio del Táchira on the Venezuelan side is easy. *Busetas* (shared taxis) depart from in front of the Ventura Plaza mall. Expect to pay about COP$2,500 for a bus ticket. Taxis will cost upwards of COP$20,000. Be sure to get off before the bridge so you can get your passport stamped by immigration officials. Visas are not required for North Americans or European Union citizens. Hotels in San Antonio del Táchira are absolutely dismal, so it's far better to either stay in Cúcuta or continue onwards to Caracas immediately. For more information on visas you can visit the Consulado Venezuelano (Av. Aeropuerto Camilo Daza, Sector Corral de Piedra, Zona Industrial, Cl. 17 Esquina, tel. 7/579-1954 or 7/579-1951, 8am-10am and 2pm-3pm Mon.-Thurs., 8am-10am Fri.).

BOYACÁ

MAP SYMBOLS

═══ Expressway	【 Highlight	✈ Airport	⚲ Golf Course
⋯⋯ Primary Road	○ City/Town	✈ Airfield	₽ Parking Area
─── Secondary Road	◉ State Capital	▲ Mountain	▱ Archaeological Site
─ ─ Unpaved Road	❀ National Capital	✛ Unique Natural Feature	⌂ Church
─ ─ Trail	★ Point of Interest		⬓ Gas Station
⋯⋯⋯ Ferry	• Accommodation	Waterfall	⤳ Dive Site
─ ─ Railroad	▼ Restaurant/Bar	⚑ Park	Mangrove
⋯⋯ Pedestrian Walkway	▪ Other Location	❶ Trailhead	Reef
⌇⌇⌇ Stairs	Λ Campground	🗼 Lighthouse	Swamp

CONVERSION TABLES

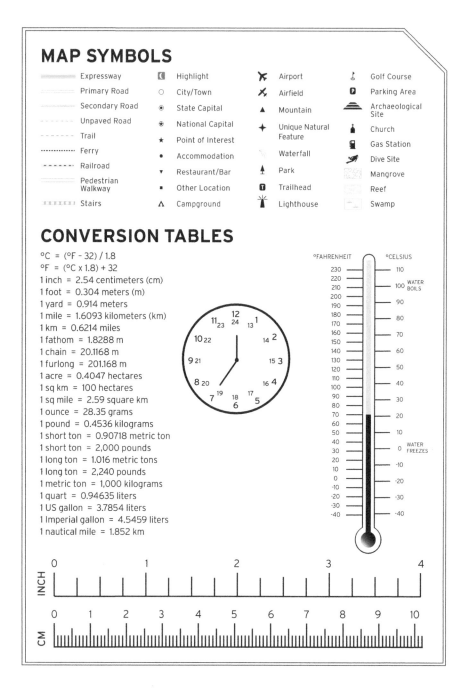

°C = (°F − 32) / 1.8
°F = (°C x 1.8) + 32
1 inch = 2.54 centimeters (cm)
1 foot = 0.304 meters (m)
1 yard = 0.914 meters
1 mile = 1.6093 kilometers (km)
1 km = 0.6214 miles
1 fathom = 1.8288 m
1 chain = 20.1168 m
1 furlong = 201.168 m
1 acre = 0.4047 hectares
1 sq km = 100 hectares
1 sq mile = 2.59 square km
1 ounce = 28.35 grams
1 pound = 0.4536 kilograms
1 short ton = 0.90718 metric ton
1 short ton = 2,000 pounds
1 long ton = 1.016 metric tons
1 long ton = 2,240 pounds
1 metric ton = 1,000 kilograms
1 quart = 0.94635 liters
1 US gallon = 3.7854 liters
1 Imperial gallon = 4.5459 liters
1 nautical mile = 1.852 km

MOON SPOTLIGHT BOGOTÁ

Avalon Travel
a member of the Perseus Books Group
1700 Fourth Street
Berkeley, CA 94710, USA
www.moon.com

Editor: Leah Gordon
Series Manager: Kathryn Ettinger
Copy Editor: Deana Shields
Graphics and Production Coordinator: Domini Dragoone
Cover Design: Faceout Studios, Charles Brock
Moon Logo: Tim McGrath
Map Editor: Mike Morgenfeld
Cartographer: Stephanie Poulain

ISBN-13: 978-1-63121-097-6

Title page photo: The Plaza de Bolívar in Bogotá.
© Andrew Dier

Printed in the United States of America

All recommendations, including those for sights,
activities, hotels, restaurants, and shops, are based on
each author's individual judgment. We do not accept
payment for inclusion in our travel guides, and our
authors don't accept free goods or services in exchange
for positive coverage.

Although every effort was made to ensure that the
information was correct at the time of going to press, the
author and publisher do not assume and hereby disclaim
any liability to any party for any loss or damage caused
by errors, omissions, or any potential travel disruption
due to labor or financial difficulty, whether such errors
or omissions result from negligence, accident, or any
other cause.

ABOUT THE AUTHOR

Andrew Dier

Andrew Dier and his Colombian partner Vio arrived in Bogotá from New York City in 2002. It was initially supposed to be a temporary move – a change of scenery for a while – but 10 years and a couple of adopted street dogs later, bustling Bogotá has become their home.

Excited to share his insider perspective on Colombia with others, Andrew is continuously astounded by the natural beauty of the country and touched by the genuine warmth of its people.

Andrew is a regular contributor to *The City Paper*, an English-language newspaper in Bogotá, and has written for a number of publications in the United States. He's also become a deft translator, mostly for local nonprofit organizations.